Loves, Lies, and Tears

An Intimate Look at America's First Ladies

Volume I

Martha Washington to Helen Taft

1789–1913

Jacqueline Berger

ROSERITA BOOKS, INC.

Published by Roserita Books, Inc.

ISBN-13 978-0-9817041-0-4
ISBN-10 0-9817041-0-7

Books are available at special discounts when purchased in bulk for premiums and sales promotions, as well as for fund-raising or educational uses. Special editions or book excerpts can be created to customer specifications. For details and further information, contact:

Special Sales Director
Roserita Press
Roserita Books, Inc.
1534 N. Moorpark Rd., #228
Thousand Oaks, CA 91360-5129
Phone: (805) 497-8994
email: firstladies.lady@verizon.net

www.firstladieslady.com

Set in Warnock
Book design and composition by Mark McGarry, Texas Type & Book Works

Printed in the United States of America

FIRST PRINTING: JULY 2008

10 9 8 7 6 5 4 3 2 1

Dedicated to my mother, Rose, the First Lady in my life,
my father, Eddie, who taught me the love of books,
and my husband, Bruce, the only man in my life.

Contents

Acknowledgments

I owe so much to so many people, it is not possible to acknowledge every individual who was involved with and championed this labor of love. However, this book would not exist without the unwavering support, encouragement, commentary and patience of several individuals, to whom I owe a mountain of gratitude.

My husband Bruce will forever remain at the top of the list. *Loves, Lies, and Tears* is a reality due to his unselfish love, support and tolerance. He has sacrificed a great deal, for a very long period of time, in order for me to fulfill this dream and I am eternally indebted. To my children Eric and Lauren Berger, Andrea and Rob Mettel, and my grandchildren Rachel, Jeremy, and Jake, I love you—always and forever.

To my women's circle, Arline Agay, Dee Decubellis, Denise Forlizzi, Dee Dee Gartman, Patricia Hackel, Fran Halpern, and Ann Rea, this book was written only because of your obstinate insistence that I could do it. I will forever adore you and cherish our friendship.

A heartfelt thank you to Pam Garvin, who remained steadfast in her vision, shared her extensive wisdom, and continually supplied enormous optimism to this project.

To Heidi Resnik, Catherine Viel, and Gray Cutler, my endless admiration and appreciation for their superb copy editing. I also want to thank those who read and reread the original manuscript: Anna Berger (who sadly did not live long enough to see this book in print), Dee Dee Gartman, Frances Griffiths, Lynda Hendon, Barbara Roach, and Rita Steinberg. Your feedback was invaluable.

Thanks go to my agent Bill Gladstone for his belief in the book and to my project manager David Wilk for never losing his patience, holding my hand and walking me through the final months of this painstaking journey. I also want to acknowledge Mark McGarry for his book design expertise and Cody Jenkins, my computer guru, for saving my life on more than one occasion.

Last but certainly not least, infinite gratitude goes to my dear friend and associate Barb Elman, who worked tirelessly and endlessly with me for months and months on end, simply out of the goodness of her heart! She saw a need, fulfilled it and refused anything more than a few tacos and a couple of ice cream sandwiches.

Words will never express my deepest and sincerest appreciation to each and every one of you.

Introduction

NOVEMBER 22, 1963, began like any other day. It was impossible to know that day's events would have an impact on the rest of my life. You see, I am often asked how or when I became interested in the First Ladies. While sometimes I have to think long and hard about what I had for lunch yesterday, some events, although over forty years old, are seared in my mind. I can recall them with crystal clarity. One such event occurred on that dreadful Friday in 1963.

I was in the fifth grade at Darby Elementary School in Southern California, receiving an introduction to US history. We were studying George Washington and the American Revolution when the fire alarm went off. Nothing appeared unusual; we had practiced those drills many times before with never any real danger.

Every student, every teacher, every employee quietly lined up and walked out onto the handball courts. The sun was shining and it began to get warm standing on the hot blacktop. Gathered together outside, everyone waited for the final bell to signal us back to our routine. Little did we know, this alarm was anything but a routine drill.

Unexpectedly, the school principal's voice was heard over the PA system. In a tense, apprehensive tone he announced: "President Kennedy had been shot." School was cancelled and everyone was excused to go home. Stunned, I didn't understand—what did that mean? I turned, wanting to ask my teacher, but she stood frozen with a horrified look on her face, unable to speak.

While the other students played outside, waiting for their mothers to pick them up, I walked the nearly two miles home, alone and confused. When I arrived home, my father, recuperating from a serious heart attack, was staring at the TV. For the next four days I sat glued to the television set, never turning it off. I am sure I slept and ate during that time; however, I have no memory of doing either or of my parents even asking me to.

My father and I sat like robots; we watched, we listened, we cried. I recall my mother and sister coming and going, but I could not move. History was unfolding before my very eyes: the motorcade, the First Lady's bloodstained suit, the new president's swearing in, the shooting of Lee Harvey Oswald, and the funeral. There were no interruptions, no commercial breaks, not even a pause. Shock and uncertainty clouded the air, making it difficult for me to breathe, yet I continued to watch.

In my eyes, the First Lady was single-handedly holding the entire country together. Although I was only eleven years old, I was mesmerized by her courage, her strength, and her sense of duty. I watched her carry on with sophisticated grace. If she could survive seeing her husband assassinated, maybe I could learn how to survive the loss of my father when the time came. I feared that event would come sooner, rather than later.

My father and I had a very special relationship. He was the one who chose my name, "Jacqueline," much to my mother's chagrin. Oh, my mother adored me, but my name—not as much. Naturally, everyone called me Jackie, with the exception of my father, who never stopped loving the name Jacqueline.

At the time, I do not remember knowing any other Jackies, certainly no other girls named Jackie. I recall Jackie Gleason and Jackie Cooper, but they were men and did not count. So three years earlier, in 1960, when a young, good-looking, charismatic senator won the presidency, my father had proudly boasted: "If the name is good enough for the president's wife, it's good enough for MY KID!"

I wanted to emulate Jackie Kennedy's poise and charm, and great strength. I remember walking around the house in my mother's three-inch-high heels, with the *Encyclopedia Britannica* balanced on my head, trying desperately to imitate the First Lady's statuesque bearing. Now, more than ever, I became curious about her life.

My fascination with the First Ladies had been set in motion. Throughout my teenage years and beyond, when life would present me with new and sundry challenges, I would turn to the First Ladies as role models. Discovering the assortment of adversities they were faced with, and how they managed to cope with misfortune and hardships, was inspiring and insightful.

The affluence, resources, and comfort many First Ladies were privy to were a few of the counterbalancing privileges afforded them. There were also the thrill of adventure and the brilliance that comes with greatness.

Our presidents' wives were a unique group of women who with courage and conviction not only endured, but more often than not also thrived during hardship, sorrow, and embarrassment. Just a fraction of the magnificence and grandeur created by a number of these women would be a lesson in itself.

Whether they actively sought membership in this prestigious club, were reluctantly inducted by their spouses, or simply found themselves there through happenstance, time and again they rose to the stature of First Lady with great dignity, compassion, and even humor.

It became my passion to discover the personalities, the intimate struggles, and the accomplishments of these women who stood as pillars for the men elected to serve as commander-in-chief of the United States of America. Although I have never personally sat down and talked with any of these ladies—as much as I would welcome and cherish the opportunity—I feel as though I know each and every one of them.

Their lives are well documented, primarily through the extensive research of others. But, more recently, First Lady autobiographies have become exceedingly popular and sought after.

Oddly enough, Jacqueline Kennedy, a lover of books and someone who became a book editor at the age of forty-six, never wrote or spoke of her own experiences. While any publisher in the United States would gratefully have given her license to share anything of her choosing, she responded: "I would rather live my life than document it." Jackie was known for being an extremely private person, and I found her comment both perceptive and poignant.

Collectively, our nation's First Ladies are truly an amalgam of strength, intelligence, and character. They are also a fascinating study in intuition, vision, and, in some cases, ambition. They are all inspiring women who led remarkable lives.

I extend my deepest, heartfelt gratitude to the First Ladies of the United States and particularly the historians and biographers who have revealed their lives to us. In my widespread study, I did not unmask some remarkable, unique tale that had never been revealed. Just the opposite: the stories and facts contained in this book have all been shared over and over again through multiple venues. They have been documented by prominent and distinguished authors whose writings I highly respect and recommend—First Lady historians such as Carl Sferrazza Anthony, Betty Boyd Caroli, Bill Harris, Robert Watson, PhD, Margaret Bassett, Edith Mayo, and Dorothy and Carl Schneider, to name just a handful—as well as presidential historians Michael Beschloss, Doris Kearns Goodwin, David McCullough, and William A. DeGregorio. This book will guide you through a compilation of my research and provide you with a glimpse into each woman's life, plus my favorite stories about them.

Whenever possible, I have tried to include quotes or documented written material on each First Lady. All printed letters within the text are shown as written with original spelling, punctuation, and grammar. To avoid excessive citations, only substantive quotations have been referenced.

Exploring the lives of America's First Ladies, you will discover ordinary women who were daughters, wives, and mothers. Some amassed enormous fortunes; others suffered devastating financial set-backs. Many experienced death, divorce, the miraculous birth and tragic loss of children, crippling illness, and dreadful repetitive wars.

They considered themselves fortunate or unfortunate—depending on their point of view—to experience the triumph and majesty that comes with "winning" the White House. None, however, were able to escape criticism and a relentless public scrutiny into their private lives.

To quote President Harry Truman: "There is nothing new in the world except the history you do not know." How very accurate he was! I now invite you to join me on my journey through history, meeting these women and seeing their remarkable lives through my eyes.

Some individuals spoke extensively in their writings, sharing their thoughts and views, even family photos, at great length. Others were more private and offered only a small glimpse into their world. Nevertheless, each woman had something distinctive to impart. At the conclusion of each biography, I share with you the insightful life lesson I gained from each woman's remarkable life. I trust you will gain a few of your own. Enjoy the journey.

PART ONE

WOMEN OF THE REVOLUTION

THE AMERICAN REVOLUTION, according to respected historian David McCullough, was one of the bloodiest wars in US history, second only to the Civil War.[1] For eight punishing and agonizing years, considerably longer than anyone anticipated, twenty-five thousand American soldiers (one percent of the population) died for freedom. Those courageous and committed men gave their lives so their families and each and every other American could be free and independent today.

Fortunately for us, George Washington, John Adams, Thomas Jefferson, James Madison, James Monroe, and John Quincy Adams—some of the country's bravest and most brilliant individuals of the era—were in the center of that revolution. There were crucial battles that required determination and leadership. There was the drafting and ratification of the Constitution, the Declaration of Independence, the Bill of Rights, and the Monroe Doctrine, not to exclude the many successful negotiations required to deliver and maintain peace. All of those critical accomplishments were the direct result of those six individuals.

Living in the shadows were Martha Washington, Abigail Adams, Martha Jefferson, Dolley Madison, Elizabeth Monroe, and Louisa Adams—their devoted and dedicated wives. These were six women who never sought fame or recognition; they stood strong, providing great men the opportunity to be successful and accomplish monumental tasks against overwhelming odds.

Abigail Adams may have said it best when she wrote to her husband in August of 1774: "The great distance between us, makes the time appear very long to me. It seems already a month since you left me. The great anxiety I feel for my Country, for you and for our family renders the day tedious, and the night unpleasant."[2]

Duty and fear were consistently in the forefront of Abigail's mind, as witnessed in another letter dated June of 1775: "I feard much for your Health when you went away. I must intreat you to be as careful as you can consistant with the Duty you owe your Country. That consideration alone prevaild with me to consent to your departure, in a time so perilous and so hazardous to your family . . . I wish you may be supported and divinely assisted in this most important crisis when the fate of Empires depend upon your wisdom and conduct."[3]

Martha Washington also had good reason for trepidation. As a major in the Virginia militia during the French and Indian War, George Washington had two horses shot from beneath him in battle and four bullets pierced his coat.[4] Now a general, Washington was elected commander-in-chief of the Army of the United Colonies.

All the turbulence, suffering, and loss experienced by those men were also shared by their equally heroic and duty-bound spouses. It was a time in eighteenth-century history when militiamen were rich in courage and resolve, yet lacked warm clothing and sturdy shoes. In the midst of the brutal winters, their feet left bloody tracks in the snow.

For those still at home it was whispered that mothers often deliberately avoided bonding with their infants because the pain of child death was so very common. Children would succumb to smallpox, dysentery, and whooping cough, and entire communities would die from yellow fever.

No common conveniences yet existed, and over 80 percent of the population lived in rural areas. Assuming you could get to the center of town, "readers" (individuals reading the newspaper aloud) broadcasted from statehouse balconies, so those who were illiterate could hear the news of the day. Correspondence took weeks, sometimes months, to be delivered. Another eighty-two years would pass before the Overland Mail Company established regular twice-a-week stage-coach mail delivery between St. Louis and far away San Francisco.

Looking back at that era, if you are not already a believer in the adage: "Behind every great man stands a great woman," get ready to change your mind. The stories of six great, essential women of the American Revolution follow.

It was a very different generation, in a very different era. Could it be true that each and every one of us is born at a precise time with a particular calling in life? If so, how do we know what our purpose or the task truly is? Do we choose, or are we chosen? And finally, is the mission a clear one, or does it only come into focus at the end of life's journey, if ever? With so much to learn and understand of life, those who lived before us can offer insightful wisdom.

1

The General's Lady

MARTHA WASHINGTON

I am still determined to be cheerful and to be happy, in whatever situation I may be; for I have also learned from experience that the greater part of our happiness or misery depends on our disposition and not our circumstances.

—MARTHA WASHINGTON

IT WAS APPARENT that when it came to philosophy, Martha Washington was a true scholar. Yet she was born in the eighteenth century, receiving minimal education that stressed only domesticity and social graces.

Her appearance was unpretentious. Standing less than five feet tall with snow-white hair, she wore rather plain dresses beneath a well-worn apron. Martha was a humble woman, warm and gracious. It was easy to understand why Abigail Adams was deeply impressed with her "elegant plainness and modest dignified manners." Martha on the other hand described herself as an "old-fashion Virginia housekeeper, steady as a clock, busy as a bee and cheerful as a cricket."

After a lifetime filled with hardship and sorrow, Martha's only desire was to retire quietly at Mount Vernon with her husband, George,

---

#1 Martha Custis Washington

Born: June 2, 1731

Birthplace: New Kent County, Virginia

Married: 1750 (Daniel Parke Custis) Died
1759 (George Washington)

Children: 4 with Custis
0 with Washington

White House Years: 1789–1797

Died: May 22, 1802

Fact: Wealthiest widow in Virginia

Aka: Lady Washington

their family, and immediate friends. However, like other unforeseen circumstances in Martha's life, economic depression and political differences now prevented her withdrawal into retirement. After years of a revolutionary war, lengthy separations, and unspeakable fears, in 1789 General George Washington was unanimously elected the young nation's first president.

The presidency was a new position, within an experimental, monarchless form of self-government. (A position which only one man in history would hold under unanimous consent.) This unheard-of concept was based on a constitution, which Washington himself confided to friends would probably last "no more than twenty years."

When that constitution was developed and written, Martha was fifty-eight years old; and she was now facing yet another novel challenge in her life—being married to the first president of the United States—a role she was neither born into, reared for, or trained in performing.

Martha's remarkable capacity to comprehend the importance of personal courage, sacrifice, and duty obviously prepared her well for the life and times in which she lived—the mid-1700s when America, or " the colonies" as it was known, was under British rule. It was a formidable, discriminatory time when monarchies ruled nations.

The indispensable ideology and story of a petite grandmother is what follows.

Martha's unforeseen journey began in 1731. Around the time of her birth, the estimated population of the colonies was approximately 500,000. Born into a prosperous family, on a five-hundred-acre plantation, Martha was the eldest of eight children. Her parents, church elder Colonel John Dandridge and Frances Jones Dandridge, were active churchgoers. Martha's upbringing, which most likely included some home tutoring, infused her with strong moral principles and simple tastes, which she retained throughout her life.

Although the history books vary somewhat on exact dates, they all agree that Martha married a wealthy man from a tobacco fortune, in his late thirties, when she was nearly nineteen years old. Her husband, Daniel Parke Custis, was said to have had a difficult and domineering father who at first opposed his son's marriage to Martha. Mr. Custis had objected to all of his son's prospective brides, possibly because of the large fortune he had amassed. Martha was the only woman able to win him over.

She and Daniel were married and settled down on a Custis estate, ironically known as the White House. It was a happy marriage, which produced four babies in seven years.* Martha gave birth to her first child around the time a scientist by the name of Benjamin Franklin published his *New Experiments and Observations on Electricity*. Although I doubt the new mother had much interest in that novel subject.

Only Martha's youngest children, son Jacky and daughter Patsy, survived. Her two older children died in early childhood, a commonplace occurrence during the eighteenth century. Nevertheless, Martha was a financially comfortable, contented wife and mother. Then, tragically, her husband died suddenly (from a possible heart attack) in 1757. Daniel's death would change her life forever.

According to experts, Martha was considered perhaps the wealthiest widow in Virginia. What is not common knowledge is the tremendous obstacles she then had to face on her own. She was responsible for raising two young children, and all that involved, along with plantation management (such as maintaining and farming extensive acreage, buying and selling products, paying bills, and administering homeopathic medicine), in addition to seeing to the well-being of dozens of people, including her slaves. (According to historian Henry Wiencek, author of *An Imperfect God: George Washington, His Slaves, and the Creation of America*, Martha also owned her illegitimate mulatto half-sister, Ann Dandridge.)

Martha maintained a courageous attitude and carried on, even though she was without formal education or male family members to

---

* Daniel Parke Custis II (1751–1754), Frances Parke Custis (1753–1757), John "Jacky" Parke Custis (1754–1781), Martha "Patsy" Parke Custis (1756–1773).

turn to for advice. (Both Martha's father and father-in-law had passed away years earlier.) Martha tackled the arduous tasks and persisted. Having learned from her experience, over three decades later Martha wrote to her niece Fanny Bassett Washington:

> I very sincearly [*sic*] wish you would exert yourself so as to keep all your matters in order yourself without depending upon others as that is the only way to be happy—to have all your business in your own hands without trusting to others . . . look upon this advice in the friendly way it is meant, as I wish you to be as independent as your circumstances will admit and to be so, is to exert yourself in the management of your estate. If you do not no one else will. A dependence is, I think, a wrached [wretched] state and you will have enough if you will manage it right.[1]

Within two years Martha met George Washington of the Virginia militia when he came to Williamsburg on public business. Both were invited dinner guests of a neighbor, and after a brief courtship, Martha and George, who was one year her junior, were married on January 6, 1759. The couple settled down at Mount Vernon, the estate her husband had inherited from his brother. Both dependable, hard-working individuals, they treasured their home and family life.

George was fond of Martha's children and they of him, calling him "Pappa." Neither sought nor welcomed public acclaim. There was no indication of temperamental clashes or substantiation of infidelity. Contrary to popular folklore (that their marriage was merely for convenience and George maintained strong feelings for Sally Fairfax, a neighbor's wife), the Washingtons' marriage showed evidence that both partners expressed true caring and devotion to one another. If their marriage lacked any passion, it was well compensated for by their mutual admiration, respect, and effective teamwork. These are invaluable characteristics I regard with high esteem.

Although the two had hopes of having more children, months

turned into years, and this was a happiness not meant to be. A year after their marriage, Martha contracted measles. It is not unreasonable to believe that she was rendered infertile by the illness. Accepting the disappointment of having no other children, Martha then learned that her dear, sweet daughter, Patsy, had epilepsy; she was given no hope that Patsy could live more than a few years. Patsy's death at seventeen, in 1773, created a void that Martha constantly tried to fill with other young girls (nieces/cousins) growing up in the family. Not long after Patsy's death, son Jacky, against advice from his stepfather, left college and married at nineteen years old.

During this time the English Parliament, in an effort to raise money, had enacted the highly opposed Stamp Act. The indignant colonists refused to pay taxes to Britain on items such as paper, legal documents, newspapers, and other printed items. Five years later, British troops arrived in Boston and were surrounded by angry colonists. Adding fuel to the colonists' expanding resentment, the British fired into the crowd, killing three Americans and wounding others, in an incident now known as the Boston Massacre. The Boston Tea Party followed—the colonists, now refusing to pay a "tea tax," dumped 342 casks of tea into the Boston harbor.

By 1775, George understood with certainty that the growing conflict with England would erupt into fighting. "Give me liberty or give me death!"—the legendary declaration by Patrick Henry—became the colonists' creed. Later that same year, after the Continental Congress appointed Martha's husband commander of the army of the United Colonies, George wrote to his wife:

My Dearest: I am now set down to write you on a subject which fills me with inexpressibly concern, and this concern is greatly aggravated and increased, when I reflect upon the uneasiness I know it will cause you . . . You may believe me, my dear Patsy, [the name Martha used] when I assure you in the most solemn manner that, so far from seeking this appointment, I have used

every endeavor in my power to avoid it, not only from my unwillingness to part with you and the family, but from a consciousness
of its being a trust too great for my capacity, and that I should
enjoy more real happiness in one month with you at home than I
have the most distant prospect of finding abroad, if my stay were
to be seven times seven years . . . I therefore beg that you will
summon your whole fortitude and pass your time as agreeably as
possible . . . my earnest and ardent desire is that you will pursue
any plan that is most likely to produce content, and a tolerable
degree of tranquility; as it must add greatly to my uneasy feelings
to hear that you are dissatisfied or complaining at what I really
could not avoid . . .[2]

There is no evidence or documentation that Martha ever complained. Not even after Thomas Hickey, one of Washington's body-
guards, along with others conspired to kidnap and possibly kill the
commander-in-chief.* Anxious as she must have been, Martha loy-
ally supported the American patriots. She wrote: "To me that has
never seen anything of war, the preparations are very terrible indeed,
but I endeavor to keep my fears to myself as well as I can."[3]

Determined to find her contentment by following her husband to
the battlefields, Martha did so for eight lengthy, punishing years.
(Troop-following was a common practice in the early wars of the century, as it was again during the Civil War.) During that period, General Washington returned to Mount Vernon only once, for just two
days, in 1781.

Meanwhile, Martha never missed an opportunity to visit her husband between battles in Massachusetts, Pennsylvania, New Jersey,
New York, and Maryland.†

Never knowing what type of quarters she would occupy with the

* Hickey was tried before a court-martial and hanged in June of 1776.
† Some of the more famous crusades Washington was involved with were known as
the battles of Long Island, White Plains, Trenton, Princeton, Brandywine, German-
town, Valley Forge, and Yorktown.

general, it is safe to say they were all remote and lacking in comfort. During the dreadful winters when fighting stopped and the passage of supply wagons was obstructed by snow, Martha, like many other wives, came to comfort and encourage her husband. Often finding George burdened by the lack of the food and clothing needed for his militia (horses starved from the shortage of provisions), she organized sewing groups to mend the soldiers' clothing and helped nurse the wounded.

Washington wrote to Martha from Valley Forge: "To see men without clothes to cover their nakedness, without blankets to lay on, without shoes, by which their marches might be traced by the blood from their feet, and almost as often without provisions as with; marching through frost and snow."[4]

The signing of the Declaration of Independence on July 4, 1776, was considered treason, and George, along with the other Founding Fathers, was now exposed to the English threat of the gallows, or torture in the Tower of London. Martha was unquestionably concerned that her husband might be captured by the British.

Before the war was over, Martha had another devastating loss to endure. Around the time of Washington's greatest victory (the decisive battle at Yorktown, which induced the British to eventually negotiate), son Jacky died of typhoid fever at the age of twenty-six, leaving four young children without a father. When it became evident that Jacky's widow could not care for all of Martha's grandchildren, the Washingtons adopted the two youngest* to raise as their own. When the war finally ended in 1783, eight grueling years after it began, no one was more relieved than Martha Washington.

If the story had ended there, Martha would certainly have earned a quiet retirement, not to mention great respect and gratitude for all that she gave and wearily bore. But the story did not end there. In an excerpt from a letter written to Mercy Otis Warren, wife of the pres-

---

* Eleanor "Nelly" Custis (1779–1852), George Washington Parke Custis (1781–1857).

ident of the provincial congress, Martha yet again exhibited good sense and a wise attitude when she told of her decision to accept her newest challenge: "I had anticipated, that from this moment we should have been left to grow old in solitude and tranquility together: that was, the first and dearest wish of my heart—but in that I have been disappointed; I will not, however contemplate with too much regret disappointments that were enevitable. I cannot blame him for having acted according to his ideas of duty in obaying the voice of his country . . ."[5]

In 1789, George Washington was unanimously elected to lead the new nation.* As the very first wife of the country's leader, with no precedents or role model to emulate, Martha provided an excellent example for all women. Yet she remained unconvinced that she was the appropriate choice: "I sometimes think the arrangement is not quite as it ought to have been; that I, who had much rather be at home, should occupy a place which a great many younger and gayer women would be prodigiously pleased."[6] Martha and every woman succeeding her would have to define the position of First Lady for herself. The role of the president's wife carried a great deal of responsibility, yet she is neither compensated nor elected. Never mentioned in the Constitution, the status of First Lady requires only one individual's acceptance—that of her spouse.

In fact, our Founding Fathers even had a debate over what to call the chief executive's wife. They felt strongly that they should not call her "Your Majesty," like the queens of Europe. Also rejecting "Your Highness," they decided simply on "Mr. President" for Washington and "Mrs. President," or "Lady Washington," for Martha. The term "Lady" was soon dropped because it too sounded like a title for nobil-

---

* Washington was the only president to be twice unanimously elected. Inaugurated in New York City (1789) and Philadelphia (1793), he was the only president who did not reside in Washington, DC.

ity. People then went back to calling the president's wife "Mrs."; the official title of "First Lady" occurred much later in history.

Martha instinctively understood the young nation's need for a balance between dignity and formality, but without the trappings of a monarchy. Her popular twice-weekly social receptions, referred to as "levees," displayed a harmony of pageantry and prudence.

With great resolve and an inherent sense of duty, Martha dedicated herself—as a strong partisan of Washington's Federalist Party and her country—to her husband's new career with much humility. Deliberately refraining from purchasing or wearing British clothing, she supported only American-made products. The many demands and complicated new protocols of her position also added to her responsibilities: "I am more like a state prisoner than anything else. There [are] certain bounds set for me which I must not depart from and as I cannot do as I like I am obstinate [and] stay at home a great deal."

After eight demanding years, Washington declined a third presidential term, setting a precedent for future presidents that would last one hundred forty-four years. (Franklin D. Roosevelt was the only president to seek and win a third then fourth presidential term.) Martha referred to her presidential years as "lost days" with "empty ceremonies of etiquette." The retiring chief executive's wife endured it all, at enormous sacrifice to herself, without complaint. Now her long-awaited and earnestly deserved retirement was finally approaching. After returning to Mount Vernon, Martha wrote: "I cannot tell you, my dear friend, [Mrs. Knox] how much I enjoy home after having been deprived of one so long, for our dwelling in New York and Philadelphia was not home, only a sojourning."[7]

But instead of the solitude and tranquility Martha longed for, she faced an endless flow of admirers, leading citizens, and visiting dignitaries who traveled to Mount Vernon to visit the distinguished former president. In addition to not having time alone with her husband, their home had been neglected for so long that it was now in great need of repair, with no time to attend to the damage. Not exactly what

Martha had anticipated, yet she gladly accepted it. Now sixty-six years old, Martha joyfully recorded: "The General and I feel like children just released from school or from a hard taskmaster, and we believe that nothing can tempt us to leave our sacred roof-tree again . . . the twilight is gathering around our lives."[8]

In 1799, a meager two years into retirement, not nearly enough time to make up for the lost days gone by, George Washington died from quinsy, a severe inflammation of the throat. (He had been fighting a fever and severe cold, which turned into laryngitis and pneumonia.) His personal secretary, Tobias Lear, recorded the general's last words: "Tis well."*

The Washingtons were married for nearly forty-one years. Because their strengths and weaknesses complemented one another, they were able to weather the toughest of storms—lengthy separations, the American Revolution, loss of family, and the demands of governing, to name just a few. Two years after the general's passing, Martha died of "severe fever" and was buried next to him at their Mount Vernon estate in 1802. An intensely private person, Martha had already burned her husband's letters to her.

She may have lived in the shadow of her great husband, but as one of her obituaries states, she was truly a "worthy partner." A woman of courage and conviction, Martha honestly and deservedly earned her place in history.

What Martha taught me:

Martha Washington survived two husbands and all four of her children. In addition to accepting the responsibility of raising two of her

---

* Martha was granted "franking privileges," the use of free postage, to assist with her exceptionally large condolence-letter responses. Washington DC, originally called the federal city, was renamed for Martha's late husband when the capital was finally established.

grandchildren, she also sacrificed much of her life to duty and the American patriotic cause.

If I were to glean only one thing from Martha's life, it would be her philosophic view regarding emotions. Her "determination to be cheerful and happy" because "happiness or misery depends on our dispositions" has shown me that attitude is far more significant than circumstances.

2

First Lady of Liberty

ABIGAIL ADAMS

We are carried step by step to endure that which we first think insupportable.

—ABIGAIL ADAMS

WHILE MARTHA WASHINGTON was a woman of her times, Abigail Adams, only thirteen years Martha's junior, was born a century ahead of her progressive beliefs. The era and circumstances of her day no doubt stifled Abigail's position as a woman in society, but they could not muffle her philosophy.

With a casual glance at a likeness of Abigail, one might see only a woman dressed in period clothing. But upon noticing her strong facial features—with her long pointed nose and determined look—one would sense that Abigail was shrewd and insightful, with a clear sense of right and wrong.

> **#2 Abigail Smith Adams**
>
> **Born:** November 11, 1744
> **Birthplace:** Weymouth, Massachusetts
> **Married:** 1764 (John Adams)
> **Children:** 5
> **White House Years:** 1797–1801
> **Died:** October 28, 1818
> **Fact:** 1st First Lady to occupy White House; 1st wife of a President and mother of another.
> **Aka:** Mrs. President

Although both Martha and Abigail were brought up with church teachings, Abigail abhorred slavery, a commonly accepted practice of her day. Condemning slavery as immoral and destructive, Abigail wrote: "It always seemed a most iniquitous scheme to me to fight ourselves for what we are robbing the Negroes of, who have as good a right to freedom as we have."* Like her predecessor, Abigail forfeited her private peace and happiness for the benefit of her country.

> July, 1776
>
> The cruel Seperation to which I am necessitated cuts of half the enjoyments of life, the other half are comprised in the hope I have that what I do and what I suffer may be serviceable to you, to our Little ones and our Country . . .[1]

But unlike her predecessor, Abigail seemed to celebrate in her sense of duty to her country, even if she doubted that she had the "patience, prudence, and discretion" of Martha Washington, whom she deeply admired.

In addition to the great respect Abigail and Martha had for one another, their mutual devotion to motherhood, comprehension of moral obligations, and commitment to patriotism strengthened their association. Abigail's commitment is documented in a letter to her husband:

> June, 1775
>
> We cannot but consider the great distance you are from us as a very great misfortune, when our critical situation renders it necessary to hear from you every week, and will be more and more so, as difficulties arise. We now expect our Sea coasts ravaged. Perhaps, the very next Letter I write will inform you that I am driven away from our, yet quiet cottage. . . . We live in continual expectation of alarms. I shall when ever I can, receive and entertain in the best Manner I am capable the Gentlemen who have so generously proferd their Service in our Army. Government is wanted in the army, and Else where. I feel a respect for the lowest Subaltern in the Army.[2]

---

* The Washingtons, Jeffersons, Madisons, Jacksons, Tylers, Polks, and Taylors all owned slaves during their tenure in the White House.

Here was another courageous woman with very little formal educa-
tion (as evidenced in her flawed spelling and lack of punctuation), yet
Abigail was well read, articulate, and knowledgeable about politics.
Her candid and forthright communication with her husband, plus her
highly advanced activist ideas regarding women and education, set
Abigail apart from her contemporaries.

March 31, 1776

I long to hear that you have declared an Independency—and by
the way, in the new Code of Laws which I suppose it will be necessary for you to make, I desire you would Remember the Ladies,
and be more generous and favourable to them than your ancestors. Do not put such unlimited power into the hands of the Husbands. Remember, all Men would be tyrants if they could. . . .[3]

Who was this principled crusader of women who wrote so innov-
atively in 1776? More important, what could I learn from this ultra-ad-
vanced, radically opinionated heroine of the American Revolution?

Her remarkable story began in November 1744, when Abigail Quincy
Smith entered the world in Weymouth, Massachusetts. Her reverend
father, William Smith, taught her strong lessons in religion and morality. Whereas Abigail's mother, Elizabeth Quincy Smith, taught her patience and submission; attributes she herself had inherited from a
long-established and respected family of the region.

A sickly child, Abigail grew up in a household with two sisters and
one brother. Although she lacked educational opportunities, she was exposed to her father's extensive library, and became an avid reader who
remained interested in learning throughout her life. She noted: "Every assistance and advantage which can be procured is afforded to the Sons,
whilst the daughters are wholly neglected in point of Literature."

At seventeen Abigail fell passionately in love with twenty-six-year-
old John Adams, her third cousin. John had graduated from Harvard,

as had Abigail's father. Be that as it may, Abigail's mother did not initially approve of the struggling village lawyer with whom her daughter was so enamored. Mrs. Smith's disapproval was possibly due to the fact John did not choose the ministry, as his father had, (John AdamsSr., was a respected deacon in the church), the preferred profession of the day. Or it could have been his cold, aloof personality that prevented him from relating well to other individuals.

Nonetheless, the couple was undeniably in love, and after a two-year courtship Reverend Smith married the devoted pair in 1764. The Adams marriage forever linked the hearts and minds of Abigail and John.

During their many years together, John was away for months and sometimes even years at a time because of his passionate commitment to the American Revolution. While her husband was away, Abigail wrote eloquently of her loneliness:

December, 1773

How many snow banks devide thee and me and my warmest wishes to see thee will not melt one of them. . . . The Roads at present are impassible with any carriage. . . . My daily thoughts and Nightly Slumbers visit thee, and thine.[4]

Sepbr. 1774

Dearest Friend

Five Weeks have past and not one line have I received. I had rather give a dollar for a letter by the post, tho the consequence should be that I Eat but one meal a day for these 3 weeks to come.[5]

october 1774

My Much Loved Friend

I dare not express to you, at three hundred miles distance, how ardently I long for your return. I have some very miserly Wishes; and cannot consent to your spending one hour in Town till at least

I have had you 12. . . . ten weeks absence knows not how to brook any longer restraint, but will break forth and flow thro my pen. May the like sensations enter thy breast . . .[6]

July 1778

In vain do I strive to divert my attention, my Heart, like a poor bird hunted from her nest, is still returning to the place of its affections, and fastens upon the object where all its cares and tenderness are centered.[7]

Due to these prolonged absences, most of the administration of their farm and business affairs fell upon Abigail. Fortunately, she proved to be a good business manager, making payments and collecting bills, while becoming quite proficient at the planting and selling of crops for a profit. "I hope in time to have the reputation of being as good a farmeress as my partner has of being a good statesman . . . I want to hear from you much oftener than I do."[8]

In addition to maintaining their business affairs, Abigail became a working mother almost immediately. Just a few days shy of her nine-month wedding anniversary, she gave birth to her first child. Within eight years, she would be the mother of five.*

Independent thinkers who agreed with each other's philosophy, both Abigail and John believed strongly that their children should be educated for public service. Communication regarding their family was another part of their correspondence. John wrote to his wife:

The Education of our Children is never out of my Mind. Train them to Virtue, habituate them to industry, activity, and Spirit. Make them consider every Vice, as shamefull and unmanly: fire them with Ambition to be usefull—make them disdain to be destitute of any usefull, or ornamental Knowledge or Accomplishment. Fix their Ambition upon great and solid Objects, and their

---

* Abigail Amelia (1765–1813), John Quincy (1767–1848), Susanna (1768–1770), Charles (1770–1800), Thomas Boylston (1772–1832).

Contempt upon little, frivolous and useless ones. It is Time, my
dear, for you to begin to teach them French. Every Decency, Grace,
and Honesty should be inculcated upon them.[9]

After teaching her children what she could, the boys would be sent
abroad or to live with relatives to complete their studies. Sadly, teaching her little ones about war was also a reality. Abigail and her seven-
year-old son, John Quincy, were seated atop an embankment from
which they watched the Battle of Bunker Hill on June 17, 1775. The
following day, Abigail wrote to her husband:

Sunday June 18 1775

Dearest Friend
    The Day; perhaps the decisive Day is come on which the fate
of America depends. my busting Heart must find vent at my pen.
I have just heard that our dear Friend Dr. Warren is no more but
fell gloriously fighting for his Country—saying better to die hon-
ourably in the field than ignominiously hang upon the Gallows.
Great is our Loss. He has distinguished himself in every engagement, by his courage and fortitude, by animating the Soliders &
leading them on by his own example a particuliar account of these
dreadful, but I hope Glorious Days will be transmitted you, no
doubt in the exactest manner.[10]

John Adams later said: "I must study politics and war that my sons
may have liberty to study mathematics and philosophy."
    Threats of war, perpetual loneliness, and separation from her chil-
dren all came at a great sacrifice to Abigail. Compounding these burdens were life-threatening illnesses; the dysentery (1775) and smallpox
(1776) epidemics struck very close to home.

August, 1775

The return of thee my dear partner after a four months absence is
a pleasure I cannot express, but the joy is overclouded, and the

Day is darkened by the mixture of Grief and the Sympathy I feel for the looss of your Brother. [John's youngest brother, Elihu, died of dysentery.] . . . May thy life be spaired and thy Health confirmed for the benefit of thy Country and the happiness of thy family is the constant supplication of thy Friend.[11]

Sepbr. 1775

Dearest Friend

I set down with a heavy Heart to write to you. I have had no other since you left me. Woe follows Woe and one affliction treads upon the heal of an other. My distress for my own family having in some measure abated; tis excited anew upon the distress of my dear Mother. Her kindness brought her to see me every day when I was ill and our little Tommy [both from dysentery]. She has taken the disorder and lies so bad that we have little hopes of her Recovery. . . . Some poor parents are mourning the loss of 3, 4 and 5 children, and some families are wholy striped of every Member.[12]

October, 1775

How can I tell you (o my bursting Heart) that my Dear Mother has Left me, this day about 5 oclock she left this world for an infinitely better. . . . At times I almost am ready to faint under this severe and heavy Stroke, separated from [thee] who used to be a comfortar towards me in afflicition. . . . My poor father like a firm Believer and a Good Christian sets before his children the best of Examples of patience and submission. . . . Tis a dreadful time with this whole province. Sickness and death are in almost every family.[13]

The Adamses' long struggle and lonesome separations continued throughout their country's battle for sovereignty. A well-respected attorney and statesman, John attended the First and Second Continental Congresses, insisting on independence for the colonies. Abigail reinforced their position, confirming that "the only alternative which every American thinks of is Liberty or Death. Is it not better to die the last of British freemen then live the first of British slaves?"[14] With honesty and resignation Abigail remained faithful in her convictions.

May 7 1776

How many are the solitary hours I spend, ruminating upon the past, and anticipating the future, whilst you overwhelmd with the cares of State. . . . All domestick pleasures and injoyments are absorbed in the great and important duty you owe your Country for our Country is as it were a secondary God, and the First and greatest parent. It is to be preferred to Parents, Wives, Children, Friends and all things the Gods only excepted. For if our Country perishes it is as imposible to save an Individual, as to preserve one of the fingers of a Mortified Hand.[15]

June 3. 1776

I can not avoid sometimes repineing that the gifts of fortune were not bestowed upon us, that I might have injoyed the happiness of spending my days with my Partner. But as it is, I think it my duty to attend with frugality and oeconomy to our own private affairs, and if I cannot add to our Little Substance yet see that it is not dimished. I should enjoy but little comfort in a state of Idleness, and uselessness. Here I can serve my partner, my family and myself, and injoy the Satisfaction of your serving your Country.[16]

One month from the date of Abigail's last letter, John was ecstatic to share what he referred to as "the greatest Question ever debated in America":

Philadelphia July 3. 1776

A Resolution was passed . . . these united Colonies, are, and of right ought to be free and independent States. . . . The Second Day of July 1776, will be the most memorable Epocha, in the History of

America.—I am apt to believe that it will be celebrated, by succeeding Generations, as the great anniversary Festival. . . . You will
think me transported with Enthusiasm but I am not.—I am well
aware of the Toil and Blood and Treasure, that it will cost Us to
maintain this Declaration, and support and defend these States.—
Yet through all the Gloom I can see the Rays of ravishing Light
and Glory. I can see that the End is more than worth all the
Means.[17]

Abigail wrote back:

Sunday july 14

. . . your Letters never fail to give me pleasure . . . yet it was greatly
heightned by the prospect of the future happiness and glory of our
Country; nor am I a little Gratified when I reflect that a person so
nearly connected with me has had the Honour of being principal
actor, in laying a foundation for its future Greatness. May the
foundation of our new constitution, be justice, Truth and Righteousness.[18]

Finally, yet not without the toil and blood Adams was convinced
would be needed, the new states simultaneously began adopting
government, with Congress's Declaration of July 4, 1776. The great
"Anniversary Festival" had begun.

Life and all its adversity continued for the courageous couple that
never forgot or abandoned their duty to their country. Abigail diligently persisted in manning the home front, deciding to have her children and herself inoculated for smallpox. Nabby, her eldest child, and
Charles, her middle son, both suffered severe, painful cases of the viral
disease. The entire family endured "very weak eyes" from a "bad inflammation" preventing them from writing or reading for a period of
time. When John finally learned of the situation, he exploded with
frustration and anger.

Philadelphia. July 20. 1776

. . . Do my Friends think that I have been a Politician so long as to
have lost all feeling? Do they suppose I have forgotten my wife and
Children? . . . Dont mistake me, I dont blame you. Your Time and
Thoughts must have been wholly taken up, with your own and your
Families situation and Necessities. –But twenty other Persons
might have informed me. I suspect, that you intended to have run
slyly, through the small Pox with the family, without letting me
know it, and than have sent me an Account that you were all well.
This might be a kind Intention, and if the design had succeeded,
would have made me very joyous. But the secret is out, and I am
left to conjecture . . . Make Mr. Mason, Mr. any Body write to me,
by every Post—dont miss one for any Cause whatever.[19]

In other correspondence, Abigail discussed the "fatal effects" of
smallpox and how "almost every person, in every town" was involved
with a hospital. She expressed how dreadfully difficult it was to "procure Labourers" and when she could, how incredibly expensive it
was. She would discuss which debts she "discharged," the severe
"Drougth," ending promising hopes of grain for their farm, and how
much she "lamented" the death of her husband's gray horse. Often
Abigail would reiterate: "We daily see the Necessity of a regular Government."

Regarding the advanced education of their children, Abigail confessed: "I find myself soon out of my debth, and destitute and deficient to every part of Education." She went on: "I most sincerely wish
that some more liberal plan might be laid and executed for the Benefit of the rising Generation, and that our new constitution may be distinguished for Learning and Virtue. If we mean to have Heroes,
Statesmen and Philosophers, we should have learned women. . . . great
benefit must arise from literary accomplishments in women."[20] At the
same time, her letters reflected some disappointment with her husband and his colleagues: "I can not say that I think you very generous

to the Ladies, for whilst you are proclaiming peace and good will to Men, Emancipating all Nations, you insist upon retaining an absolute power over Wives."

When all was said and done, with the "patience and submission," her mother so wisely taught her, Abigail accepted the male-dominated society she was born into, and continued to live within its constraints. Even she conceded: "But Rome was not Built in a day."

Along with the crucial items of the day, Abigail also included local gossip in her correspondence, although she was apprehensive that someone other than her husband might read the information: "I expected Mr. Gerry would have set off before now, but he finds it perhaps very hard to leave his Mistress—I wont say harder than some do to leave their wives. Mr. Gerry stood very high in my Esteem—what is meat for one is not for an other—no accounting for fancy. But hush—Post, dont betray your trust and loose my Letter. "[21]

By September 1776, Abigail was nearing the end of her wits. John was still in Philadelphia on Senate business while the family remained in Braintree, Massachusetts. They had closed their home in Boston, fearing a British invasion of the city.

> I wish any thing would bring you nearer. I am not apt to be intimidated you know . . . whilst you are engaged in the Senate your own domestick affairs require your presence at Home, and that your wife and children are in Danger of wanting Bread. . . . unless you return what little property you possess will be lost. . . . the House at Boston is going to ruin. When I was there I hired a Girl to clean it . . . The House is so exceeding damp being shut up, that the floors are mildewd, the sealing falling down, and the paper mouldy and falling from the walls. I put it into the best state I could. . . . I know the weight of pub lick cares lye heavey upon you that I have been loth to mention your own private ones. . . . We are no ways dispiritted here, we possess a Spirit that will not be conquerd.[22]

John obtained a leave of absence from the Senate and temporarily returned to his family. In January 1777, Abigail learned she was pregnant with her sixth child. Once again, her husband was returning to his congressional duties and she was left to bear their child alone. When her husband had been away for prior births, Abigail's mother remained close by to help fill the void. With her mother now gone, Abigail felt particularly forlorn during this pregnancy.

Two months later, Abigail was writing of severe weather: "Snow banks five and six feet high. A Cry for Bread, never before Heard, and miserabley poor meat." By July, she was nearing the end of her pregnancy and unable to hide her apprehensions:

July 9 1777

I have been very unwell for this week past, with some complaints that have been new to me, tho I hope not dangerous. I was last night taken with a shaking fit, and am very apprehensive that a life was lost. I would not Have you too much allarmd. I keep up some Spirits yet, tho I would have you prepaird for any Event that may happen.[23]

John could only respond with his own anxiety and pain:

Philadelphia July 10. 1777. Thursday

My Mind is again Anxious, and my Heart in Pain for my dearest Friend . . . Three Times have I felt the most distressing Sympathy with my Partner, without being able to afford her any Kind of Solace, or Assistance. When the Family was sick of the Dissentery, and so many of our Friends died of it. When you all had the small Pox. And now I think I feel as anxious as ever. . . . Before this shall reach you I hope you will be happy in the Embraces of a Daughter, as fair, and good, and wise, and virtuous as the Mother, or if it is a son I hope it will still resemble the Mother in Person, Mind and Heart.[24]

Abigail continued to record her experiences for her faraway spouse:

July 10 [1777] 9 o clock Evening

Tis now 48 Hours since I can say I really enjoyed any Ease . . . Slow, lingering and troublesome is the present situation. . . . I pray Heaven that it may be soon or it seems to me I shall be worn out.

July 11

I got more rest last night than I expected, this morning am rather more ill than I was yesterday. This day ten years ago master John [their son John Quincy] came into this world. May I have reason again to recollect it with peculiar gratitude. Adieu.

On July 13, 1777, John Thaxter Jr., a cousin of Abigail's, wrote to John:

Sir

The day before Yesterday Mrs. Adams was delivered of a daughter; [but] it grieves me to add, Sir, that it was still born. It was an exceeding fine looking Child. Mrs. Adams is as comfort-able as can be expected. . . . Every thing in my power that respects her Comfort, or that respects the Children, shall be attended to by Sir, Your most obedient Servt.,
    J. Thaxter Junr.

Mr. Thaxter was a law student of and later became John Adams's pri-vate secretary, as well as tutor to John Quincy Adams.

This was the second daughter Abigail would mourn. One-year-old Susanna had died seven years earlier. Abigail reported that no one was more affected than twelve-year-old Nabby, "who mourned in tears for Hours" over the loss of her sister. Regarding her own sadness, Abigail wrote: "I have so much cause for thankfulness admidst my sorrow, that I would not entertain a repineing thought."[25]

Returning home in November for what John believed to be his last separation from his family, he immediately resumed his law practice in order to begin replenishing the family finances. It did not take Congress long, however, before it elected Adams commissioner to France. Abigail wrote a letter to the Massachusetts delegate on the Committee for Foreign Affairs:

December 15 1777

Can I Sir consent to be separated from him who my Heart esteems above all earthly things, and for an unlimited time? My life will be one continued scene of anxiety and apprehension, and must I cheerfully comply with the Demand of my Country?[26]

The answer, as you might expect, in conjunction with all the other demands inflicted upon Abigail by her country, was yet again yes. This time John set sail for France with their ten-year-old son, John Quincy. Abigail now conveyed her sentiments, first to her son and again to her husband:

June 1778 (circa)

. . . 'Tis almost four months since you left your native land . . . It is a very difficult task, my dear son, for a tender parent to bring her mind to part with a child of your years, going to a distant land; nor could I have acquiesced in such a separation under any other care than that of the most excellent parent and guardian who accompanied you. . . . improve your understanding by acquiring useful knowledge. These are mature standards to set before a boy of ten, but greater demands follow. Great learning . . . will be of little value, unless virtue, honor, truth and integrity are added to them . . . I would rather you should have found your grave in the ocean you have crossed than to see you an immoral, profligate or graceless child. Be assured I am most affectionately yours.[27]

May 18 1778

Difficult as the Day is, cruel as this War has been, seperated as I am on account of it from the dearest connextion in life, I would not exchange my Country for the Wealth of the Indies, or be any other than an American ... My Soul is unambitious of pomp or power. I have been calld to sacrifice to my Country, I can glory in my Sacrifice, and derive pleasure from my intimate connextion with one who is esteemed worthy of the important trust devolved upon him.[28]

Over the next ten years, John's diplomatic missions to Europe took him to Paris, London, and Holland, as minister to the Netherlands, then minister to England. He did sail home for a three-month visit with his family in 1779, this time returning to Europe with another son, Charles. While John Quincy blossomed in a Paris school and later in an Amsterdam university, eleven-year-old Charles became exceedingly homesick and returned to the United States.

According to historian Sandra Quinn-Musgrove, the ship Charles was traveling on spent several months drydocked in Spain for repairs. Stranded and undoubtedly fearful, Charles was unable to communicate with his family. Abigail was grateful to see her son again after four anxious months, for she had believed him lost at sea.[29] It was not long before Charles and his younger brother Thomas went to live with family for further educational studies.

October 1 1782 [Their wedding anniversary.]

Eighteen years have run their circuit since we pledged our mutual faith to each other and the hymeneal torch was lighted at altar of Love. Yet it burns with unabating fervor. Old Ocean has not quenched it, nor old Time smothered it in his bosom. It cheer me in the lonely hours; it comforts me even in the gloom which sometimes possesses my mind. Who shall give me back time? Who shall compensate me for the years I cannot recall? You have obtained

honor and reputation at home and abroad . . . Do you look like the
miniature you sent? Gracious Heaven! . . . restore to me the original and I care not who has the shadow.[30]

Anxious to be reunited with his wife and daughter after several
years of separation, John encouraged and then begged Abigail to join
him with Nabby. In poor health and fearful of crossing the Atlantic
without a male companion, Abigail nonetheless embarked with her
daughter on their month long journey to Europe in June 1784. Her
younger boys remained with family to continue their schooling.

The next four years proved to be an eye-opening experience for
the puritanical, dedicated, and thrifty American mother. Aware of the
French prostitutes who worked the dirty streets of Paris, and unable
to speak the language, plus the financial demands imposed by
Abigail's social obligations were all added challenges in her new life in
Europe.

While in France, John worked closely with Thomas Jefferson, another minister on a diplomatic mission, to create some of their nation's
most important legislation. Although Jefferson and Abigail had some
differing political views, they shared a mutual interest in their country's
independence and developed a friendship while living in Paris.

Abigail managed to maintain a correspondence with Jefferson after
moving with her husband to his next post in England. There the king
received the couple somewhat less than cordially. Historian Margaret
Bassett reports that Abigail was "firmly snubbed by the Queen." One
must bear in mind that Abigail and John represented the American
rebels, but regardless of how they were treated, both attended court
as required by etiquette.

Before returning to the United States in 1788, Abigail cared for Jefferson's younger daughter Polly after she and Sally Hemings, a fourteen-year-old slave, arrived in England. The young girls, both
motherless, were to eventually meet Jefferson in Paris.

The following year, Abigail felt a sense of pride and entitlement
when John was elected the country's first vice president: "I will take

praise to myself, I feel that it is my due, for having sacrificed so large a portion of my peace and happiness to promote the welfare of my country which I hope for many years to come will reap the benefit, tho it is more than probable unmindfull of the hand that blessed them."[31]

Abigail moved to New York, the original capital city, where her friendship with Martha Washington was fostered. There Martha's dignity and grace (and perhaps her limited education) helped her avoid controversy. Abigail, on the other hand, had considerable political knowledge, European experiences, familiarity with other nations and cultures, and a history of frankness with her spouse. She expressed her fears when it came to being hushed, as you might say, out of necessity: "I have been so used to freedom of sentiment that I know not how to place so many guards about me, as will be indispensable, to look at every word before I utter it, and to impose a silence upon myself, when I long to talk."[32]

As the young government struggled to materialize, differing views among politicians were predictable and unavoidable. Although she still believed in liberty, Abigail began to doubt Americans' ability to govern themselves: "I am sometimes led to think that human nature is a very perverse thing, and much more given to evil than good."[33] The question remained: should the nation be ruled by a powerful federal government made up of irreproachable elite intellectuals (like her husband), or consist of autonomous states governed by individuals of dubious integrity?

Plagued with chronic illness during much of her husband's vice presidency, Abigail was saved from much of the internal bickering and backbiting. Eventually she was forced to return to their home in Massachusetts. On top of her deteriorating health, Abigail was once again separated from her husband for lengthy periods of time.

When Washington refused a third presidential term, it was only natural that Adams would succeed him. Abigail was still at home, now caring for her dying mother-in-law, when John achieved the presidency. On the day of her husband's inauguration, Abigail wrote: "My feelings are not those of pride or ostentation, upon the occasion. They are . . . a sense of the obligation, the important trust, and numerous duties connected with it."[34] Shortly thereafter, the new president wrote back: "I never wanted your Advice and assistance more in my life. The Times are critical and dangerous, and I must have you here to assist me." John greatly respected his wife's opinion and told her: "I think you shine as a stateswoman."

In 1797, Abigail joined her husband, then in Philadelphia (the temporary capital city after New York). She eventually moved to Washington, DC, where the federal government permanently located after the president's home was constructed there in 1800. Abigail's trip to the new capital city was intensely emotional, as she stopped to visit her gravely ill thirty-year-old son, Charles, on her way.

Knowing Charles would never visit his parents at the White House, the mother in Abigail understood that she would never see her son again. Charles had been an alcoholic and was now on his deathbed. Visiting him for the last time, the politician in Abigail understood the necessity and obligation of her move to the new executive mansion.

Surrounded by forests, Washington was still located in the wilderness; not yet a city, streets did not exist and the roads remained deep in dust and mud. Abigail wrote to her family back in Massachusetts, describing the new house. The First Lady described the still-unfinished rooms, the need to build great fires in the fireplaces to dry out the wet, plastered walls, and her use of the large reception room (today known as the East Room) to hang her laundry.

Mrs. President—as Abigail was branded because of her influence over her husband, her promotion of women's rights, and her partisanship of the Federalist Party—sadly wrote to her sister when Charles died: "Weep with me, over the grave of a poor unhappy child who cannot now add another pang to those which have pierced my heart for several years."

It was only a matter of a few short months before Abigail was again packing, this time to return to Massachusetts, as President Adams did not win his bid for reelection. She accepted the defeat with more resignation than disappointment: "I have learned to know the world and its value. I have seen high life. I have witnessed the luxury and pomp of state, the power of riches, and the influence of titles. Notwithstanding this I feel that I can return to my little cottage and be happier . . . and if we have not wealth, we have what is better—integrity."[35] She held no resentment against Thomas Jefferson, once a very good friend of the family, but now a bitter political enemy of her husband and the presidential victor.

Retirement brought Abigail the "lost time" she could now spend with her husband. For the first time in thirty-six years, she could tend to her family and garden without the anxiety and loneliness incurred by her husband's absences. In 1804, Abigail initiated a new correspondence with Thomas Jefferson when his daughter Polly (whom she had cared for in London) died during his administration. They continued to correspond, despite Adams' and Jefferson's estrangement, for eight more years until the men finally renewed their friendship.

During this time, Abigail remained well acquainted with illness. Not just her own, but her children's health as well. Having seen one son die from alcoholism, she now watched another son become an alcoholic, and witnessed her daughter's painful battle and death from a then unnamed disease in her breast. Research indicates that Nabby suffered from cancer. Long before anesthesia was developed or mastectomies were heard of, the only way doctors knew to eradicate the disease was by removing Nabby's breast. The operation was preformed in the family home. The mutilation, and ultimate loss of her daughter two years later in 1813, were all further sorrows Abigail had to bear.

Toward the end of her life Abigail wrote: "I am determined to be very well pleased with the world, and wish well to all its inhabitants. Altho in my journey through it, I meet with some who are too selfish, others too ambitious, some uncharitable, others malicious and envious, yet these vices are counterbalanced . . . I always thought the laughing phyosopher a much wiser man, than the sniveling one."[36]

Abigail's inner strength was tested right up until her death from typhoid fever in 1818. Although she received great gratification in seeing son John Quincy's distinguished service to the nation, sadly she did not live long enough to experience the joy of seeing her son inaugurated president twenty-four years after his father left that distinguished office.

Abigail Adams was one of the earliest American women to demonstrate strength, intelligence, and insight. Her son John Quincy Adams may have said it best: "Her life gave the lie to every libel on her sex that was ever written."

Abigail and John shared a true, loving partnership as equals; this was exceptionally noteworthy as they lived during a time when men and women were not equal. Their marriage was tested by numerous and lengthy separations while John was off negotiating America's battle for liberty. Abigail supported her husband's patriotic cause and understood the great sacrifices that would be required.

Fifty-four years after marrying the love of his life, John was left behind to live out his eight remaining years without the counsel and support of the person he called "My Dearest Partner, My best, worthiest wisest friend in this world."

John Adams died on July 4, 1826, fifty years to the day after he signed the Declaration of Independence.* He was laid to rest beside his wife in a basement crypt at the First Unitarian Church in Massachusetts. A memorial tablet to him states: "Abigail, His beloved and only wife . . . During a union of more than half a century, they survived, in harmony of sentiment, principle and affection."

What Abigail taught me:

Equally committed to independence as her spouse, Abigail's devotion to her principles of freedom, morality, conduct, and education gave her a serene certitude. Those convictions, particulary to freedom and liberty, held authority over her personal safety and security. To quote her: "If we

---

* Unknown to Adams, Thomas Jefferson died on the same day.

have not wealth, we have what is better—integrity." By example, Abigail Adams demonstrated a sincere commitment to education and public service for herself and her family.

Abigail taught me the wisdom of a "laughing philosopher" versus a "sniveling one," particularly in the face of perceived failure. When her husband lost reelection, it was Abigail who said: "If I did not rise with dignity, I can at least fall with ease, which is the more difficult task."

Charles Francis Adams, son of John Q. Adams, the grandson of Abigail and John Adams, fortunately became the family archivist. While Abigail Adams was still alive, she refused publication of her letters, believing it improper for a woman. A world of gratitude is due to Charles for publishing a selective volume of his grandparents' correspondence. He began in 1840 with *Letters of Mrs. Adams*. Then later in 1876, nearing seventy, Charles celebrated the nation's centennial with *Familiar Letters, of John Adams and His Wife*.

In 1975, Butterfield, Friedlaender, and Kline edited *The Book of Abigail and John: Selected Letters of the Adams Family 1762–1784*, providing many of the selections quoted above. The editors have allowed us an intimate look at a remarkable relationship and an exclusive view of our country during the time of the American Revolution. Abigail's letters ring true—with honor, integrity, and morality.

3

Never to Be First Lady

MARTHA JEFFERSON

[She] was remarkable for her beauty, her accomplishments,
and her solid merit . . .

—DESCRIPTION OF MARTHA JEFFERSON IN
THE PIONEER MOTHERS OF AMERICA

AFTER HAVING READ Abigail Adams' tender and revealing letters, which have enlightened historians as to her life and times, in contrast Martha Jefferson remains a vague and obscure personality. No picture of her likeness or written documentation of Martha's words have survived.

Frankly, if it had not been for Thomas Jefferson's affair with his black slave Sally Hemings, one wonders if anyone would even bother to read the tiny bits of history we do have about Martha's life. Conversely, life being stranger than fiction, when it was discovered that Sally was in fact Martha's half-sister, interest in Martha increased.

> **#3 Martha Skelton Jefferson**
>
> **Born:** October 19, 1748
> **Birthplace:** Charles City County, Virginia
> **Married:** 1766 (Bathurst Skelton) Died
> 1772 (Thomas Jefferson)
> **Children:** 1 with Skelton
> 6 with Jefferson
> **White House Years:** 1801–1809
> **Died:** September 6, 1782
> **Fact:** Died 19 years before husband
> became President

As for me, I was more curious about the characteristics and qualities of the individual who was capable of filling her husband's heart so fully that it prevented him from ever considering marriage to another woman.

What might indeed sound fictional is the recorded information we do have on Thomas Jefferson's never-to-be First Lady. Ironically enough, had Martha Jefferson lived longer, her husband may well have never become president. After you read Martha's story, which begins in 1748, you will understand why.

Everything was set into motion when Martha Eppes married John Wayles, a prominent land owner and barrister.* She brought to her marriage a female African slave and the woman's half-black, half-white daughter, Betty Hemings, as part of her dowry. The couple's only child, also named Martha, was born on the family's large Virginia plantation in October 1748. Two weeks after giving birth, Martha senior died, then not an uncommon occurrence.

Mr. Wayles went on to marry two more times, producing several half-siblings for his eldest daughter. Growing up Martha had two step-mothers and four half sisters. The number of Martha's younger half-siblings became more convoluted as time went on.

As it turned out, Mr. Wayles outlived all three of his wives. When his third wife passed away, Wayles took Betty Hemings, a slave's daughter still in the family, as his concubine and had six more children (three girls and three boys) with her. So much for the theory that history is boring!

As Martha grew up she was described as an outgoing beauty, with "striking auburn hair" and hazel eyes. Said to have had many suitors, at eighteen she married a successful lawyer named Bath-hurst Skelton. Skelton happened to be an acquaintance of Thomas Jefferson, who like him had graduated from William and Mary College. Medicine being what it was, within two years Martha's husband died, leaving her with a young son.† When Thomas Jefferson began to court the twenty-two-year-old widow, their mutual passion for music inevitably played some part. Martha sang and played the pianoforte, while Thomas accompanied her on the violin.

---

* A British attorney qualified to represent clients in higher law courts.
† John Skelton (1767–1771)

They also read to one another, quiet pleasures they shared together.

Thomas proposed both marriage and guardianship to Martha's child; however, the wedding was postponed for a six-month period of mourning, due to the sudden death of her four-year-old son, John. When the couple did finally marry, on New Year's Day in 1772, the newlyweds moved to Jefferson's mansion, Monticello, which remains to this day a wonderful historic site.

Legend has it that en route to their new home, the road was deep in snow and their horse-drawn carriage broke down. Riding horseback the last eight miles up a steep mountain road, the newlyweds arrived at Monticello very late at night. With the servants asleep in their quarters, the Jeffersons found a bottle of wine and warmed themselves in the barn overnight.

Just nine months later, Martha gave birth to their first child.* In the meantime, Martha continued to gain half-siblings as her father had more and more children with his concubine, Betty Hemings. In 1773, Sally Hemings, Martha's youngest half-sister, was born. All of Betty's children retained her last name, although by including her in his will John Wayles provided evidence that Betty was in fact his mistress. Wayles also stipulated that in addition to other property and slaves Martha would inherit Sally Hemings, who was then still a young girl.

Only three years into the Jefferson marriage, the Revolutionary War began. During a British invasion near Monticello, Martha, frail and in poor health, was twice forced to escape danger by leaving her home, with a toddler and second infant in tow.

The little evidence that exists suggests that Thomas devoted himself to his wife and her care throughout their happy ten-year marriage. During that time, Martha's health was broken by grief and multiple childbirths—six in ten years. It would have been impossible for Martha not to feel anxious with every pregnancy. She knew childbirth had caused her mother's premature death at thirty-five, and four of

---

* Martha Washington (1772–1836), Jane Randolph (1774–1775), an unnamed son (1777–1777), Mary aka Marie or Polly (1778–1804), Lucy Elizabeth (1780–1781), another daughter also named Lucy Elizabeth (1782–1785).

her children had already died in early childhood. Gravely ill following the birth of her last child, Martha died (with no specific known diagnosis) four months later. She was only thirty-three years old.

Upon hearing of his wife's death, Thomas collapsed and remained in his room for weeks, inconsolable in his grief. Their eldest daughter, Martha (aka Patsy), never forgot the depth of her father's despair. Remembering her mother's demise, Patsy wrote: "The violence of his emotion, when . . . I entered his room by night, to this day I dare not describe to myself."

Martha did, however, live to see her husband draft the Declaration of Independence and win his reelection bid for governor of Virginia.

Martha was buried in the family plot at Monticello. Jefferson had these lines inscribed on his wife's gravestone:

> *If in the melancholy shades below,*
> *The flames of friends and lovers cease to glow,*
> *Yet mine shall sacred last; mine undecayed*
> *Burn on through death and animate my shade.*

According to slaves who attended to Martha in her final days, she asked her husband to promise he would never marry again. Some believe it was because she grew up with two stepmothers of her own. Whether that tale is accurate or not, Jefferson lived as a widower for over forty-three years, never remarrying.

Surely for Jefferson the loss of his wife was very great. Yet in all his writings, he left exceptionally little information about his spouse. One can only make guesses about Martha's personality and her relationship with her husband. But like her predecessors, she appears to have been a fitting complement to the truly brilliant, albeit imperfect, Renaissance man Jefferson was.

It should be noted that Jefferson resigned from Congress to care for his ill wife. Eight weeks after Martha's death, Jefferson made it known to his political friends that he was ready to return to government. If Martha had lived longer, it is conceivable Jefferson would not have returned to Washington so quickly.

Had he not, Congress might never have elected Jefferson to succeed Benjamin Franklin as minister to France. It is also plausible that Jefferson may not have accepted his diplomatic missions to Paris and London, (leaving his frail wife in the United States), which led to his appointment as secretary of state and ultimately the presidency.

Eighteen years after his wife's death, Jefferson went to the White House a confirmed widower. When his daughter Patsy was unable to fulfill a First Lady's duties, Dolley Madison, wife of Secretary of State James Madison, served as hostess in the executive mansion.

Although Jefferson never remarried, he did have other relationships. Historians commonly mention two women, Betsey Walker and Maria Cosway, both married, in connection with him. But his relationship with Sally Hemings, considered scandalous at the time, is the most widely known.

In 1998, DNA testing indicated that Jefferson fathered at least one, and perhaps all, of Sally's six children. Only one quarter black, she was depicted as "mighty near white . . . very handsome, long straight hair down her back." All of her children were light-skinned and three of them lived as "members of white society."[1]

What Martha taught me:

The life of Martha Jefferson exemplified for me that some things are simply out of our control. Had medical science been more advanced, Martha might well have lived to see her husband succeed further in his political career. On the other hand, had she lived longer, her husband might be remembered for being a great inventor instead of our third president.

The lesson I learned from Martha is that I needed to become skilled at serenity. "God grant me the serenity to accept the things I cannot change, the courage to change the things I can, and the wisdom to know the difference."

4

Bountiful Hostess to All

DOLLEY MADISON

> There is one secret, and that is the power we all have in forming our own destinies.
>
> —DOLLEY MADISON

WHETHER THE actual birth certificate read Dorothea, Dorothy, or simply Dolley, as some historians believe, they all agree that Dolley Madison was one of our nation's most popular hostesses. She was also the courageous individual responsible for saving Gilbert Stuart's famous portrait of George Washington during the War of 1812.

But perhaps more important than the former president's picture were the meticulously maintained notes that her husband, James Madison, now recognized as the Father of the Constitution, recorded behind closed door Continental Congress meetings. In order to save her husband's significant congressional papers, Dolley had to magnanimously sacrifice her own personal belongings.

The year was 1814, and former secretary of state James Madison had succeeded Thomas Jefferson as our fourth president of the

#4 Dolley Payne Todd Madison
Born: May 20, 1768
Birthplace: Guilford County, North Carolina
Married: 1790 (John Todd) Died 1794 (James Madison)
Children: 2 with Todd 0 with Madison
White House Years: 1809–1817
Died: July 12, 1849
Fact: Raised Quaker, became national hostess
Aka: The Presidentress

United States. The Constitution, which Founding Father George Washington had feared would survive only two decades, was now twenty-three years strong. Britain's continued denial of the colonies' independence only strengthened America's resolve to protect the Constitution and continue the fight for autonomy. A two-year battle ensued, now known as the War of 1812, during which the British attacked America, gutted Washington, DC, and left the White House a burned-out shell.

In her own handwritten letters, Dolley documented her refusal to leave the executive mansion until the very last minute. She did not depart until literally all her friends, acquaintances, and even guards stationed to protect her had left the city.

Tuesday Aug. 23, 1814.

Dear Sister.

My husband left me yesterday [morning] to join Gen. Winder. He enquired anxiously whether I had courage, or firmness to remain in the President's house until his return . . . on my assurance that I had no fear but for him and the success of our army, he left . . . he desires I should be ready at a moment's warning to enter my carriage and leave the city; that the enemy seemed stronger than had been reported and that it might happen that they would reach the city, with intention to destroy it. . . . I am accordingly ready; I have pressed as many cabinet papers into trunks as to fill one carriage; our private property must be sacrificed, as it is impossible to procure wagons for its transportation. I am determined not to go myself until I see Mr. Madison safe, and he can accompany me, as I hear of much hostility towards him . . . My friends and acquaintances are all gone; Even Col. Col. C— with his hundred men, who were stationed as a guard in the enclosure . . . (Wednesday)

Our kind friend, Mr. Carroll, has come to hasten my departure, and is in a very bad humor with me because I insist on waiting until the large picture of Gen. Washington is secured, and it requires to be unscrewed from the wall. This process was found too tedious for these perilous moments; I have ordered the frame to be broken, and the canvass taken out . . . And now, dear sister, I must leave this house, or the retreating army will make me a prisoner in it. . . . When I shall again write you, or where I shall be tomorrow, I cannot tell!![1]

In addition to Dolley's courage and patriotism during the war, she will always be remembered for her warm and gracious hospitality, as well as her bountiful and extravagant meals. It was people, not politics, that mattered most to her. In a letter to her sister, Dolley wrote: "Politics is the business of men. I don't care what offices they may hold, or who supports them. I care only about people."[2] Dolley's policy of nonpartisanship was genuine, and she made each and every guest feel like the most important person in the room.

With the ability to never forget a name, coupled with her poise and nonjudgmental graciousness, Dolley proved indispensable in the world of politics. Individuals who met her were quoted as saying that she was "all things to all men" and "you cannot discover who are her husband's friends or foes."

Dolley would carry the latest book with her, often using it to put people at ease when there was a lull in the conversation. She once wrote to a niece asking: "Do you ever get hold of a clever novel, new or old, that you could send me? I bought [James Fenimore] Cooper's last [presumably *The Water Witch*], but did not care for it, because the story was so full of horrors."[3]

Her popularity was so immense that Dolley was often credited with her husband's presidential reelection in 1813. Reportedly, James' opponents complained of having to run "against both Madisons." In the end, former president John Adams marveled that Madison somehow managed to establish "more Union, than all his three Predecessors." I trust he meant the president and Dolley Madison.

The woman who brought the "First Ladyship" out of the president's shadow and into its own status had a unique talent for sharing her generosity and kindness with the entire nation. It was only her heartache and grief that Dolley kept to herself. Learning the rest of her story made it possible for me to truly appreciate her accomplishments.

Born the eldest daughter of eight children in 1768, Dolley was raised in a strict yet loving Quaker family. In her early childhood, she lived on her mother's family plantation and attended a Quaker school. Wearing dull Quaker clothes and adhering to all the church's principles, Dolley and her family were spared the bloodshed of the Revolutionary War, as their religion forbade fighting.

When her father, John Payne, went bankrupt, the Quaker community disowned him. Within three years, he died a penniless recluse, and her mother, Mary Coles Payne, was forced to open a boardinghouse to support the family. Nonetheless, Dolley remained devoted to the Quaker restrictions and continued to live within its restrictions.

After turning down several proposals of marriage, she finally accepted the hand of John Todd, a bright Quaker lawyer who had pursued her for several years. Some say she accepted partly out of gratitude to him and partly out of respect for his personal qualities. It was John Todd who had rescued the Payne family from hopelessly poor conditions, providing lodging and food from his own pocket when it was most needed.

Four months before her twenty-second birthday, she and John were married. The Todd marriage proved happy and successful, producing two sons.* Then the terror of yellow fever erupted in 1793 and entire cities began dying. John sent his wife and babies away, gallantly staying behind to write wills for those who were infected and caring for his own parents when they were stricken.

When John himself became ill, Dolley returned to care for him; he soon died in her arms. Isolated, Dolley and her newborn son became

* John Payne Todd (1790–1852), William Temple Todd (1793–1793).

incapacitated, infected with the fever as well. She recovered, but baby William did not.

A widow at twenty-five, with only one surviving son, Dolley was growing into the next phase of her life. She sought the advice of Senator Aaron Burr (who later became Thomas Jefferson's vice president), a former boarder in her mother's boardinghouse and longtime friend. People speculated that Burr was courting her, but it was James Madison, the devoted bachelor and well-established lawyer and statesman, who won her heart.

James, standing only five foot four inches tall and weighing scarcely a hundred pounds, known as the "Great Little Madison," was smitten from the minute he met the blue-eyed, jet-black-haired, five-foot-six Quaker. It was Martha Washington who encouraged Dolley: "If it is so, do not be ashamed to confess it; rather be proud; he will make thee a good husband, and all the better for being so much older [by seventeen years]. We both approve of it; the esteem and friendship existing between Mr. Madison and my husband is very great, and we would wish thee to be happy."[4]

Dolley gave up her devout commitment to Quakerism at twenty-six when she married forty-three-year-old James, in her sister's (Lucy Payne Washington) home. (Lucy had eloped at fifteen with President George Washington's nephew.) Upon their marriage, Dolley wrote to a friend: "I give my hand to the man who of all others I most admire . . . In this union, I have every thing that is soothing and grateful in prospect and my little Payne will have a generous and tender protector." Madison was an Episcopalian, and Dolley understood that the Quaker community would disown her; however, Dolley's new commitment was now to the man she admired, more so than to her religion.

The plain, reserved Quaker housewife James married blossomed into a national icon. Already a seasoned member of the U. S. House of Representatives, the very shy yet brilliant Madison was on a visibly unstoppable career path. What is not clear is whether James wanted more children. It is probably fortunate that the couple never had any children, as it soon became apparent that Dolley's son, John Payne

Todd (always called Payne), proved to be more than either of them could handle.

Within seven years, Thomas Jefferson would appoint Madison his secretary of state. Because both President Jefferson and Vice President Aaron Burr were widowers, Dolley would frequently step in as White House hostess. (Years later, when Madison ran for the presidency on the Democratic-Republican ticket, Federalist newspapers—the political party of Washington and Adams—went so far as to imply that Dolley had been intimate with Jefferson.) Dolley loved being center stage and would light up a room with her charm, dimpled cheeks, and warm laughter.

Quickly becoming a fashion statement with Empire-waist dresses made of silk and satin, Dolley became known for her exquisite velvet and satin turbans with towering bird feathers. Even her use of snuff, which she carried in a gold and enamel snuffbox, became fashionable. It was the tobacco addiction of the day.

While Dolley was emerging as a skillful, competent stateswoman, her son Payne was growing up to be a self-indulgent, dishonest, drunken playboy whom she was constantly bailing out of debt. Imprisoned for an unknown period of time for gambling debts, Payne was a constant misery and public disgrace to his parents. His stepfather estimated that they had spent forty thousand dollars (an exceptionally large sum of money in the early 1800s) in efforts to help him.

In 1809, Madison was elected the country's fourth president on the Democratic-Republican ticket and Dolley effortlessly waltzed into the role she was born to live. Soon her penchant for bountiful entertaining was renowned. It was said of the First Lady that she thought "abundance was preferable to elegance; that circumstances formed customs, and customs formed taste."[5]

Wanting to convey her country's prosperity, Dolley did so by demonstrating its resources. (Resources were so plentiful that more and more individuals sought refuge in the new nation. By 1810 the third national census recorded 7,239,881 people living in the United States.) She enjoyed informal entertaining where she could move from room to room, greeting her guests and attending to their needs. The First Lady hosted a large weekly invitation-only dinner party, and every Wednesday opened her drawing room to everyone. Even her husband's enemies were greeted with gracious hospitality.

Less than ninety days prior to the United States declaring war on Britain (the War of 1812), Dolley arranged the first wedding ever held in the executive mansion. It celebrated the union of her widowed sister, Lucy Washington, to Supreme Court Justice Thomas Todd (no relation to her former brother-in-law John Todd). The country's most illustrious hostess was simply repaying the favor for being married in Lucy's home eighteen years earlier.

Within two weeks of Madison's declaration of war, the first interest-bearing treasury notes in the United States were authorized to help support the military. Fighting soldiers were naturally concerned as to how the First Lady's Quaker training would affect them. "[I] have always been an advocate for fighting when assailed,"[6] Dolley assured them.

Very early in the war, the United States suffered a series of defeats at the hands of the British. Add to that the country's continual struggle with the Indians, and soon each conflict became crucial. Britain's early successes motivated many Indian tribes to attack remote military outposts to help defeat the Americans.

The Battle of Fort Harrison, fought in Indiana territory, was considered the first land victory for the United States in the War of 1812. For his gallant conduct in defending the fort, a young captain (and future president) by the name of Zachary Taylor received his first honorary acknowledgments from his government.

The war raged on for two years. After witnessing a British attack Francis Scott Key composed the celebrated song, "The Star Spangled Banner." Just three months later, in 1814, a peace treaty with Britain was signed.

Following the war, with the president's home now destroyed, the first family moved into a nearby townhouse, where Dolley's receptions remained the nucleus of Washington society until the end of her husband's term. When the British burned Washington, DC, which included the destruction of the Library of Congress, the members of

Congress decided to purchase former president Thomas Jefferson's personal library and begin anew.

While the administration was rebuilding, Jane Austen wrote *Pride and Prejudice*, Washington Irving wrote *Rip Van Winkle*, and the Grimm Brothers published children's books entitled *Little Red-Riding Hood, Snow White, Cinderella*, and *Tom Thumb*, which they called "fairy tales." Both the stethoscope and kaleidoscope were invented; and, considering that the number of cotton mills quadrupled in one year, totaling 269, it is understandable that the United States' leading export became cotton.

It was also during Madison's term that the public debt first exceeded a hundred million dollars. Mordecai Manuel Noah was appointed the first Jewish diplomatic representative of the United States, to Tunis. And, although New York City had become the largest city in the United States, Baltimore, Maryland, was the first city to be lit by gas.

In 1817, after eight years of officiating as First Lady, Dolley retired with James to Montpellier, their estate in Virginia. Although she would have liked to travel, and missed keeping up with the latest fashions, her husband's declining health prevented it. Dolley also cared for her elderly mother-in-law, Nelly Rose Madison, who lived to be ninety-eight years old.

Instead, Dolley devoted herself to organizing and preserving Madison's papers for publication. Although she was surrounded with constant visitors, the heartache she silently bore—her ne'er-do-well son—remained with her throughout her life.

Dolley's extraordinarily happy marriage of nearly forty-two years came to an end when James died at eighty-five. She was forced to sell her property and, penniless from her son's continued debts, the third and concluding phase of her life began. After a nineteen-year absence, Queen Dolley returned to Washington to make yet another new life for herself.

Over the next dozen years she maintained a residence across the street from the White House at Lafayette Square, living in a state of absolute poverty. Fortunately for her, Dolley's universally generous hospitability had not been forgotten. When foreign or domestic officials visited the White House, their trip was not complete until they visited Dolley Madison. Additionally, old friends and former acquaintances would stop by and leave food and other items for her.

She remained a constant visitor and unofficial consultant in the president's home. Chief executives Martin Van Buren, John Tyler, and James K. Polk (whose presidential years collectively ran from 1837 to 1849) all welcomed her presence, while their youthful female hostesses viewed her as a mentor. Dolley recalled her experience in relation to Julia Tyler, President John Tyler's second wife, when she wrote: "I had some small part in elevating a girl in her twenties into the ranks of us old ladies who remember our own days [in the White House]."

The entire House of Representatives also welcomed her with open arms; a resolution was unanimously passed in the House, assuring Dolley a seat within the hall whenever it was her desire to visit.

Congress was eventually persuaded to buy a portion of Madison's records, from the Continental Congress confidential meetings, for thirty thousand dollars. Payne again squandered that amount of money from his mother's assets, plus much more. When Congress purchased the remaining papers for an additional twenty thousand dollars, the money was placed into a trust fund to ensure the proceeds would not fall into her son's hands.

Dolley refused to wilt into old age. Although Dolley was no longer the fashion statement of her youth—her once fashionable clothing and overflowing wardrobe now consisted of shabby old gowns—she maintained the prestige of being a grande dame of etiquette. The former First Lady struggled to keep up appearances and devoted herself to guarding her husband's fame and reputation.

Chairing the drive to raise funds for the Washington Monument, Dolley was present at the laying of its cornerstone on July 4, 1848. Later that same month, fifty-nine years after George Washington was elected the country's first president, women in Seneca Falls, New York, attended a women's rights convention.

Dolley's final grand appearance was at President Polk's last gala before he retired from the presidency. She was received on the dais with her dear friend, outgoing First Lady Sarah Polk. Too weak to attend incoming president Zachary Taylor's inauguration, Dolley received the newly elected chief executive at her residence. He had come to seek her blessing.

Having outlived all her siblings, Dolley had become matriarch to her whole family of nieces and nephews. At eighty-one, she was distressed to hear that President Polk had passed away, just after leaving office. Barely one month later Dolley suffered a stroke, went into a coma, and died.

It was at Dolley's funeral that the earliest public use of the term "First Lady" was documented. President Zachary Taylor referred to Dolley in his eulogy, saying: "She will never be forgotten, because she was truly our First Lady for a half-century." It would still be many years before "First Lady" would become a household term.

Payne Todd shocked the public one last time when he tried to cut his own cousin Annie out of his mother's will. Annie, considered an adopted daughter, was Dolley's niece and constant companion throughout Dolley's widowhood. Payne lost in court and died at the age of sixty, three years after his mother.

What Dolley taught me:

Looking back on Dolley Madison's life, I am reminded of a comment the wonderfully talented late actress Bette Davis made: "Old age isn't for sissies." The older I get, the more piercingly accurate her comment becomes. Consider what Dolley lived through, all before reaching her forty-seventh birthday.

She survived the deadly yellow fever, while watching her closest loved ones die from it. Although she honored Quaker restrictions for twenty-five years, her entire life up to that point, the church excommunicated her because she chose to marry outside its beliefs. She then endured a war that destroyed not only her home, but the majority of her personal belongings as well.

In addition to all the predicable losses that go with living a long life, one would hope that the senior years would at least bring some level of financial security. Yet Dolley lived her senior years in a state of complete and total financial ruin. Dolley taught me that rather than surrendering to loss, participating in life to whatever degree possible remains the more constructive and rewarding choice.

5

European Formal Lady

ELIZABETH MONROE

The drawing room of the president, was opened last night to a beggarly row of empty chairs.

—NATIONAL INTELLIGENCER,
DECEMBER 18, 1819

TO FOLLOW on the heels of Dolley Madison, the nation's favorite hostess, had to be an impossible task. No one could have been so loved or admired—at least not immediately. Add to that an entirely different upbringing and persona, and the challenge is magnified. Could an exquisite woman from considerable wealth, skilled in European metropolitan high society, fill the First Lady's shoes? This is the story of the woman who found herself at that exact impasse.

> **#5 Elizabeth Kortright Monroe**
>
> **Born:** June 30, 1768
> **Birthplace:** New York, New York
> **Married:** 1786 (James Monroe)
> **Children:** 3
> **White House Years:** 1817–1825
> **Died:** September 23, 1830
> **Fact:** Credited with saving Mme. Lafayette's life
> **Aka:** La Belle Américane; Queen Elizabeth

Captain Lawrence Kortright was a prominent merchant and an officer in the British army during the French and Indian War (1754–1763). A loyal Tory merchant, he lost most of his fortune during the American Revolution and remained with his family in the United States after that war.

Daughter Elizabeth Kortright was one of his five children, all born in New York City. Elizabeth was only nine when her mother, Hannah Aspenwall Kortright, died. Raised in New York society by her wealthy paternal grandmother, Elizabeth was well read, but no other information about her education or childhood is known. Unfortunately, no documented quotes from Elizabeth Monroe have survived.

What is evident from the two pictures that exist is that Elizabeth was a great beauty. She had raven-black hair, violet eyes, and was petite, standing about five feet tall. Growing up with privilege and social position, she blossomed into a cultured, sophisticated, and self-confident young woman.

At sixteen, Elizabeth met James Monroe, a handsome Virginia delegate to the Continental Congress. Ten years her senior, James was in New York City, then the capital, on business. It is not known exactly how they were introduced to one another.

The two Episcopalians were immediately captivated with each other. Considering that Elizabeth's father chose not to return to Britain after the war, it is only reasonable that she would eventually marry an American. The particular American Elizabeth fell in love with was wounded in battle fighting for his country, then promoted to the rank of captain by General George Washington for his bravery under fire when Elizabeth was still a child of eight.

The youthful teenager and seasoned American diplomat courted only a brief time before they married the following year at Trinity Episcopal Church in New York. Although it may have appeared to be an unlikely match in the beginning (considering her husband's and father's differing loyalties), the two maintained a devoted marriage for nearly forty-five years. Unlike some of her predecessors, who were separated from their spouse for excessive periods of time, Elizabeth traveled with her husband on all of his diplomatic missions.

Their first child, Eliza, was born the same year they married. Thirteen years would pass before Elizabeth gave birth again, this time to a son, who fell victim to whooping cough at the tender age of two. The Monroes had been married seventeen years when Elizabeth delivered her last child, a daughter named Maria.*

---

* Eliza Kortright (1786–1840), James Spence (1799–1801), Maria Hester (1803–1850).

During that time, the United States elected its first president. And farmers in Pennsylvania, opposed to paying tax on liquor, initiated the Whiskey Rebellion of 1791. James had been elected governor of Virginia, and according to the 1800 census, the population in America had risen to approximately 5.3 million people.

One of the most well-known public figures of her time, Elizabeth Monroe is almost completely unknown today. If her name is recognized at all, it is only because she was the wife of the individual who became the United States minister to France, the successful negotiator of the Louisiana Purchase, a minister to Great Britain, secretary of state, the author of the Monroe Doctrine, and ultimately the fifth president of the United States.

The Monroes moved to Paris in 1794 after President Washington appointed James plenipotentiary minister to France. There Elizabeth learned to speak French and developed a deep appreciation for French styles and formal social customs. Because of her beauty and grace, and her obvious admiration for the French, the local people called her *la belle américaine.*

While in France, Elizabeth associated with European royalty; her eldest daughter, Eliza, went to school with Hortense de Beauharnais (the future queen of Holland) and Caroline Bonaparte, Napoleon Bonaparte's sister (the future queen of Naples).

During her stay, Elizabeth was also credited with saving the life of a Frenchwoman and became highly respected for her courage. The Monroes had come to Paris at the height of the Reign of Terror, a period during the French Revolution characterized by brutal tyranny. Just days before their arrival, one hundred government officials had been beheaded. Additionally, the Marquis de Lafayette, a French nobleman and personal friend of George Washington, had been imprisoned in Germany for his support of the American Revolution. His wife, Madame Lafayette, and other family members were being held in a French prison.

Madame Lafayette watched as her mother and grandmother were taken to the guillotine. It was then that Elizabeth requested she be taken to the prison in the minister's official carriage, with only her servants to accompany her. Upon her arrival, she asked to speak with the prisoner Madame Lafayette.

Thinking she was being called to her death, Madame Lafayette broke down in tears when she saw the wife of the US minister. The crowd that had gathered outside was so moved that they spread word of the two women's meeting and their apparent friendship. Not wanting to offend its American allies, the French government used Madame Monroe's visit to spare Madame Lafayette's life and release her from prison.

Eventually, Elizabeth became very successful in blending European style and elegance with American values and democratic behavior. Slowly the European powers began to recognize America as an independent country.

After fourteen years of diplomatic missions in Europe, the Monroes returned to the United States, and James went back to the Virginia legislature. When Thomas Jefferson was elected president in 1801, he appointed his good friend James as his secretary of state. Monroe remained a cabinet member throughout President Madison's administration as well.

When Monroe was elected to the chief executive position in 1817, Elizabeth did not appear at her husband's swearing-in ceremony, nor did she greet guests at the subsequent reception (both took place in her home), setting a new tone for First Lady protocol. Had the restoration of the White House been completed, after its destruction during the War of 1812, Elizabeth could have remained secluded upstairs, a practice some later First Ladies chose. However, in her own home, Elizabeth's absence felt more personal to Washington society and therefore more offensive.

Once the presidential couple moved into the newly renovated executive mansion, it was the president who took charge of its furnishings. Influenced by their many years of European living (reportedly, the Monroe family spoke only French at home), coupled with their preference for French style, the mansion was painted white and decorated in gilded French Empire furniture. Several items from the "Monroe period"—Louis XVI furnishings and Empire chairs decorated with gold eagles in crimson satin—remain in the White House today.

During her White House years, Elizabeth became debilitated by frequent illnesses; some historians believe she suffered from rheumatism, headaches, and fevers. Some say she suffered from "the falling sickness" (epilepsy), a perplexing and mysterious disease in those days. If this is true it would explain Elizabeth's lack of energy and her desire to withdraw from public view. A local resident confirmed the Monroes "are perfect strangers not only to me but all the citizens,"[1] despite the fact that they lived in Washington for seven years prior to occupying the White House.

Elizabeth's lack of socializing in general—she was rarely seen other than at official functions—and her preference for European traditions (which did not include making or returning visitors' calls) prevented her from cultivating many friendships, at least in the United States. She had established a wide circle of friends in Paris. (The Monroes had been guests at Napoleon's coronation in France.) Elizabeth's behavior, so completely opposite that of Dolly Madison's, gave her the appearance of being aloof and haughty; not to mention, it infuriated Washingtonians.

Whereas Martha Washington was known as "Lady Washington," Abigail Adams as "Mrs. President," and Dolley Madison affectionately called "the Presidentess," Elizabeth Monroe was referred to as "Queen Elizabeth."

Seeking an advocate, Elizabeth received the support of the secretary of state's wife, Louisa Adams, who had been born and educated in Europe. Elizabeth deemed formality an important attribute needed to impress European diplomats and essential for saving her strength.

Eldest daughter Eliza Monroe Hay, who resided at the White House with her husband and children, acted as the official White House hostess for her physically weak mother. However, unlike future White House hostesses who would fill in for ailing First Ladies, Eliza's European training and her friendships with royalty seemed to offend Washington society even more and exacerbated Elizabeth's lack of popularity.

This became very evident when, at seventeen, youngest daughter Maria fell in love with her first cousin Samuel Gouverneur. Samuel, the son of Elizabeth's sister, had come to work as a presidential secretary at the White House.

Eliza announced that her sister's wedding would be a small, private affair "for only forty two personal family and friends"; no diplomats or any other officials were invited. Gifts were specifically indicated as not wanted. This was not a politically correct move, as Elizabeth and many other First Ladies would soon discover. This pronouncement angered both the groom and Washingtonians alike. It caused a breach between Eliza and Maria, and many of the social ladies of the capital boycotted future White House parties, believing the president's wife to be snobbish and aristocratic.

As First Lady, Elizabeth may have been envied for her beauty and elegance, but she was not necessarily liked. Her predecessor left behind some rather large shoes to fill. Elizabeth Monroe's reserved formality was no match for Dolley Madison's spontaneous warmth.

Ironically, Monroe was such a popular president that only one elector out of 232 voted against him in his reelection campaign. Some say the elector cast his opposing vote as a protest against a unanimous election; he believed George Washington was the only man worthy of that honor. Others contend the elector was in fact opposed to the Virginia presidential dynasty. Either way, George Washington remains the only unanimously elected president.

During this period, known as the "era of good feelings," the first American steamship, the *Savannah*, crossed the Atlantic Ocean, and the first high school opened in Boston. Good feelings maybe, only not directed toward the First Lady. Elizabeth's health continued to deteriorate during her husband's second term, and her public appearances grew even more infrequent. This only reinforced the public's mistaken impression of the First Lady.

By the time John Quincy Adams was inaugurated in 1825, Elizabeth was too ill to travel. The Monroes remained in the White House for an additional three weeks before leaving Washington for their home in Oak Hill, Virginia. Spared the hordes of visitors who had inundated Martha Washington and Dolley Madison, Elizabeth lived quietly in retirement with her husband for five years. Subject to several serious illnesses, at one point, Elizabeth was severely burned after collapsing near an open fireplace.

By 1830, Elizabeth was too frail to persevere. She died at age sixty-two, nearly one year before her husband passed away. A close friend of James Monroe described his grief: "I shall never forget the touching grief manifested by the old man on the morning after Mrs. Monroe's death, when he sent for me to go to his room and with trembling frame and streaming eyes spoke of the long years they had spent happily together."[2]

Elizabeth was buried at their modest estate at Oak Hill, only thirty miles away from Washington. Seventy-three years later, her body was moved to Hollywood Cemetery in Richmond, Virginia, to lie beside her husband's body, which was moved there from New York, twenty-two years after his death.[*]

What Elizabeth taught me:

Elizabeth Monroe was strong and insistent when it came to her ideals. Even when her actions were met with public disapproval, she maintained her point of view regarding her stewardship of the White House. By doing so, she demonstrated the importance of taking positive, constructive measures—even when those measures may appear to benefit only oneself. Elizabeth taught me the importance of self-preservation.

By refusing to bow to burdensome social obligations, which was necessary for her own best interest, Elizabeth set a new precedent. In doing so, she aided many appreciative future First Ladies who would follow her lead.

---

[*] When former president James Monroe died on July 4, 1831, he was the third president to pass away on the anniversary of America's Declaration of Independence.

6

Foreign-Born Culture

LOUISA ADAMS

The woman selected for your wife [Abigail Adams] was so highly gifted in mind, with powers so vast, and such quick and clear perception, altogether so superior to the general run of females, you have perhaps formed a too-enlarged opinion of the capacities of our sex . . . and having never witnessed their frailties, are not aware of the dangers to which they are exposed, by acquirements about their strength.

—LOUISA ADAMS, IN A LETTER TO HER
FATHER-IN-LAW, FORMER PRESIDENT JOHN ADAMS

THE AMERICAN REVOLUTION and all the sacrifices it entailed had to be particularly difficult for a young woman born in London and raised in France. Add to that a husband who tells you he loves you, but he loves his country more, and a mother-in-law who happens to be the articulate, politically astute Abigail Adams—the First Lady of Liberty— and you might begin to wonder how you found yourself living in the United States.

It is not unreasonable to think Louisa Adams asked herself that question many times during her marriage. She noted in her journal: "The more I bear, the more is expected of me, and I sink in the efforts I make to answer such expectations. Thus sickness passes for ill temper and suffering for unwillingness and I am decried an incumberance."[1]

> **#6 Louisa Johnson Adams**
>
> **Born:** February 12, 1775
> **Birthplace:** London, England
> **Married:** 1797 (John Quincy Adams)
> **Children:** 4
> **White House Years:** 1825–1829
> **Died:** May 14, 1852
> **Fact:** Only First Lady to be born outside of United States
> **Aka:** The Madam

At the age of forty, looking back on her life from her upstairs bedroom in the White House, it is very plausible that Louisa finally recognized just how sheltered she had been as a young girl. At twenty-two, filled with self-doubts and insecurities, she chose to marry a mature, disciplined thirty-year-old foreigner. Not surprisingly, she had been impressed with John Quincy Adams when they first met in London; but over a quarter of a century had passed since then.

Was it his position that attracted her? After all, he was on a diplomatic mission in her country, and his father was the vice president of the newly created United States. Or was it John's intelligence? He was highly educated, an attribute very attractive to Louisa. On the other hand, John was also cold, reserved, demanding, and insensitive to others; unattractive qualities that only amplified with age. Considering the countless arguments they had during their courtship, not much had changed over the years. John remained impatient and continued to disregard Louisa's needs.

Had Louisa insufficiently focused on their dissimilarities and lack of shared interests? Would the relationship have dissolved had another man come along? Should Louisa have waited for another romance, and what if another one had never come? Considering her loathing for the White House—"There is something in this great unsocial house which depresses my spirits beyond expression and makes it impossible for me to feel at home or to fancy that I have a home any where"—would no romance have been better? Undeniably, it was too late for Louisa to be considering these questions. By understanding more of her life and recognizing some of the pitfalls she failed to recognize, the real question for me was, could much of her unhappiness have been avoided?

Louisa was born in 1775, the second eldest of nine children, to an American father, Joshua Johnson, and British mother, Catherine Nuth Johnson. Barely over five feet tall, with curly hair and a fair complexion, Louisa was tender, sensitive, and shy.

Raised in France, Louisa lived a privileged life and received an impressive education. She developed a love of books, theater, and music; she wrote poetry, sang, and played both the piano and harp; and she spoke English, French, Latin, and Greek.

Yet all the culture and education Louisa received could not equal the lessons that only maturity and life experience bring. In contrast, even before meeting her future daughter-in-law, John's perceptive mother, Abigail Adams, understood the situation: "He [John] must not let Louisa's beauty blind him to her inexperience, the difference in their temperaments, and her European upbringing."

With widely different personalities, tastes, and opinions, John and Louisa were ill suited to one another from the beginning. Yet despite sound advice to the contrary, they were married in London in 1797. To complicate matters more, Louisa's father was now failing in business, while John's father had just been elected to the US presidency.

John's political career came before everything else in his life, and it was inevitable that Louisa would one day be residing in the United States. After four years of marriage living in various parts of Europe, the Adamses set sail for America with their infant son. After meeting her in-laws, the confirmed dedicated loyalists, Louisa, who underestimated her own intellect and talents, said of Abigail: "[She] was in every point of view a superior Woman . . . the equal of every occasion in life who forms a most striking contrast to poor me."

Abigail (at this time the nation's First Lady) had hoped that since her daughter-in-law's father was originally from Maryland, Louisa would feel as strongly about the American Revolution as she and her family did. Louisa, however, was unlike her American father and nothing at all like her mother-in-law. She had no interest in politics, nor did she appreciate her new country's revolution, confirming: "I was not patriotic enough to endure such heavy personal trials for the political welfare of the nation, whose honor was dearly bought at the expense of all domestic happiness." Considering how similar John was to his mother, and how mismatched Louisa was with her husband, it was no surprise that the two women would be in such conflict with one another.

Unlike the aristocratic European circles in which she felt comfortable, Louisa found herself by her own admission "a forlorn stranger in the land of my Fathers." With her parents now living in Washington, DC, impoverished and humiliated, Louisa was feeling embarrassed and self-conscious. She feared people would think that her father had deceived John Adams into marrying his destitute daughter.

Louisa also found herself repeatedly pregnant. According to one account, she had five miscarriages before delivering her first child and was pregnant eleven times during her first thirteen years of marriage.[2]*

Suffering from depression (in all probability due to feelings of inferiority, a disapproving mother-in-law, and devastating miscarriages) poor health (migraine headaches, frequent fainting spells, and difficult deliveries), and locked into a deteriorating marriage as her husband grew more critical and intolerant, Louisa was yet to face her greatest challenges.

Without consulting his wife, John accepted a diplomatic post as minister to Russia. Louisa was horrified, to say the least. Leaving ahead of her, John insisted that Louisa follow with their youngest son, two-year-old Charles Francis. The two older boys (six and eight years old) were to remain in Massachusetts to pursue their educations. Louisa wrote: "In this agony of agonies, can ambition repay such sacrifices? Never!!!"[3]

To Louisa, abandoning her children and responsibilities as a parent was a sin she would never be able to forgive her husband. Making the dangerous transatlantic voyage in 1809, long before today's luxurious ocean liners, with a maid, her niece, and infant son, was noteworthy in itself. She later wrote: "To the end of time, life to me will be a succession of miseries only to cease with existence."

Living in remote, frigid Russia, with no friends and no ability to see her sons during her six-year absence, was merely the beginning of the obstacles Louisa faced. While she was away, both her mother and older sister died. Additionally, Louisa received inadequate pay to run her

---

* George Washington (1801–1829), John II (1803–1834), Charles Francis (1807–1886), Louisa Catherine (1811–1812).

household and perform her hostess duties. She noted in a diary: "Debt and meanness is the penalty imposed by the salary of an American Minister."[4]

Louisa's only morsel of happiness came when she bore another child, a baby girl she named Louisa Catherine after her maternal grandmother (Louisa) and mother (Catherine). When Louisa Catherine died of dysentery at thirteen months old, Louisa's grief was immeasurable: "My heart is almost broken and my temper which was never good suffers in proportion to my grief. . . . My heart is buried in my Louisa's grave and my greatest longing is to be laid beside her."[5]

As if losing her child were not enough, John was then reassigned to London. Expecting to return within a year, he went alone, leaving Louisa in St. Petersburg. It appears from reviewing her correspondence during the separation that Louisa was melancholy about how her marriage had evolved. She wrote to her husband and spoke of her sadness, particularly regarding the lack of happiness between them. Then, to Louisa's astonishment, John summoned her to meet him in Paris, where he was negotiating a treaty between Britain and the United States to end the War of 1812. When John's business in France was completed, they would go to London together and send for their two older sons to join them.

Delighted and filled with hope, Louisa first had to sell most of their possessions, close up their house, and package and ship their books before venturing across war-torn Eastern Europe. She was expected to make this journey by carriage, in the middle of winter, with Charles, now a seven-year-old. She brought along with her a maid and two male servants.

The travelers carried their own food with them, which froze solid and needed to be melted by the heat of candles; and the snow was so deep that a few times they had to be dug out. After losing their way, her exhausted horses needed care, and ill-fitting broken carriage wheels required repair. Adding insult to injury, destitute lodgings were the only accommodations available to them.

At times they crossed over ice so thin that the men had to walk ahead to test its safety. During one stop, Louisa learned of a murder that had taken place on the road the preceding evening. She wrote that "from a proud and foolhardy spirit" she decided to go on. Concerned with thievery, she attempted to hide her money in hopes it would not be lost or stolen.

Louisa continued through Prussia, where she saw fields covered with corpses from the Napoleonic War. Learning that Napoleon had returned to France, after they arrived in Frankfurt her two male servants deserted her. She courageously continued on with only a fourteen-year-old Prussian messenger as escort.

Making a detour in her route to avoid soldiers rallying to Napoleon, Louisa was further delayed when she was mistaken for a Russian because of her Russian carriage. Thinking quickly, Louisa waved an American flag and cried out: *"Vive Napoleon, Vive l'Empereur."* She was able to push on through drunken, undisciplined mobs.

Louisa then learned that forty thousand troops had assembled around Paris, where a battle was impending. She wrote: "This news startled me very much, but on cool reflection I thought it best to persevere . . . I was sure that if there was any danger Mr. Adams would have come to meet me." After six hazardous and treacherous weeks, remarkably, they arrived safely.

Louisa's courage and determination earned her newfound admiration from her husband and respect from her mother-in-law. Abigail apologized for having misjudged her, and Louisa noted in her diary that she should have listened to Abigail's efforts to instruct her. She acknowledged her failure to realize what "a kind and affectionate mother" Abigail could be. Decades later, Louisa wrote of her adventure, entitling it *Narrative of a Journey from St. Petersburg to Paris, 1815.*

When President Monroe appointed John his secretary of state in 1817, the Adamses returned to the United States and the political life that Louisa detested. "It is understood, that a man who is ambitious to become President of the United States must make his wife visit the Ladies of the members of Congress first."[6]

Feeling powerless to protest, Louisa rose to her responsibilities and placed her public duty above her happiness. "Oh these visits make me sick many times, and I really sometimes think they will make me crazy."[7] Paying and receiving innumerable social calls at her husband's insistence, with her hospitable manner Louisa (unlike Elizabeth Monroe) cultivated many relationships.

The Adamses purchased the former home of Dolley and James Madison, where Louisa was praised for her gracious entertaining. One splendid event was given on the tenth anniversary of the Battle of New Orleans. One thousand guests attended to honor General Andrew Jackson for his defeat of the British. On other occasions, Louisa would play the piano and harp, or recite her own poems for her guests. Captivating those who once brought charges of snobbishness, her warmth and charm balanced her husband's dullness.

Sadly, Louisa and John continued to squabble. They fought over money and the lack thereof, how to raise their sons, and where to live. Louisa never stopped battling with her husband's practice of censuring women in general, and herself in particular. At one point, Louisa wrote: "Hanging and marriage were strongly assimilated."[8] Marriage and politics remained the noose around Louisa's neck: "For myself, I have no ambition beyond my present situation . . . the exchange to a more elevated station must put me in a Prison." So when Adams defeated Andrew Jackson in the 1824 presidential election, it was not only the two men who became embittered, but Louisa as well.

Failing to receive the majority of the popular vote, John was charged with winning the election unfairly. He was accused of cutting a deal with the House leader, Henry Clay (who was later appointed Adams' secretary of state), to win the electoral college.

John became depressed by the continued charges that he stole the election, in addition to frustrations within his administration. His already foul disposition only worsened. Louisa advised her husband to ignore his political enemies' attacks, suggesting he "put a little wool in your ears and don't read the papers."[9]

The White House years did nothing to improve Louisa's situation either. John's refusal to discuss any of his business matters with her only reinforced Louisa's insecurity and created a greater wedge between the couple. By now, their marriage was going through a period of estrangement.

Barely speaking to each other, the president and First Lady went so far as to take separate summer vacations. Growing more envious of women who shared relationships of equality with their spouses, like her mother's and mother-in-law's relationships with their husbands, Louisa regrettably felt only "the scorn of her companion."

Believing she was doing something constructive, Louisa took in a niece, Mary Catherine Hellen (her deceased sister's daughter), to live in the White House with the family. Instead, the gesture caused further emotional chaos, creating havoc with her three sons. Mary, a bit of a flirt, was first attracted to her cousin Charles. Soon after she fell in love with Charles's brother, her cousin George, and the two announced their engagement.

Unhappy with this state of affairs, both the First Lady and president opposed the pending marriage between Mary and George. Meanwhile, third brother John II (named after his grandfather, the former president) was expelled from Harvard and returned home. Mary quickly turned her attention to him. In the end, Mary and John II were married in the Blue Room of the White House in 1828. Both George and Charles declined to attend. It was the only time in history, that a president's son married in the White House.

When the president lost reelection to his old nemesis Andrew Jackson, Louisa was only too happy to leave the White House. Unfortunately, Louisa's boys continued to be a source of anxiety and heartache. It was believed that eldest son George used opium to sleep and fathered a child with a maid, middle son John II became an alcoholic, and youngest son Charles kept a working-class mistress. While their father shouted demands and wrote piercing letters to his three sons instructing them on how to conduct themselves, it was their mother who connected with them emotionally.

The gravest news came only one month after the Adamses left the executive mansion. Twenty-eight-year-old George was on board a steamer bound for Washington, DC, when he allegedly committed suicide by jumping overboard and drowning. Ironically, their son's death gave Louisa and John a sense of deep mutual sorrow, something they could at last share together.

Within three years of retiring, the former president returned to the political arena. Upon learning of her husband's decision to seek congressional election, Louisa was reminded that "family is and must ever be the secondary consideration to a zealous Patriot." Forever the fervent patriot, John spent the last seventeen years of his life representing Massachusetts in the House of Representatives.

During that time, Louisa lost another son: John II died from alcoholism at the age of thirty-one. She did receive some joy from assisting her daughter-in-law (and former niece) in raising her two granddaughters when John II's family returned to live with her.

Drawing on her own life experiences, Louisa wrote a play, *The Metropolitan Kaleidoscope.* It was the story of a harsh politician consumed by ambition and his suffering wife. Later, Louisa was the first First Lady to write her memoirs, entitled *Adventures of a Nobody*, which a grandson published years after her death.

That same grandson, who affectionately called his grandmother "the Madam," went on to say of Louisa: "Try as she might, the Madam could never be Bostonian, and it was her cross in life." Another struggle Louisa would never overcome was the shame of her father's financial collapse. She reminded her children: "The injury Mr. Adams received by his marriage with me was the loss of the 5,000 pounds and the having connected himself with a ruined house."[10]

Just prior to their fiftieth wedding anniversary, John experienced a paralyzing attack that confined him at home for four months. The seventy-nine-year-old statesman recuperated and returned to his life's work.

A year and half later, the former president suffered his second paralyzing attack, most likely a stroke. Befitting a proud dedicated supporter of the American Constitution, John collapsed and died on the floor of the Speaker's Room in the House of Representatives.

When Louisa died in 1852 at the age of seventy-seven, four years after her husband, Congress adjourned to attend her funeral. Little comfort, if any, for a marriage filled with disappointment; nonetheless, a small acknowledgment for the woman who endured misery and distress for the land of her fathers.

What Louisa taught me:

Louisa Adams was well educated, spoke four languages, and demonstrated talent as a musician, author, and poet. Her courage in crossing war-torn Europe was in itself a notable accomplishment. Yet she failed to give herself credit for her achievements. Louisa's aptitude and capability far surpassed many of her contemporaries; in spite of the fact, she felt her abilities and talents did not equal those of others. This is simply a fact of life for all of us.

Louisa illustrated for me that focusing too heavily on our limitations can prove destructive and poisonous. Paradoxically, it was Louisa who said it best: "Under all circumstances we must never desert ourselves."

PART TWO

WOMEN OF THE FRONTIER

WHEN THE UNEDUCATED, sometimes barbaric former general Andrew Jackson was elected president in 1829, it was the end of the Virginian presidential dynasty. Andrew Jackson was the first president born west of the Allegheny Mountains. He had seen many changes in the United States, including the expansion and movement into western territory. The United States had practically doubled in size with the $15 million Louisiana Purchase twenty-six years earlier. In addition to the 846,000 square miles former president Thomas Jefferson bought from Napoleon, future president General William Henry Harrison negotiated treaties to obtain three million additional acres of Indian land.

It was only natural that future White House residents would be born or have lived on the frontier, where schools were scarce, and fashion and etiquette lacked sophistication. Frontier wives appeared to have the greatest distaste for politics and the least desire to occupy the executive mansion.

Of the next three presidential wives, Rachel Jackson and Anna Harrison, two frontier women with minimal aspirations, would see their husbands elected president. Yet they, along with Hannah Van Buren, would not occupy the president's home.

The stories of these three very diverse yet oddly similar women follow.

7

A Scandalous Youthful Blunder

RACHEL JACKSON

To think that thirty years had passed in happy social friendship with society, knowing or thinking no ill to no one—as my
judge will know—how many prayers have I offered up for their
repentance.

—RACHEL JACKSON,
REFERRING TO HER HUSBAND'S POLITICAL ENEMIES

The frontier, so new, and comprising so many hardships and lack of
refinement, was certainly not the ideal place for every woman. It took
a unique female possessed of distinct
qualities (often grounded in religion)
to withstand the loneliness and difficulties of the wilderness. Rachel
Donelson was one such woman.

Rachel was born in June of 1767;
the exact date remains open to conjecture. Some say she was the tenth,
others the ninth, of eleven children.
What historians seem to agree on is
that Rachel came from one of the

#7 Rachel Donelson Jackson
Born: June 1767
Birthplace: Halifax County, Virginia
Married: 1784 (Captain Lewis Robards) Divorced; 1791 and 1794 (Andrew Jackson)
Children: 1 adopted; raised others
White House Years: 1829–1837
Died: December 22, 1818
Fact: 1st First Lady to be divorced
Aka: The Adulterer

largest families in the region and was named after her mother, Rachel
Stockly.

Her father, Colonel John Donelson, was a planter, a surveyor, and
a member of the Virginia House of Burgesses. According to family
folklore, when Rachel was a young girl she spent time at the homes of
George Washington and Thomas Jefferson, political colleagues of her

father. But most of Rachel's early childhood was spent on the family plantation in Virginia, where she received a basic home education that focused primarily on domestic skills and religion.

Described as short, with brown hair and brown eyes, Rachel was an accomplished horsewoman and good dancer. She enjoyed reading, primarily the Bible and other religious works, as well as an extensive collection of poetry.

When she was twelve years old, Rachel's father decided to join a group of men taking up land and moving their families to the Cumberland settlements later known as Tennessee. Husbands and fathers went ahead to survey the land and prepare shelter. The routes safest from Indian attacks were the rivers, yet they were also the slowest. Colonel Donelson, along with some thirty men acting as guards, was in charge of transporting 150 women and children on flatboats down the Holton River to the Tennessee River, down the Tennessee to the Ohio River, then up the Ohio River to the Cumberland River; there they established the first white colony in what today is Nashville.

These early settlers needed courage, stamina, and patience to make their journey. The long, harrowing, and tedious voyage proved strenuous and uncomfortable. Young Rachel proved herself a true frontier woman by coping well with her unsettled surroundings.

Having survived a surprise Cherokee Indian attack, many settlers became sick from exposure or smallpox when a food-filled cargo canoe overturned in a set of rapids they were crossing. To survive, buffalo hunting parties were organized and other game was trapped. The kill was dragged back to camp for food; fat was rendered for oil and animal hides and pelts were made into clothing.

Once the arduous four-month, nearly thousand-mile expedition was completed, the job of making a home in the wilderness began. Older, more experienced settlers helped immigrants build log cabins and start crops. Although attacking Indians proved they were not going to accept the invaders without a fight, Rachel was courageous and happy, content to live in the wilderness.

Soon it became necessary for the new settlers to carry guns and be on constant guard. Eventually, the warfare between the Indians and pi-oneers drove Donelson to move his family to a larger community in Kentucky.

While in Kentucky, seventeen-year-old Rachel married twenty-seven-year-old Captain Lewis Robards, an insanely jealous and abu-sive man. With the marriage soon in trouble, Robards sent Rachel back home to live with her mother. Mrs. Donelson, now a widow, as her husband had been murdered by an unknown gunman the year Rachel married, was running a boardinghouse to help support her-self and her family. Having male occupants around discouraged In-dian invaders. One of her boarders was Andrew Jackson, an attorney who became fast friends with Rachel.

It was not long before Robards demanded Rachel return to their marriage. After a brief reconciliation with her husband, Robards again sent his wife back to her mother and told her he was filing for divorce. Unlike in modern times, divorce was once widely condemned. Whether a husband had the lack of dignity to leave his wife, or a wife shamefully left her husband, it was the woman who was denounced, and her reputation denigrated.

Humiliated by her circumstances, Rachel returned to her mother's boardinghouse and rekindled her friendship with Andrew. When their friendship turned into genuine love, in the face of Rachel's dis-graced divorce, the two married in 1791. They lived happily together for a couple of years before Robards notified Rachel that he had never filed the final divorce decree. Mortified, Rachel was charged with adultery; her divorce was finalized in 1793. The Jacksons remarried immediately in January 1794. But the damage was done. Rachel, a re-ligious woman, would forever be labeled an adulteress by the press and disapproved of by her contemporaries.

Life went on and, as was common for her day, Rachel managed the household, the farm, production of food and clothing for the couple, and their many slaves. Despite the fact that Rachel bore no offspring of her own, she raised several children (some from her family, some not) left in her care for one reason or another. In 1809, the Jacksons also adopted a twin nephew of hers, whom they named Andrew Jackson Jr.

Years later, when a Creek Indian boy named Lyncoya was orphaned after an attack led by Jackson, then commander of the Tennessee militia, Andrew brought the two-year-old home to be raised with his family.

A fierce American patriot, Jackson was often absent from home, fighting battles against either the Indians or the British. Missing her husband, a discontented Rachel wrote: "Do not, my beloved husband, let the love of country, fame and honor make you forget that you have me. With you I would think them all empty shadows. You will say this is not the language of a patriot, but it is the language of a faithful wife, one I know you esteem and love."[1]

During the War of 1812, unaware that a peace treaty had been signed, Jackson crushed the British at the Battle of New Orleans. In doing so, he returned home a national war hero. When not at war with armies, Jackson would duel anyone who maligned his wife.

Many times during the course of their thirty-seven-year marriage, Andrew was called upon to defend Rachel's honor, as she was frequently depicted as an adulteress and worse. Jackson challenged more than one man to a duel, and when Charles Dickinson, believed to be one of the best pistol shots in the United States, made disparaging remarks about his wife, Jackson heroically confronted him as well. Jackson was hit in the chest first; wounded from his opponent's bullet, which grazed his breastbone and broke some ribs, Jackson then fatally shot Dickinson. Until his final breath, years later, Jackson carried that painful reminder of his love for his wife, inside his body. It appears that a bullet could not kill Jackson, nor the malicious rumors and attacks against his wife. They too continued until her death.

Meanwhile, Jackson's law career was shifting to politics. He served as a delegate to the Tennessee State Constitutional Convention and as a member of the House of Representatives; he did a short four-month stint as governor of Florida (the reason for leaving he simply explained was: "Mrs. Jackson is anxious to return home") and then went on to become a US senator. Jackson was planning to retire from public life when his friends urged his candidacy for president of the United States. Rachel expressed her frustration in a letter to her niece: "I do hope they will leave Mr. Jackson alone . . . He has done his share for his country. How little time he has had to himself or his own interests in the thirty years of our wedded life. In all that time he has not spent one fourth of his days under his own roof."[2]

Andrew won both the popular and electoral votes for president in 1824, but not by the majority needed for election. Both he and Rachel traveled to Washington to be present as the House of Representatives chose the new chief executive. Stunned and embittered when the House elected John Quincy Adams president, Jackson and his supporters believed Adams stole the election.* Soon after, Jackson began to prepare for the 1828 presidential campaign.

The rematch between the two candidates four years later proved to be a particularly malicious and spiteful campaign. In addition to insults directed at Jackson, President Adams's supporters also unmercifully attacked Rachel's reputation. She was referred to as an adulteress and was portrayed as a coarse old woman who smoked a clay pipe, had lived in a log cabin, spoke with poor syntax, and misspelled her words.

Technically, you could say the above was true, yet those idiosyncrasies were not particularly relevant to Rachel's character. Nor did any of the disparaging comments made about her have anything to do with her husband's ability to govern the nation.

Other things were also true: Rachel stayed informed regarding her husband's career, her letters straightforwardly conveyed her opinions, she possessed a rare ability to remember the names and titles of visitors, addressing each one appropriately, and she also hosted regular gatherings of her husband's political supporters at the Hermitage, their 425-acre estate. The Hermitage had evolved over the years, and Rachel

---

* Jackson ultimately became the first president who received a plurality of popular votes but failed to win the election.

had a direct role in the management and design of the plantation; additionally, she supervised the many slave families working there.

The year 1828 proved to be very distressing and painful. In addition to an anti-Jackson pamphlet called "Truth's Advocate" containing an enormously shameful depiction of Rachel as an adulterer, bigamist, and divorcée, a newspaper editorial asked the question: "Ought a convicted adulteress and her paramour husband to be placed in the highest offices of this free and Christian land?" Then, suddenly, while working at the Hermitage, Rachel's sixteen-year-old adopted son, Lyncoya, died.

Soon after, Rachel learned of her husband's political triumph over his archrival John Quincy Adams; being the religious woman she was, she said: "For Mr Jackson's sake, I am glad, but for myself I had rather be a doorkeeper in the house of my Lord than to live in that palace [the White House] in Washington."

Despite Jackson's desperate attempts to shield her, Rachel did learn of the offensive insults directed at her after he won the presidential election. Devastated by the cruel comments, she wrote to a friend: "The enemies of the General have dipped their arrows in wormwood [poison] and gall and sped them at me. Almighty God was there ever any thing to equal it." Rachel went on and told a niece: "Listening to them, it seemed as if a veil was lifted and I saw myself, whom you have all guarded from outside criticism and surrounded with flattering delusions, as others see me, a poor old woman. I will not go to Washington, but stay here as often before in Mr. Jackson's absences."[3]

As fate would have it, Rachel never did go to Washington. In fact, several of her family and friends, including her husband, believed the shameful depictions of Rachel literally killed her. Just two months prior to Jackson's swearing in, sixty-one-year-old Rachel died from what appeared to be a broken heart, most likely a heart attack.

Rachel was laid to rest in the white gown she had planned to wear to her husband's inauguration. Newspapers across the country reported her death. On Christmas Eve 1828, ten thousand people attended the First Lady–elect's funeral. Speaking at his wife's ceremony,

Jackson said: "I am now President of the United States and in a short time must take my way to the metropolis of my country; and if it had been God's will, I would have been grateful for the privilege of taking her to my post of honor and seating her by my side; but Providence knew what was best for her. For myself, I bow to God's will, and go alone to the place of new and arduous duties."

Before entering the White House a broken, lonely widower, the president said: "May God almighty forgive her murderers as I know she forgave them. I never can."[4] On Rachel's grave he placed a tablet that read: "A being so gentle and so virtuous slander might wound, but could not dishonor."

In deep mourning throughout his presidency, Jackson always carried a locket with a cameo picture of his wife. Placing it on his night stand every evening, his wife's face was the last thing he saw before retiring, and the first thing he saw every morning.

What Rachel taught me:

Identifying with Rachel Jackson's life, I remember as a young girl reciting the popular nursery rhyme "Sticks and stones may break my bones, but words can never hurt me." I also recall not being totally convinced of that.

Why did mere words hurt so much? Was it because the words were so maliciously offensive, or because there was some truth in them? Rachel taught me not to allow scandal and gossip to define who I am. Embarrassment and shame should come as a result of one's intentions and actions, not malicious gossip.

I have learned you can prevent things that may cause regret in the future by making better choices in the present. But if a situation has already occurred, the best you can do is rectify it, apologize for it if appropriate, and by all means learn and grow from the experience. After all, is that not the main purpose of life?

8

Matt's Dutch Sweetheart

HANNAH VAN BUREN

Her loving, gentle disposition emphasized her modest, even timid manner.

—DESCRIPTION OF HANNAH VAN BUREN
BY HER NIECE MARY CANTINE

AS WITH MARTHA JEFFERSON, relatively little is known about Hannah Van Buren's life, and there is no surviving documentation of her words. This lack of information is probably due to the fact that both she and Martha died eighteen years before their husbands, Thomas and Martin, became president. Also it was considered an insult to refer publicly to a lady during the early 1800s.

> **#8 Hannah Hoes Van Buren**
>
> **Born:** March 8, 1783
> **Birthplace:** Kinderhook, New York
> **Married:** 1807 (Martin Van Buren)
> **Children:** 4
> **White House Years:** 1837–1841
> **Died:** February 5, 1819
> **Fact:** Died 18 years before husband became president
> **Aka:** Jannetje

Neither husband mentioned his wife in his written communications (Van Buren's eight-hundred-page autobiography focused exclusively on politics and public affairs), and each man remained a widower for forty-three years after his wife's passing.

Ironically, the two women shared other similarities as well. At twenty-three, both married lawyers and were reported to have happy yet short-lived marriages of less than twelve years. Both died in their early thirties, but not before they had experienced the heartache of losing a child.

Here were two would-be First Ladies with similar life experiences, yet neither knew of the other's existence. Hannah Van Buren was born just six months after Martha Jefferson passed away. Nonetheless, their fleeting lives remain linked in history.

Hannah Hoes was born in Kinderhook, New York, in 1783. Attractive, small, and fragile, she was deeply involved with the Dutch Reformed religion. Completely devoted to the church's charitable works, both the needy and poor were said to know Hannah better than anyone outside her own family. Hannah and Martin, distant cousins (like Abigail and John Adams before them and Eleanor and Franklin Roosevelt after them) only a few months apart in age, grew up in the same Dutch community. They were childhood sweethearts who attended the same village school.

The Hoes, Van Burens, and Van Alens, all of Dutch descent, had a history of intermarriage. Martin Van Buren's mother, Maria, was born a Hoes and initially married a Van Alen.[1] After giving birth to three children, she was widowed. Maria then married Abraham Van Buren and had five more children with him. Succeeding generations from the Kinderhook region, where the three families lived, were all more or less kin.

Although Jannetje (Hannah) and Matt (Martin), as they called one another, pledged themselves to each other early on, though they did not marry until Martin was an established lawyer. Hannah was then twenty-three years old. We know the couple spoke Dutch in their home, as did the other members of their community; and Hannah bore four sons during her nearly twelve-year marriage.* Some early historians, like Laura Holloway and Mary Whitton, speculate that Hannah had a fifth son who died in infancy the same year she passed away.

The Van Burens lived in Albany, New York, where the winters were particularly cold and wet, which may have contributed to Hannah's poor health. Tuberculosis cut this young mother's life short at the age of thirty-five.

Historian Laura Holloway obtained a description of Hannah's

---

* Abraham (1807–1873), John (1810–1866), Martin Jr. (1812–1855), Smith Thompson (1817–1876).

death given in 1880 by her seventy-plus-year-old niece, Mary Cantine: "Hours before Aunt Hannah's death . . . her youngest child still an infant [purportedly a son who also died that same year] . . . Hannah called her four juvenile sons [ages two to ten years old] into her room and with utmost composure bade them farewell."[2]

Hannah requested that the customary mourning scarves be eliminated from her funeral and the money that would have been spent on them be given to charity. Her obituary read in part: "Modest and unassuming, possessing the most engaging simplicity of manner, her heart was the residence of every kind affection, and glowed with the sympathy for the wants . . . of others. No love of show . . .no ambitious desires . . . no pride of ostentation."[3] Her gravestone reads: "A sincere Christian, dutiful child, tender mother and most affectionate wife; precious shall be the memory of her virtue."[4]

Van Buren remained a widower and brought all four of his adult sons to live in the White House with him in 1837. Eldest son Abraham became President Van Buren's private secretary. His wife, Angelica Singleton Van Buren (a cousin to Dolley Madison), was a young, attractive woman with dark curly hair and a fair complexion; she came from a wealthy family and had attended prestigious schools.

Angelica, described in the *Boston Globe* as "a lady of rare accomplishments, vivacious in her conversation and universally admired," served as White House hostess during Van Buren's administration. It is Angelica's portrait, not Hannah's, which hangs in the White House.

What Hannah taught me:

Hannah Van Buren's core values were revealed in her request for the elimination of mourning scarves from her funeral, proposing instead that the money be given to charity. By living her values, I believe a young mother was granted the inner peace and composure to remain strong to the very end of her ephemeral life. This valiant, kindhearted woman taught me to live my values—merely having them is insufficient.

9

Frontier Matriarch

ANNA HARRISON

I hope my dear, you will always bear upon your mind that you are born to die and we know not how soon death may overtake us, it will be of little consequence if we are rightly prepared for the event.

—ANNA HARRISON, IN A LETTER TO HER SON WILLIAM AFTER HIS YOUNGER BROTHER'S DEATH

ONLY ONE THING distinguishes Anna Harrison from her frontier sisters. Of the thousands of courageous and devout frontier women of her generation, Anna had the good fortune to receive an unusually good education. Considered intelligent with broad teachings, she was the first wife of a president to have had public schooling.

> **#9 Anna Symmes Harrison**
>
> **Born:** July 25, 1775
> **Birthplace:** Morristown, New Jersey
> **Married:** 1795 (William Henry Harrison)
> **Children:** 10
> **White House Years:** 1841
> **Died:** February 25, 1864
> **Fact:** Never saw the White House; gave birth to the greatest number of children
> **Aka:** Ma

Virtually unknown, Anna spent the shortest amount of time as First Lady in history. In fact, she never set foot in the White House. Unlike Martha Jefferson, Hannah Van Buren, and Rachel Jackson, who did not live long enough to see their husbands inaugurated president, Anna survived her husband by twenty-three years. She also bore more children than any other presidential wife and is the only First Lady to also be the grandmother of a president.

Anna was born in 1775, the year before Thomas Paine published his classic work *Common Sense*—the first attempt to challenge the authority of the British government in plain, passionate language for the people of the colonies. Now forgotten, Anna's story contains tragedy, sadness, and most important—a vital life lesson.

Anna Tuthill Symmes was introduced to death at a very young age. Her mother, who had the identical name, died one year after her daughter's birth. (Some believe Anna was three years old; in either case, she was deprived of knowing her biological mother.) What's more, young Anna lived to bury the majority of her family and loved ones. So when she spoke to her fifteen-year-old son William of his baby brother's death, her depth of understanding came from her own painful experiences.

Anna had only one sister, Maria, thirteen years her senior. When she was still a young child her father, Judge John Cleves Symmes, took his younger daughter to live with her maternal grandparents in New York. The tale passed down through history is that, disguised as a red-coat, the nearly fifty-year-old Symmes stuffed Anna into a saddlebag and maneuvered around enemy camps in order to get her from New Jersey to Long Island.

While Anna was being safely cared for by her grandparents, Symmes, a member of the Continental Army, returned to fight as a colonel in the American Revolution. During her father's absence Anna's grandparents provided her with the finest education. By the time she was eight years old, Noah Webster had written his *Blue-Backed Speller*, which standardized the teaching of spelling and grammar for generations of future Americans.

Anna attended Clinton Academy and later a boarding school in New York City. As the family were devout Presbyterians, religious training was included in her daily routine. This foundation of faith sustained Anna through times of sorrow.

When the Revolutionary War ended, Anna's father was appointed to the Continental Congress and they moved to New York City. After Judge Symmes married his third wife, he decided to return to the Northwest Territory (now Ohio) and settle there with Anna, who had developed a very close relationship with her stepmother. Anna's older, and now married sister, Maria, was living in Lexington, Kentucky.

At nineteen Anna was petite, about five foot one, with dark hair, large brown eyes, and a cleft chin. While visiting Maria in Kentucky, Anna met Lieutenant William Henry Harrison, a seasoned soldier who had been forced to drop out of medical school and join the army when his funds ran dry. Harrison served under George Washington in the Continental Army and his own father, Benjamin Harrison V, was a signer of the Declaration of Independence. When her sweetheart was sent back to war, Anna began what was to become an integral part of her life: waiting anxiously for Harrison to return.

Harrison did return home, now a captain, and asked Judge Symmes for Anna's hand in marriage. Concerned the career soldier could not properly provide for her, the judge answered with a resounding "No!" Against her father's wishes, the independent twenty-year-old Anna waited for her father to leave home before she walked down to the local justice of the peace and married her military officer.

When Symmes learned of the marriage, he confronted his new son-in-law by asking, "How do you plan to support my daughter?" "With my sword, sir, and my good right arm," replied Harrison. Having been a soldier himself, Judge Symmes appeared to appreciate William's spirit and offered his hand in friendship. Even so, he wrote to a friend in frustration: "If I knew what to make of Captain Harrison, I could easily take proper arrangements for his family, but he can neither bleed, plead, nor preach, and if he could plow I should be satisfied."[1]*

A couple of years into the marriage, Captain Harrison resigned from the army when President John Adams appointed him secretary of the Northwest Territory at a salary of twelve hundred dollars a year. He became very successful at negotiating treaties with the Indians and was later appointed superintendent of Indian Affairs and territorial

---

* During that time "bleed, plead, and preach" referred to occupations. Doctors "bleed" their patients, attorneys "plead" their clients' cases, and ministers "preach" to their congregation. Finally, Judge Symmes would have been happy had his new son-in-law been a farmer who could "plow" a field.

governor of Indiana. Harrison held that position for thirteen years, under presidents Adams, Jefferson, and Madison.

Frontier life in the 1800s was strenuous, crude, dangerous, and financially barren, yet Anna and William's marriage proved to be a solid and happy union. Anna remained in the wilderness, having one child after another, almost every two years like clockwork, totaling ten altogether.*

It was not uncommon for many wives to return to the East, specifically because of the many difficulties existing in the territories; Indian raids were a large concern. Anna stayed, however, believing in her husband's duty to his country. Revealing just how isolated she felt, in a letter to a cousin she inquired: "I should like to know, wether your Father is still living, & how many brothers, & Sisters you have, indeed any thing, & every thing, that relates to any of my relations, friends, or acquaintance, will be truly grateting to me, in this far off Country."[2]

Embracing responsibility for her children's religious and secular education, Anna also managed the family's land and finances. Financial record keeping proved to be her weakness, and money became an incessant concern. Predictably, expenses mounted with college tuition and weddings as Anna's sizeable family grew older. The Harrisons always lived humbly, and financially assisted their children's families as well. "Money is very scarce and hard to be got," she wrote to one son.

William, whom Anna addressed as "Paw," remained loyal to the military and returned repeatedly to lead various battles. During the long war years, and there were many of them, Anna had to prepare herself for the possibility that she might never see her husband again.

William defeated the Indians at Tippecanoe, a river running through Indian territory, and during the War of 1812, now as a brigadier general, Harrison fought the British at the Battle of the Thames. Returning a national war hero, William now spent even more time away from home when he became a member of Congress and then the Senate. At long last, William retired in 1829 to their farm in Ohio.

---

* Elizabeth "Betsy" Bassett (1796–1846), John Cleves Symmes (1798–1830), Lucy Singleton (1800–1826), William Henry Jr. (1802–1838), John Scott (1804–1878), Benjamin (1806–1840), Mary Symmes (1809–1842), Carter Bassett (1811–1839), Anna Tuthill (1813–1845), James Findlay (1814–1817).

Grateful to finally have her absent spouse home, Anna was strongly opposed to William's decision to run for president in 1836. Although she was accustomed to supervising many individuals and hosted official functions as the governor's wife, she felt unqualified to serve as First Lady, for several reasons. Not least of these was the fact that both she and her husband were in their sixties and the stress of politicking concerned her. Although William campaigned all week long, Anna persuaded him to refrain on Sundays. When he lost the presidential election to Martin Van Buren she was not disappointed.

Harrison decided to run in a rematch against Van Buren in the 1840 campaign, and this time his supporters were better prepared. Portraying their candidate as a national war hero who lived in a log cabin built with his own hands, their presidential slogan read "Tippecanoe and Tyler Too," thus reminding voters of Harrison's victory over the Indians and including his vice presidential running mate, John Tyler.

Harrison had indeed once lived in a log cabin and defended his country many times; however, he and his family had long ago moved to a lovely three-story brick home with over thirteen rooms. Anna did have memories of protecting her children from frightening Indian raids while her military husband was away, but, thankfully, almost thirty years had passed since his victory at Tippecanoe.

More reluctant than ever, Anna became seriously ill. By then she had lost five adult children (all in their twenties and thirties) to various unnamed causes and found little peace in her husband's political ambitions. Considering all the illnesses and deaths in her life, one wonders if Anna ever regretted that her husband never finished medical school. Harrison completed sixteen weeks of a thirty-two-week course at the University of Pennsylvania. After the death of yet another child, Anna wept openly when her husband won the presidency. "I wish that my husband's friends had left him where he is, happy and contented in retirement," [3] she bemoaned.

On William's sixty-eighth birthday, he traveled to Washington, DC, aboard the Baltimore and Ohio Railroad. Because of her illness, Anna did not attend William's inauguration, although she did plan to travel to Washington in May when the weather was more clement.

The newly elected president rode a white horse to his March 1841 in-auguration at the Capitol building in typically cold and stormy Wash-ington weather.

After delivering the longest inaugural address on record, one hour and forty-five minutes, President Harrison attended three balls. The first was the Native American Inaugural, the second was known simply as the Presidential Inaugural Ball, and the third, attended by a thousand people all paying ten dollars each, was the People's Tippecanoe Ball.[4]

Anna was reluctantly packing up her home when she received word that her husband had died from pneumonia after only thirty-two days in office. Unable to arrive in Washington in time for his fu-neral service and burial, she remained in Ohio. This was the first time in history that a vice president succeeded to the presidency. It was also the first time there were three presidents in the same year (on this point history would repeat itself forty years later). After President Van Buren concluded his four-year term in March 1841, President Harrison was inaugurated and died one month later; President John Tyler was then inaugurated in April of the same year.

At the time of President Harrison's death his estate was in debt. According to a nephew "the numerous creditors [were] . . . howling in every direction for their money."[5] Anna's religious devotion may have grown more passionate with her husband's passing, yet her fi-nancial situation never improved.

Even with the twenty-five-thousand-dollar one-time pension voted her by Congress (some of which went to pay off creditors), like her predecessor, Dolley Madison, Anna sadly needed to scrimp and borrow money throughout her widowhood.

Anna remained in her home for the next seventeen years and con-tinued to keep up with current events. She strongly opposed slavery and had policy differences with the two men, John Tyler and James K. Polk, who immediately succeeded her husband in office.

Even if Anna had occupied the White House, it is unlikely that any of her children would have joined her there, had the president sur-vived. Of Anna's ten children only four were still alive when their fa-ther was elected, and they were then between the ages of twenty-eight and forty-five. Within four years of her husband's death Anna also lost her three remaining daughters.

In the end only one son, John Scott, the father of her grandson Benjamin Harrison, our twenty-third president, survived Anna. This gave her the distinction of being the wife of a president and grandmother of another.

Anna also had the greatest number of grandchildren, forty-eight, and the greatest number of great-grandchildren, 106.[6]* She remains the First Lady who bore the greatest number of children; however, her husband could not claim to be the president with the greatest number of offspring—more information follows in the next biography.

Only after her farm and home burned down did Anna, then eighty-three, move in with her sole surviving child, John Scott. In her mid-eighties when the Civil War broke out, despite her many bereavements, Anna supported her grandson's decision to join the Union army to fight slavery. After burying nine children and her lifelong sweetheart, with whom she had eloped nearly seventy years earlier, Anna died in her son's home at the age of eighty-eight.

What Anna taught me:

Anna Harrison was only First Lady in absentia. Although she neither felt prepared nor desired the position, considering her educational background, strong religious and work ethics, and the empathy she gained from personal losses, it is conceivable Anna would have made an admirable First Lady. As it turned out, she was simply an admirable woman.

Undoubtedly, Anna believed in duty, but it was her husband and family that she was devoted to above all else. Anna taught me that we are all born to die and how very important it is to become skilled at appreciating life in all its fragility. Someday it *will* be gone and for many of us sooner rather than later.

* Thomas Jefferson's descendants, tracked to modern times, are reported to number over 1,200.

PART THREE

WOMEN OF TRANSITION AND EXPANSION

PRESIDENT William Henry Harrison's sudden death took the country by utter surprise. A vice president had never before succeeded to the presidency upon the death of the chief executive. Once again, the still youthful, evolving United States Constitution was going to be debated and challenged for the umpteenth time in its fifty-two-year history.*

It would take two days for Vice President John Tyler to arrive in Washington to be sworn into office. The chief clerk from the Department of State had to hand deliver notification of the president's death to the Tyler's home in Virginia. Since the job of vice president was so minimal, Tyler had returned to his home and family immediately following his inauguration, where he could at least attend to his plantation and personal affairs.

The next eight years would see new developments in the White House. To begin with, John Tyler had never expected to live in Washington, DC, with his eight children and wife of twenty-eight years, let alone get remarried while living in the executive mansion.

---

* Many individuals interpreted the Constitution as intending the vice president to serve as acting president only until a new chief executive could be elected. John Tyler, however, assumed the presidency and unwaveringly exercised all of the privileges and powers associated with the position. He was determined to remain in the White House until the end of Harrison's term.

Within six months of Tyler taking the oath of office the entire cabinet, with the sole exception of the secretary of state, would resign. Within eighteen months, a second unprecedented death would occur in the president's home. Additionally, the United States territory would expand to include Utah, Nevada, Arizona, New Mexico, California, and parts of Colorado and Wyoming.

During this time of transition, Tyler proved to be so autonomous in his thinking that a resolution to impeach him was introduced. Although the nine charges against him were rejected, Tyler was referred to as the "acting president" or "His Accidency." By the end of the term, Tyler's Whig Party did not nominate him as their candidate for re-election; when Tyler left office he was known as "the man without a party."

James K. Polk, the newly elected president in 1845, believed the United States should fulfill its Manifest Destiny, so when a new border dispute erupted, it triggered yet another war. The twenty-eighth (Texas), twenty-ninth (Iowa), and thirtieth (Wisconsin) states were admitted to the Union by the end of Polk's four-year term; the country reached from ocean to ocean. In 1848 alone, a hundred thousand immigrants entered the United States, a historical first.[1]

"Go West, young man" was a commonly repeated phrase, which many heeded. However, making the move was demanding, time consuming, and dangerous. The primary causes of death for those traveling were smallpox and cholera.* Often the location of a pioneer settlement was determined by whether the area was considered healthy enough to live in.

With more and more illness, and considering that women were the primary caregivers in the family, it only made sense that they would eventually go into medicine. Elizabeth Blackwell, well ahead of her time, was the first American woman to earn a medical degree; she

---

* Smallpox, one of the most feared and contagious diseases, is a virus that forms blisters on the skin; the blisters are also found in the mouth and throat, which sometimes prevent breathing. Cholera is another highly contagious disease that causes nausea, vomiting, and chills.

graduated from the Geneva Medical College of New York in 1849. Blackwell, who had to overcome considerable prejudice in her chosen profession, was the individual who reinforced and supported Florence Nightingale's desire to go into medicine.

During that time of social evolution, three vastly different women—an invalid, a want-to-be-queen, and an ambitious politically informed hard worker—would live in the White House with two new chief executives. Undeniably, the year 1841 began fortuitously and the stories of Letitia Tyler, Julia Tyler, and Sarah Polk were about to be written into the history books.

10

Upstairs White House Invalid

LETITIA TYLER

I could not hold up for you a better pattern for your imitation
than . . . presented to you by your Dear Mother.

—JOHN TYLER, TO HIS CHILDREN

IT HAD BEEN twelve years since a presidential wife acted as White
House hostess. Presidents Jackson, Van Buren, and Harrison all
resided in the executive mansion
without their spouses. Prior to that
Louisa Adams was First Lady only
under protest and Elizabeth Monroe
had delegated her official duties to her
daughter.

Enter Letitia Christian Tyler, a
woman whose husband believed there
was no better model to emulate. This
was understandable considering Letitia was a true product of the times.
She followed the tradition of automatically accepting the values of her
Southern father, and later her Southern husband. Described as
"scrupulously attentive to every wish expressed by her husband,"[1] Letitia acquiesced to the wishes and thinking of the men in her life without question.

How this submissive Southern belle answered her call to the White

> **#10A Letitia Christian Tyler**
>
> **Born:** November 1, 1790
> **Birthplace:** New Kent County, Virginia
> **Married:** 1813 (John Tyler)
> **Children:** 8
> **White House Years:** 1841–1845
> **Died:** September 10, 1842
> **Fact:** 1st First Lady to die in White House
> **Aka:** Dear Mother

House is a story more of seclusion than inclusion. Some might believe Letitia's life ended at her property line, while others might say her life began and ended in her bedroom.

Letitia was one of twelve children born into a wealthy Virginia plantation family; it is presumed her early years were typical of her status. This would have included the minimal education given to females— sewing, embroidery, household management, daily Bible readings, and prayer. Not to be overlooked was the supervision and managing of slaves, another integral part of Letitia's training, and a custom she was born into. The year was 1790, and the national census recorded 700,000 slaves (over 50 percent living in the South) out of 3.9 million people.

How slavery and religion became compatible can never be explained. All the same, Letitia was a religious person throughout her life; the Bible and prayer books were the only material she was said to read. She was described as refined and modest, with large black eyes and dark curly hair; her oval face incorporated a rather long nose and delicate features.

Letitia meet John Tyler, an eligible law student from a similar upper-class Southern background, at a private plantation party when both were eighteen years old. They courted for nearly five years before marrying on John's twenty-third birthday. Legend says that John never even dared to so much as kiss his fiancée's hand until three weeks before their wedding.

Many years later, one of the couple's sons described his parents' courtship: "[Father] was much more formal than [men] . . . of today. He was seldom alone with [Mother] . . . before marriage . . .When he visited . . . he was entertained in the parlor where the members of the family were assembled."[2]

Just two years after marrying, Letitia had her first child. Over the next fifteen years, she gave birth to eight children, seven of whom survived childhood.* Life for Letitia consisted of caring for her children

---

* Mary (1815–1848), Robert (1816–1877), John (1819–1896), Letitia (1821–1907), Elizabeth (1823–1850), Anne Contesse (1825–1825), Alice (1827–1854), Taxzewell (1830–1874).

and supervising plantation affairs. Seldom leaving her home, she never had a desire to venture beyond the world and standards she had inherited. Her entire life's vocation consisted of her duties as a wife, mother, and mistress of slaves.

With so many mouths to feed, John was fortunate to have married a woman from a prominent and influential Virginia family. Not that he was without pedigree. His father, John Tyler the elder, had been governor of Virginia; John himself had always wanted to pursue his own interest in politics. When both her parents, Robert and Mary Christian, died shortly after her marriage, Letitia's inheritance provided the financial cushion the family needed.

During all the years her husband was involved in government (legislature, Congress, governor, and Senate), there is no evidence that Letitia took any interest in politics or for that matter anything outside her domestic circle. Other than her family and household, it is probably fair to say Letitia had no other pastimes. "She was perfectly content to be seen only as a part of the existence of her beloved husband; to entertain her neighbors; to sit gently by her child's cradle, reading, knitting or sewing."[3]

Letitia's health began to decline immediately following the birth of her last child; a deteriorating and weakened physical condition was not uncommon for women who had experienced multiple childbirths. By the age of forty-nine Letitia had suffered a major, partially paralyzing stroke. From then on she remained in her bedroom, confined to a wheelchair where she continued to manage the household and read her Bible.

Shortly after Letitia became debilitated, her eldest son, Robert, wed Priscilla Cooper Tyler, a former actress who gave up the theater for marriage. Even though Priscilla's profession was considered scandalous for a woman in the early 1800s, Letitia became very close with Priscilla who wrote of her mother-in-law: "Notwithstanding her very delicate health, Mother attends to and regulates all the household affairs . . . all the clothes for the children, and for the servants, are cut out under her immediate eye, and all the sewing is personally superintended by her . . . all the cake, jellies, custards, and we indulge largely in them, emanate from her."[4]

The following year, Letitia's husband successfully ran for the vice presidency under William Henry Harrison, hero of the massive Indian defeat at Tippecanoe. As vice president, John expected to remain in Williamsburg. In fact, immediately after being sworn into office he left the capital city and was at his home, Sherwood Forest, when the president became ill. It was not until a messenger rode all day and through the night, waking the vice president at dawn, that Tyler learned he was the new chief executive. President Harrison's unexpected death necessitated the Tyler family's move to Washington, DC.

A frail invalid, Letitia arrived at the White House with her three youngest children. She had lost her infant, and her four eldest were all in their twenties and now married. Secluded in her upstairs White House bedroom, Letitia continued to live an entirely private life. The only time she was ever carried downstairs was for her daughter Elizabeth's (aka Lizzie) private wedding. Protecting his wife's privacy, the president was very careful to not satisfy public curiosity about either his wife or her health.

As tradition required, White House entertaining continued, and again the president's home was in need of a hostess. Daughter-in-law Priscilla Tyler graciously stepped into the role, aided by former First Lady Dolley Madison, while Robert served as his father's private secretary. During the three years Priscilla and Robert lived in the White House their second daughter was born.

Very few people outside her immediate family knew Letitia, and we can only speculate as to what her life in the White House was like. With the minuscule amount of information we do have, it is not hard to surmise that Letitia continued to worry about the family finances, just as she had done on the plantation; the household's financial management had always been her responsibility. The Tylers may have been land rich, but they, like George and Martha Washington, were cash poor.

We can also surmise the First Lady had regrets regarding her inability to participate in her husband's social life, as author Arden Davis

Melick suggests in her book *Wives of the Presidents*. With these added encumbrances, in 1842 Letitia suffered a second devastating stroke, destroying any good health she had left.

Meanwhile, her husband's entire cabinet resigned, with only one exception, in protest of his policies. Tyler, a strong supporter of individual states' rights, was burned in effigy by opposing groups that advocated national government.* His adversaries referred to him as "His Accidency." Witnessing her husband's distress on top of her own failing health must have caused Letitia great mental anguish.

Seventeen months into her husband's presidency, Letitia died; she was only fifty-one years old. Letitia was the first First Lady to pass away while her husband was still in office. A funeral for her was held in the East Room of the executive mansion, the same room she had been carried down to for her daughter's wedding the preceding year. Letitia left behind a very lonely husband and seven children, two under the age of fifteen.

What Letitia taught me:

Letitia Tyler was somewhat of a White House phantom. She was for the most part invisible, tacit, and seldom mentioned. In spite of that she was a beloved wife and mother to her family. Letitia taught me that being an invalid does not mean you cannot be in control of your life. Despite her physical limitations, Letitia was able to direct the management of her home and maintain authority over her private environment, feats the most able-bodied person can have difficulty accomplishing.

---

* President Tyler left the Democratic Party because of political differences. Although he was elected vice president on the Whig ticket, he had no alliances to any party or specific group. When the new president began to make policy decisions that did not comply with the Whig political platform, and vetoed a bill they wanted passed, his cabinet resigned.

11

Downstairs White House Romance

JULIA TYLER

After I lost my father I felt differently toward the President. He seemed to fill the place and to be more agreeable in every way than any younger man ever was or could be.

—JULIA TYLER

FOLLOWING LETITIA TYLER, invalid mother, homemaker, and sheltered, secluded wife, was Julia Gardiner, an enticing single socialite who had once lived abroad. Despite their many differences and discrepancy in age Letitia and Julia shared much in common, although their lifestyles were not among those things.

Julia Gardiner lived a fairy-tale life. She was born in 1820 on an island that bore her family name, and both her parents were wealthy and influential. Her father, David Gardiner, was a Yale graduate who practiced law; he was also a former New York senator. Julia's mother, Juliana Gardiner, was the heiress to a wealthy brewmaster.

#10B Julia Gardiner Tyler
Born: May 4, 1820
Birthplace: Gardiner's Island, New York
Married: 1844 (John Tyler)
Children: 7
White House Years: 1841–1845
Died: July 10, 1889
Fact: 1st First Lady to marry a sitting president
Aka: The Rose of Long Island or Her Loveliness

One of four children, Julia was educated in a New York finishing school, and by the time she was fifteen years old she was already thinking of an ideal husband. Julia noted in her diary that she was looking for "a very fine young man" with "considerable property and conversational powers."

Considered a beauty with an hourglass waist, she stood five foot three with dark hair and dark eyes; she was slightly plump and full busted. She loved being on center stage and entertained gentlemen callers by singing and playing the guitar. Always a compulsive flirt, Julia could also be daring and indiscreet. At nineteen, she appeared in an unprecedented advertisement for a retail dry goods store. The caption, which read "The Rose of Long Island," was enough to identify the young socialite.

Her parents were mortified by the vulgarity. A woman's "name" was rarely seen in print during the early nineteenth century, much less her likeness. Hoping the scandal would die away in their absence, the Gardiners took both Julia and her younger sister Margaret (their two older sons were away at school) off to Europe for a yearlong excursion.

Upon Julia's return from Europe, her family's wealth as well as her father's political influence granted her access to Washington's elite society. She and her sister attended congressional debates—more to be seen than for their informative value. Invited to a White House reception, Julia could be found downstairs flirting with President John Tyler while his invalid wife, Letitia, remained upstairs secluded in her bedroom.

Quite the charmer, Julia besieged Washington politicians, and proposals of marriage were in abundance. She received offers from at least two congressmen, a Supreme Court justice, and after his wife's death, from President Tyler himself. Julia said she admired the elegance of the president's conversation, "the incomparable grace of his bearing," and the "silvery sweetness of his voice."[1]

At a White House ball, the president again proposed. Julie later wrote: "I had never thought of love, so I said 'No, no, no,' and shook my head with each word, which flung the tassel of my Greek cap into his face with every move."[2] Despite her refusal of marriage and their thirty-year age difference, Julia continued to socialize with the president.

Early in 1844, Dolley Madison arranged a social cruise down the Potomac aboard the USS *Princeton* gunboat. The president, members of his cabinet, diplomatic corps, and members of Congress and their families were all invited guests. Julia and her father were also asked to join in the festivities. While passing Mount Vernon, the home of former president George Washington, during the firing of new cannon, a gun exploded killing Secretary of the Navy Thomas Walker Gilmer, Secretary of State Abel Parker Upshur, Julia's father, and several others.

Legend has it that upon learning of her father's death, Julia fainted into the president's arms. While she was still unconscious, Tyler carried her off the damaged ship. Julia awoke on the rescue vessel still in the president's clutches.

This tragic accident drew Julia and the president closer together. Within four months of her father's death, Julia accepted the president's repeated proposals. Tyler, the first president to get married while still in office, managed to do so in complete privacy. Their New York church wedding included only Julia's family and a handful of the president's political friends.

No word of the wedding leaked out, surprising the nation and several of Tyler's children when they finally did hear of it. According to historian Carl Sferrazza Anthony, Tyler's son John Jr. was his best man, and eldest son, Robert, with his wife, Priscilla, joined the couple for dinner on their way back to Washington.[3] The *New York Herald* joked in a headline: "Ratified without the consent of the Senate."

Younger than most of her stepdaughters, it was a number of years before Julia won their friendship. But she eventually made amends with her husband's children, with the exception of one: Letitia Tyler, named after her deceased mother, carried hatred toward her stepmother to the grave.

At twenty-four, Julia was younger than any First Lady before her. Wealthy, with no children to care for, living in a mansion with servants and with a nation of admiring fans, Julia adored her role as First Lady, cherishing every regal aspect of it. She orchestrated the Tyler White House as though it were a royal playhouse.

She engaged the showmanship of her sister Margaret, two cousins, and her husband's youngest daughter, Alice, to act as her ladies-in-waiting. They would be a court of four "maids of honor" who broke precedent and stood in the receiving line headed by the president. Julia remarked: "I determined upon and I think I have been successful, in making my Court interesting in youth and beauty. Where ever I go they form my train." Her sister Margaret recalled: "They fell back facing us until we could see a crowd of admiring faces."

With only eight months left in her reign, time was of the essence. Julia made "Hail to the Chief" an official introduction for the president, and it was played whenever the chief executive entered a public function. Musically inclined, Julia played the guitar; the president was a trained violinist. Additionally, the new First Lady introduced waltzes and the polka, dances she loved to perform.

Mentor Dolley Madison was asked her advice, but in the end Julia preferred the more grandiose style of European court customs. Wearing extravagant gowns and jewelry—including jewels above her forehead that gave a crown-like appearance—she would seat herself on a raised platform during formal affairs. This habit earned her the nickname "Her Loveliness."

According to her sister, Julia even secretly employed a press agent to sound her praises "far and near in Washington." Not everyone was enchanted, however. The forever-harsh former president John Quincy Adams wrote: "The Tylers were the laughingstock of official Washington, but they made wonderful copy for reporters." Finally, Julia was not above requesting government appointments or presidential favors for any and all of her immediate or distant relatives.

Family and those who believed that Julia only married for ambition soon discovered she was deeply enamored of her husband. Praising everything John did and defending him against all criticism, Julia was an adoring, supportive wife. The First Lady would go so far as to use her flirtatious mannerisms to encourage support for her husband's policies (for instance, his efforts to annex Texas), and there is no question that she made the president happy.

When the Whig party nominated Henry Clay as their presidential candidate in 1844, Tyler wanted to return to live on his plantation. Before the Tylers left the White House, over three thousand people attended Julia's last presidential ball, prompting Tyler to quip: "No one could now say I am a President with no party!"[4]

Even after leaving the White House and moving to her husband's Richmond, Virginia, plantation, Julia was forever to remain "Mrs. Ex-President Tyler." Maintaining her luxuriant tastes, Julia wrote to her mother: "The full extent or nothing is almost my motto now." She continued to entertain lavishly and extensively, frequently traveled with her husband, and bore him seven children.*

Luckily for Julia, she was blessed with robust health. John Tyler, now the father of fifteen children from two wives, was seventy years old when his last child was born. It appears the former president was also blessed with robust health.

In addition to being caretaker of her family, Julia was now a plantation mistress and needed to spend time and energy supervising and caring for some seventy slaves. Determined to leave her Northern consciousness behind and embrace the Southern slave-owner philosophy, Julia told her brother: "I have turned my back upon New York and aim to become a thorough Virginian." Her advocation of states' rights and the perpetuation of slavery created a rift between herself and her Northern family who supported the Union. In particular, her older brother David disagreed with and fought Julia vehemently.

At the onset of the Civil War, Julia believed the South would prevail. She wrote: "I am utterly ashamed of the State in which I was born, and its people." In her attempt to defend slavery Julia maintained: "Our slaves live better than the poor of London."[5]

Former president Tyler believed in the Union and continually tried to preserve it. He went so far as to lead a peace conference, attended by 133 commissioners from twenty-two states. In the end, remaining devoted to the principle of states' rights, Tyler supported the South's secession from the Union.

The only president who supported the Confederacy, Tyler was

* David Gardiner (1846–1927), John Alexander (1848–1883), Julia (1849–1871), Lachlan (1851–1902), Lyon Gardiner (1853–1935), Robert Fitzwalter (1856–1927), Pearl (1860–1947)

elected to the Confederate Congress. Only one thing could prevent him from taking his congressional seat—just shy of his seventy-second birthday, and before the Confederate Congress assembled, John Tyler died. Buried with a Confederate flag over his coffin; there was no governmental announcement or official notice of his death.

Now a heartbroken forty-one-year-old widow with seven children (ages two to fifteen) to raise and educate, and a plantation with slaves to manage, Julia's princess life was coming to a close. While living in the middle of a bloody civil war zone, Julia had debts on her extensive land holdings to confront, as well as lengthy and bitter legal battles with her family over her mother's estate. She also fought Congress for the five-thousand-dollar annual pension received by other former First Ladies. Needless to say, Congress did not look favorably on her Confederate sympathies.

For more than ten years Julia fought one battle after another. Her plantation was completely vandalized from the war, and she needed to borrow money for living expenses and her children's education. Lawsuits from creditors loomed over her head as well. By 1871, her twenty-two-year-old daughter Julia died, leaving her a baby granddaughter (also her namesake) to raise.

During the depression that followed the Panic of 1873 there was a period during which Julia was in desperate financial straits. Around this time she converted to Roman Catholicism, which appeared to bring her some religious, if not financial, comfort.

Eventually, Julia won her five-year battle with Congress and received the annual five-thousand-dollar presidential widow's pension. As the widow of a veteran—Tyler served briefly with the militia in the War of 1812, never encountering the enemy—Julia claimed an additional eight dollars per month. Her mother's estate was eventually settled, splitting the Gardiner's fortune among several heirs, with Julia receiving some land holdings.

Assisted by her mother's estate, Julia resumed her luxurious lifestyle during the last half-dozen years of her life. Prior to her passing in 1889, she buried her thirty-five-year-old son John and saw another son, Lyon, become a distinguished historian and president of William and Mary College, his father's alma mater.

Twenty-seven years after her husband's death, Julia suffered a cerebral stroke at the age of sixty-nine. Oddly enough, she died in the same Richmond hotel room the former president had passed away in.[6] She was buried in the Hollywood Cemetery in Richmond next to the love of her life, a man she believed had "incomparable grace of . . . bearing."

What Julia taught me:

Julia was a champion of sorts. Not a heroine in the ranks of Martha Washington or Abigail Adams but rather a campaigner for the privileged and wealthy. Historians Dorothy and Carl Schneider called her a "prototype of the self-centered, somewhat spoiled, wealthy young woman." Indeed, that appears to be a fair description. On the other hand, Julia was not malicious.

I am in no way making excuses for her reprobate point of view regarding slavery. But putting aside her Southern beliefs, Julia's other failing could have resulted from her youth. Falling in love with a powerful man old enough to be her father had to have made a serious impression. At a more mature age, under different circumstances, it is feasible that Julia might not have made some of her queenly royal mistakes.

Julia Tyler's life illustrated and reinforced for me how life is ever changing. At various periods in my life I recall wishing that time could be frozen forever, while during others it could not move fast enough. Julia taught me that circumstances never remain the same. In fact, the only thing you can count on in life, thankfully, is change.

12

The CEO's Secretary

SARAH POLK

I have not sought anything. I have not traveled. I have remained at home and received what came to me. And I am satisfied with it, and am not anxious for anything more.

—SARAH POLK

SARAH POLK may well have been satisfied with her life and not anxious for anything more. However, had she been born at a time when women were afforded more opportunities, I wonder if she would have felt the same. Highly intelligent, with political sophistication and ambition, Sarah spent her entire adult life, including the forty-two years she was a widow, devoted to her husband's career.

Sarah's life focus did not resemble that of her immediate predecessors. Never having had children (her husband was believed to be sterile from an early illness), politics was Sarah's surrogate child and fixation. When the other women retired to the parlor, her preference was to remain behind in order to discuss state and government affairs with the men. Serious minded and politically well informed, idle conversation was not her strong suit.

After the fun-loving, juvenile imprudence of Julia Tyler, the coun-

> **#11 Sarah Childress Polk**
>
> **Born:** September 4, 1803
> **Birthplace:** Murfreesboro, Tennessee
> **Married:** January 1, 1824 (James Knox Polk)
> **Children:** none
> **White House Years:** 1845–1849
> **Died:** August 14, 1891
> **Fact:** Acted as presidential secretary
> **Aka:** Sahara Sarah

try was ready for a more mature and principled First Lady. Sarah's position on being a homemaker was clear—one hundred forty-eight years before Hillary Clinton was criticized for commenting, "I suppose I could have stayed home and baked cookies and had teas"—Sarah said: "If I get to the White House, I will neither keep house nor make butter."[1] Her journey to the White House began forty-one years earlier in Murfreesboro, Tennessee.

Born the third of six children, Sarah Childress, like Rachel Jackson, was raised on the frontier. The difference was that it was an entire generation later, and Sarah lived in luxury and dressed in beautiful silks and satins. Her father, Colonel Joel Childress, was a successful tavern keeper, merchant, and militia officer. Sarah's love of politics grew out of acquaintance with her father's social and business circle of friends. Her mother, Elizabeth Whitsett Childress, supported Sarah's religious and moral training, which emphasized manners and respectability.

From early childhood, Sarah learned the value of high principles and received an excellent education for the times. After completing her elementary schooling, she was tutored and then went on to board at Moravian Female Academy, known as the best girls' school in the South. An eager student, she remained an avid reader her entire life.

Sarah's final education was cut somewhat short, unfortunately, when her father died abruptly. Sixteen-year-old Sarah, Spanish looking and fairly tall, with dark eyes and black hair that she wore in formal ringlets on both sides of her oval face, returned home to help her mother. It was not long after that Sarah met James Polk, a young lawyer who had been a schoolmate of her brother. A promising politician himself, although at the time he was only earning six dollars a day as a Senate staffer, James became a good friend and advisor to Andrew Jackson. It was Jackson who advised his young protégé to marry Miss Childress, for several reasons.

To begin with, Jackson liked Sarah immensely, finding her intelligent and ambitious besides being financially self-sufficient. Then a senator, Jackson also believed Sarah was the type of woman "who will never give you [Polk] trouble."[2] Sarah was equally fond of Jackson, whom she called "Uncle Andrew."

After a four-year courtship James, a twenty-eight-year-old Methodist recently elected to the state legislature, and Sarah, a twenty-year-old Presbyterian, had an elaborate New Year's Day wedding ceremony in her mother's home, with eight attendants and a seven-course meal. In attendance was one of James's new colleagues from the legislature. He was the American folk hero known today as "the king of the wild frontier," Davy Crockett. The wedding may well have been sophisticated, but it lacked dancing and the traditional couple's toast: two things Sarah never partook in, as they went against her religious and moral standards.

James began his seven terms in the House of Representatives; for fourteen years Sarah traveled back and forth from Columbia, Tennessee, to Washington, DC. While they were in Washington Sarah and James resided at a boardinghouse with other congressmen. From session to session, they would share meals and discuss political issues with their fellow politicians in the social area of the boardinghouse, referred to as the parlor.

Free from household duties and child-rearing responsibilities, Sarah served as her husband's secretary, advisor, confidante, nurse, observer, and reporter six days a week for his entire career. Sundays, however, were reserved for her religious life; nothing was permitted to interfere with church.

So important was she to her husband's career that a Nashville newspaper called Sarah a "membress of the Congresselect." She was quoted as saying: "I always take a deep interest in State and national affairs."[3] When James campaigned for governor of Tennessee, Sarah organized the campaign, scheduled his speeches, handled his correspondence, and kept him abreast of newspaper reports.

Before long, Sarah's knowledge of politics equaled that of her husband's. And being an efficient manager of the household expenses

proved to be one of her major assets—when Polk won the governorship in 1839, his annual salary was two thousand dollars and their rent
was five hundred dollars a year.

By 1844, James was a dark horse candidate* for president. When
told of his nomination, Polk replied: "It has been well observed that
the office of President of the United States should neither be sought
nor declined. I have never sought it, nor should I feel at liberty to decline it, if conferred upon me by the voluntary suffrages of my fellow
citizens."[4]

With her social graces and clever conversation, socialites and
politicians alike held Sarah in high esteem. A true asset to her husband, Sarah was a particular favorite among the men. The only criticism of her was that she possibly "dominated" her husband. Polk's vice
presidential running mate, George Dallas, said: "She is certainly mistress of herself and I suspect of somebody else also."

After James won the election, Sarah carried her unwavering principles with her to the White House. She continued on as her husband's
personal secretary, assisted with his speeches, took full charge of all
White House papers, and managed the domestic affairs.

Never compromising her values, Sarah asked James to refuse visitors
on Sunday. When she realized this was a favorite time for his political
cronies to see him, she graciously invited callers to join them at church.
Sarah continued this policy until it was apparent to all that Sundays
were off limits—unless of course they wished to attend services.

During previous administrations, both indoor plumbing (1834)
and central heating (1837) were installed in the executive mansion.
Although funds were given to the First Lady to refurbish the White
House, Sarah was careful to save on expenses. She chose not to re-

---

* A dark horse candidate is not expected to even place, let alone come in second or
first in a race. Not considered a contender, James K. Polk's name was not mentioned on the first seven ballots during the Democratic convention in 1844. However, the nomination for president was at a stalemate, and as a compromise
candidate Polk won unanimously on the ninth ballot. He went on to be the first
dark horse candidate elected president.

vamp the private quarters, but did install gas lighting in 1846. As fate would have it, the gas lights failed to operate during the first reception. Both sensible and practical, Sarah was prepared. Just on the off chance the lights did not work, she had thought to provide candles.

A most proper mistress, on one occasion when her husband could not accompany her, the First Lady refused to attend a party where two bachelors—one of whom was James Buchanan, then secretary of state—would be present. Nor would she attend horse races or card parties, as it would "lower the stature of the First Lady."[5] The White House was also void of hard liquor, dancing, and balls. Sarah said: "To dance in these rooms would be undignified, and it would be respectful neither to the house nor the office."[6] Instead, she encouraged the diplomatic exchange of essential state and government business.

One particular item of heavily contested business was the annexation of Texas, then under the Mexican government. Polk's strong defense of the annexation resulted in the Mexican-American War. While the issue was still being debated, Polk wrote a letter to a large contingency of citizens opposed to the annexation:

> . . . having once been a part of our Union, it should never have been dismembered from it. The Government and people of Texas, it is understood, not only give their consent, but are anxiously desirous, to be re-united to the United States. If the application of Texas for a re-union and admission into our Confederacy shall be rejected by the US, there is imminent danger that she will become a dependency, if not a colony, of Great Britain—an event which no American patriot, anxious for the safety and prosperity of this country, could permit to occur without the most strenuous resistance. . . . I should be explicit in the declaration of my opinions.[7]

The president signed it: "I am, with great respect, your obedient servant." Not everyone in the US House of Representatives agreed with the war. Congressman Abraham Lincoln wrote: "I suspect he [Polk] is deeply conscious of being in the wrong—that he feels the blood of this war, like the blood of Abel, is crying to Heaven against him. ...He is a bewildered, confounded, and miserably perplexed man."

The First Lady was in full agreement with her husband's decision. When the war ended in 1848, Mexico received $15 million—less than half of the original offer that the United States proposed for the expansive territory (which is now California, Nevada, Utah, and parts of Colorado, Arizona, New Mexico, and Wyoming) before the hostilities erupted.

One issue the president disagreed with his wife on, although "respecting her viewpoint," was the question of a national bank. James favored "hard money" and did not support the rechartering of the Second Bank of the United States. Sarah favored paper money or bank notes. "Don't you see how troublesome it is to carry around gold and silver?" she asked her husband.*

Freely expressing her opinions privately, Sarah was careful to never publicly discuss subjects considered unladylike or ill-mannered. Politicians admired and respected her ability to remain the consummate female. Dressed in the low-cut gowns popular in her day, when Sarah did discuss political issues she would add, "Mr. Polk believes . . ." or "Mr. Polk suggested . . ." Congressman Franklin Pierce bragged that he preferred discussing politics with Mrs. Polk to any man.

Clearly preferring the company of men to women, Sarah completely identified with her husband and rarely left the White House. Borrowing from her good friend Dolley Madison's handbook, she neither gossiped about nor criticized any individual, making friends even with her husband's enemies.

Believing that being elected meant "hired to work," both Sarah and James were reluctant to waste time in empty socializing, being far more interested in political issues. Out of a desire to maintain rev-

---

* Eventually, in 1863 The National Bank Act would make banks an integral part of American life.

enue for their retirement (the president was expected to use personal funds for entertaining), the First Lady served no food or drink at her twice-weekly receptions. Yet despite her descriptive reputation as "Sahara Sarah" (referring to her ban on hard liquor), guests found her charming and hospitable.

After working in the White House side by side, day and night for four strenuous years, the Polks were ready to return to Nashville for retirement. As they were preparing to leave the executive mansion, the First lady received compliments for dignifying the office.* The *Nashville Union* reported: ". . . a salutary influence . . . By exclusion of frivolities and her excellent deportment in other respects, she [Sarah] has conferred additional dignity upon the executive department of our government."[8]

Immediately after leaving the White House, James wrote the following in his diary:

March 4, 1849

I feel exceedingly relieved that I am now free from all public cares. I am sure I shall be a happier man in my retirement than I have been during the four years I have filled the highest office in the gift of my countrymen.[9]

Sincerely believing he would be happier—"As a private citizen, I will have no one but myself to serve"[10] —James did not realize just how much the presidency had drained him. Literally working himself to death for his country, Polk died a short three months after leaving office. On his deathbed, James told his wife: "I love you Sarah, for all eternity, I love you."[11]

After her husband's passing, Sarah said: "Life was then a blank." Only forty-six years old at the time, she chose to live as a recluse throughout her long widowhood, wearing a widow's cap and black

* Sarah Polk was the first First Lady to be photographed with her husband.

clothing. Remaining a shrewd businesswoman, Sarah took over the long-distance management of her cotton-raising plantation in Mississippi, and after some good years and some bad, ultimately sold it for a profit.

Frugal with public money, Sarah was generous with her own funds, which she used to support orphanages both during and after her White House years. She also gave freely to charity and the construction of public monuments.

When the Civil War broke out, many families—like those of Julia Tyler, Mary Todd Lincoln, and Julia Grant—had divided loyalties. Sarah's own family took the Southern side. Sarah probably did as well, because she too was a slave owner; however, convinced that her late husband would have remained loyal to the Union, she declared herself and her domain totally neutral.

Her position being so clearly reasonable, Sarah received both Union and Confederate officers at her home, all of whom respected her position and her property. The people of Nashville were so trusting and confident in the former First Lady that both public and private treasures were brought to her for safekeeping. With war raging around her that destroyed homes, businesses, and personal lives, Sarah's home and property were miraculously undamaged.

When federal forces took possession of the town, Sarah refused to take an oath of allegiance to the United States. Her position was that, as the widow of a man who had been president of the entire United States, she could not support one party over the other.

Regarding the slavery issue, Sarah simply said: "The war settled all that."[12] Years later, the former First Lady told historian John Robert Irelan: "When it came to actual conflict, and the lives of people with whom I always lived, and whose ways were my ways, my sympathies were with them; but my sympathies did not involve my principles. I have always belonged, and now belong, to the whole country."[13]

Becoming somewhat of a Southern icon, Sarah lived her later years at home, leaving only to attend church. She invited her great-niece (whom some believe she adopted) Sarah Polk Jetton and her family to live with her at "Polk Place," which had become a shrine to James K. Polk. Eternally the devoted wife, Sarah carefully preserved the former president's papers, memorabilia of his career, letters, and even his private diary as a memorial to her late husband.

At Polk Place Sarah continued to graciously acknowledge every visitor or delegation that came to see her. Over thirty years after she left the White House, presidential couples Rutherford and Lucy Hayes and Grover and Frances Cleveland paid their respects to the former First Lady.

Sarah's thriftiness, loyal family, and five-thousand-dollar annual presidential widow's pension from Congress enabled her to live on at Polk Place until her death in 1891, one month shy of her eighty-eighth birthday. She was laid beside her husband in his official burial site at Polk Place; ultimately, the couple was entombed on the Nashville State Capitol grounds.

What Sarah taught me:

Sarah Childress Polk was not only religious, highly principled, and intellectual, she was bright enough not to flaunt her intelligence. She never lost sight of "her place" or the place of women in society during her era. Satisfied with the cards she was dealt, Sarah demonstrated for me how to pursue personal interests and passions even when they are not readily offered to you. By being the consummate lady, Sarah taught me it was possible to successfully blend her private desires with the reality of her life and the world she lived in.

PART FOUR

WOMEN OF THE SLAVERY ISSUE

❧

JAMES K. POLK kept his campaign promise not to seek a second term. By doing so, he could make any policy decision necessary without concern for future political support. As it turned out, he would never have survived an additional four-year tenure. Known as one of the hardest-working presidents we have ever had, Polk consistently worked twelve- to fourteen-hour days and never took more than three days' vacation during his time in the White House. Not that any president ever really gets a vacation. It is a 24-hours-a-day, 7-days-a-week, 365-days-a-year job regardless of which political party is in office.

Now more than ever it was essential that the nation receive strong, principled government. The country was growing embittered and dangerously divided by the immoral issue of slavery. The Union was being torn apart by the abolitionists, who advocated the annulment of slavery, and slave-state politicians, who were fighting to preserve it.

Three pieces of legislation were introduced to stave off conflict between the "free" and "slave" states.

1. *The Compromise of 1850*
   This act provided that the territories of New Mexico, Nevada, Arizona, and Utah be organized without mention of slavery; the territories' inhabitants would decide the slavery

issue later when they applied for statehood. California would be admitted as a free state.

2. *The Fugitive Slave Act*

   This legislation was intended to pacify those favoring slavery; it required citizens to assist in the recovery of fugitive slaves and denied fugitives the right to a jury trial. Additionally, more federal officials would be responsible for enforcing the law.

3. *The Kansas-Nebraska Act*

   This legislation provided for the creation of two new territories—Kansas and Nebraska—the inference being that one territory would be "slave" and the other "free." This contradicted provisions of the Missouri Compromise, whereby slavery would have been barred from both territories. Antislavery forces were enraged, and a bitter three-month congressional debate ensued. All hopes for a peaceful solution to the slavery question were precluded when the act was finally adopted. Opponents of the bill then founded a new political organization, the Republican Party, and the United States was propelled toward civil war.

The ensuing twelve years required equally dedicated, politically minded spouses to champion the chief executive's success, as well as the success of the nation. History accounts the lives of three long-forgotten distracted wives, and the niece to our only bachelor president.

The first two wives are Margaret Taylor and Jane Pierce. No two more reluctant First Ladies would ever occupy the executive mansion. Both prayed fervently that their husbands would lose the presidency. Margaret Taylor was the military wife of a career officer who, because of his constant travels, never once cast a vote in an election. The other, Jane Pierce, was a mentally distraught mother who believed her only surviving child was sacrificed to her husband's political career.

The third wife of this period, Abigail Fillmore, was yet another less than enthusiastic occupant of the executive mansion. A former teacher who married a student nearly two years her junior, she gladly delegated some White House social obligations to her eighteen-year-old daughter. The fourth First Lady, Harriet Lane, was a young relation whose role was solely that of hostess.

Did these women influence history at all during their tenures in the White House? Irrefutably, history influenced them, as you will see in the following stories.

13

The Better Soldier

MARGARET TAYLOR

Return my husband home safely from the Mexican War, and I
shall never go into society again.

—MARGARET TAYLOR, IN A PRAYER TO GOD

A WOMAN not unfamiliar with war, Margaret Taylor was the daughter of a Continental army major who had been a commander during the American Revolution. She married a professional soldier who spent forty years in military service, was the mother of a military son, and had three daughters who married military men. It is no wonder Zachary Taylor once said of his wife: "She was as much of a soldier as I."

Margaret was a good soldier. For over half her life she accompanied her husband from one hardship wilderness post to another. Away from family and friends, she shared the dangers, deprivations, and loneliness of duty in the frontier backwoods. While her husband fought fierce battles with the Indians, Margaret would pray for his safe return. She made a home in winter cabins or summer tents and coped with the diseases indigenous to the various areas they settled in.

> **#12 Margaret Smith Taylor**
>
> **Born:** September 21, 1788
> **Birthplace:** Calvert County, Maryland
> **Married:** 1810 (Zachary Taylor)
> **Children:** 6
> **White House Years:** 1849–1850
> **Died:** August 18, 1852
> **Fact:** Never wanted to be nor acted as White House hostess
> **Aka:** Peggy

Having managed to survive illness, personal loss, and misfortune, and with her husband now sixty-two years old, Margaret supposed the war with Mexico in 1846 would be Zachary's final fight. He had already received the brevet rank of major for gallant conduct, and brevet brigadier general for distinguished service. If he came home safely from this closing battle, Margaret could finally share a quiet retirement with the man she had fallen in love with thirty-six years earlier.

Outnumbered by Mexican troops, Taylor won an important victory at the Battle of Buena Vista and did return home safely. When the war ended General Taylor, nicknamed "Old Rough and Ready," received the written thanks of Congress "for the fortitude, skill, enterprise and courage, which have distinguished the recent operations on the Rio Grande."[1]

Margaret's original prayer—that God send her husband home safely from the Mexican War—was a very common appeal. Individuals everywhere would whisper a silent prayer in times of great trepidation and anguish. Those who did pray were also known to offer something in return, in proof of their sincerity: "If you will honor my request, then I will do something just as substantial in return." It was far more unusual for those praying to hold up their end of the bargain. Margaret Taylor was one of those rare, earnest individuals.

While Margaret stood ready to make good on her word—to never go into society again—Zachary found himself a national war hero. Like those before her (Martha Washington, Anna Harrison, Rachel Jackson) and those after her (Julia Grant and Mamie Eisenhower), Margaret discovered that her country loved to make its war heroes president of the United States.

Just when Margaret believed all her prayers had been answered, the thought of living in the White House instead of the family farm in Kentucky was inconceivable. Her slave-owner husband, who had never voted in an election, had suddenly and unpredictably become a viable candidate for the presidency.

Yet again Margaret found herself praying nightly for her husband's safety. Only this time the battle was being fought on a very different kind of battleground. Would she once more have to be a good soldier? With every fiber of her being she pleaded no. How Margaret found herself at this threshold is a story in itself.

Margaret MacKall Smith was born in 1788 and raised on a Maryland plantation. Both her parents, Walter and Ann, came from wealthy families. Her mother died when Peggy, as her family always called her, was only ten years old, and her father when she was sixteen. Very little is known of Peggy's childhood and history has only a depiction of her physical appearance. It has been said, that she was the youngest of seven siblings and reportedly she was a childhood acquaintance of Nelly Custis, Martha Washington's granddaughter.

Considering her parent's wealth, it is fair to assume that she received the usual educational tutoring that emphasized the administration of domestic household activities. It was also the custom for young women to visit or go to live with relatives in larger, more populated towns, in order to provide them a greater opportunity for marriage.

When her parents died, Margaret went to live with an older married sister who lived in Louisville, Kentucky. It was there that she met and married, at the age of twenty-one, army lieutenant Zachary Taylor, then twenty-five. As a wedding gift Zachary's prosperous father gave him 324 acres of farmland in Kentucky. It proved to be the Taylors' only other dwelling, when Margaret and Zachary were not living at their primary lodging: military forts.

Within a year of marrying, Margaret gave birth to her first daughter, followed by three more over the next eight years.* Around the turn of the nineteenth century, life on isolated outposts could be harsh, providing very few comforts. Medical science was still in its infancy

---

* Anne Margaret (1811–1875), Sarah Knox (1814–1835), Octavia Pannel (1816–1820), Margaret Smith (1819–1820)

and no match for the various diseases that attacked those living in the territories stretching farther and farther west.

One such violent endemic fever took the lives of Margaret's two youngest daughters (one and four years old) in 1820 and endangered Margaret's life as well. Zachary wrote of his wife's illness: "At best her constitution is remarkable[y] delicate . . . my loss will be an irreparable one."[2]

Margaret recovered, although never to the extent that her family ceased to worry about her fragile health. Fortunately, her two older daughters survived, and years later Margaret went on to give birth to another daughter and one son.*

When all her surviving children became old enough, Margaret endured long separations and financial sacrifices to send them east for a better education. Upon the children's return home, she often felt estranged from her now independent daughters. Her son, Richard, eventually went on to Yale.

After Margaret's eldest daughter, Anne, married an army doctor, it made things more difficult for Anne's younger sister, Sarah Knox (born at Fort Knox in Vincennes, Indiana, and always referred to as "Knox"), to do the same. At eighteen, Knox announced she was in love with army lieutenant Jefferson Davis. Her father swore: "I will be damned if another daughter of mine shall marry into the Army. I scarcely know my own children or they me." Three years later when Knox reached the age of consent she married her lieutenant sweetheart without (by some historians' accounts) her parents' blessing or their attendance at her wedding.

Like her mother had done before her, the newlywed moved to be with her military husband. In letters Knox begged her parents' understanding; historians Dorothy and Carl Schneider assert that Knox confirmed in a note to her mother: "Just received your affectionate letter . . . you may readily imagine the pleasure it afforded me."[3]

---

* Mary Elizabeth "Betty" (1824–1909), Richard (1826–1879)

Unfortunately, the greatest heartbreak of this romance was soon to come. Three short months after marrying, Knox contracted malaria and died. Oddly enough, her death occurred within miles of her two younger sisters' deaths from severe fever fifteen years earlier. Questioning the wisdom of their own conduct, both Margaret and Zachary experienced the severest grief of their lives.

It was many years before the Taylors reconciled with their estranged son-in-law. Eventually they accepted Jefferson Davis as a son and his second wife, Varina Davis, as daughter. Embracing Jefferson and Varina in her life and heart could never replace what Margaret lost, but it added to what she still had.

What remained and the only thing Margaret had any interest in was her husband and her remaining family. Eleven years had passed since Knox's death, and Margaret knew only one life. That life was the military, daily hardships, and the danger of war. Not surprisingly, although undoubtedly not Margaret's preference, her only son became a lieutenant general in the Confederate army.

In Margaret's world military battle was the only thing that existed. Although a treaty had been signed in which the Seminole Indians agreed to move to reservations west of the Mississippi River, many of them refused to go. Committed to national policy, General Taylor was sent in to defeat them. After being acknowledged for distinguished service, Taylor assumed command of Fort Jesup in the Louisiana wilderness.

In the world outside of Margaret's life, construction of the Baltimore & Ohio Railroad had begun, and within a year the first steam-powered locomotive for railroad use was put into service. The gas stove was manufactured and the electric clock was invented. The country's first college of dental surgery was incorporated and the sewing machine was patented. While the first news dispatch was being sent by telegraph, medicine was also advancing, and soon the American Medical Association was organized.

Yet while these advances were occurring, war raged on; in Texas, the defenders of the Alamo had been slaughtered. President Andrew

Jackson (the only president to date to do so) paid off the federal debt; two short years later increased inflation and shrinking credit caused widespread bank failures and unemployment. The federal government then authorized ten million dollars in treasury notes, to relieve the financial panic in 1837.

By 1846, the United States formally declared war on Mexico, and Margaret's husband was again facing life-threatening combat. Margaret prayed for her husband's safe return; unknown to her, her own delicate body would survive the end of the Mexican War by only another six years.

Relieved and elated to have Zachary home, the retirement Margaret had so fervently prayed for was unraveling before her eyes. According to the national census records, the population now consisted of 23 million, with the slave population counted at 3.2 million. It appeared that a great many of those who could vote wanted war hero "Old Rough and Ready" as their next president.

Ironically, in 1848 Taylor never responded to notification from the Whig Party that he was their presidential nominee. Back then, the post office carried "collect letters"—letters without prepaid postage marked "postage due." Since Taylor made it a policy not to accept any unpaid mail, he never saw the Whig notification, and the letter was returned "unpaid."

Despite Margaret's wishes, Zachary Taylor was elected the country's twelfth president. Margaret basically refused to fully accept that she too had a position to fill as the president's wife. Beginning with their initial trip to Washington, she took a different route than the new president-elect to avoid all celebration extended to him. She went so far as to send her regrets to departing First Lady Sarah Polk's dinner invitation, prior to her husband's inauguration. Margaret was also absent from the two public inaugural balls.

Delegating all White House ceremonial functions to her youngest daughter, twenty-five-year-old Betty Bliss, Margaret pleaded poor health. Betty was married to Lieutenant Colonel William Bliss, who became her father's most trusted advisor. Granted, Margaret's health was never robust, yet she nevertheless attended Episcopalian church daily, enjoyed the company of relatives and friends, and presided over all private dinner parties.

George Custis and Nelly Custis Lewis, former First Lady Martha Washington's grandchildren, were welcome visitors, as was frequent guest Varina Davis. Varina was fond of Margaret and wrote: "I always found the most pleasant part of my visit to the White House to be passed in Mrs. Taylor's bright pretty room, where the invalid, full of interest in the passing show in which she had not the strength to take her part, talked most agreeably and kindly to the many friends admitted to her presence."[4] Margaret simply had no interest in the social scene, and, being the honorable woman she was, she never forgot her pledge to God during the Mexican War.

While the First Lady remained out of sight, Washington society gossip exploded. Our nation's First Ladies had always been criticized, some more publicly than others; none had escaped rumor, gossip, or innuendo. Those from the west, such as Margaret, were particularly considered outsiders. The newspapers ridiculed her as a corncob-pipe-smoking, dialect-speaking, illiterate hick.

Although her grandson later stated that tobacco smoke made her "actively ill," the insults continued. It was reported that Margaret Taylor was too uncouth and ignorant to be seen in public. In truth, Margaret had the capability to serve as First Lady; she merely declined to do so.

In early 1849, gold was discovered in California; within one year, thousands of prospectors seeking their fortunes flooded into the territory. (Within four years, its inhabitants increased fifteen fold.) With California's population now permitting application for statehood, President Taylor wanted the territory to enter the United States as a non-slave, or "free state." He threatened to veto the Compromise of 1850—legislation designed to resolve the slavery issue between the North and South—because he believed it favored the slave states.

Notwithstanding the fact the president himself was a slave owner, he wanted to keep peace between the extensively divided nation. The Taylors were the last presidential family to own slaves; the president preferred to keep his slaves out of sight, assigning them to the family quarters of the White House.

After no more than sixteen months in office, the president died suddenly from cholera morbus (acute indigestion) five days after participating in ceremonies at the Washington Monument on July 4, 1850. Upon her husband's death, Margaret collapsed. Varina Davis described the emotional event: "The tearing Mrs. Taylor away from the [president's] body nearly killed me—she would listen to his heart, and feel his pulse, and insist he did not die without speaking to her." Regarding the state funeral, Varina said of the president's widow: "She trembled silently from head to foot as one band after another blared the funeral march."[5]

Margaret refused to have her husband's body embalmed, or allow a customary death mask to be made. She also wanted her husband buried in Louisville at a private ceremony. Immediately following the state funeral, on the same evening, Margaret moved out of the executive mansion and never spoke of the White House again.

After Margaret left Washington, rumors immediately began to circulate that she might have poisoned her husband. This hearsay was passed down in history until the president's body was exhumed 141 years later and the rumors scientifically proven false.[6]

Living with her daughter Betty and Betty's family, Margaret survived her husband by only two years. At the end of her life, in very poor health, a broken yet deeply religious Margaret told a worried niece: "My dear, do not trouble yourself about it; there is nothing in this world worth caring for."[7] Margaret passed away quietly at sixty-three with little notice from the public.

Her obituary in the *New York Times* never even mentioned Margaret's first name. It read simply: "Mrs. General Taylor, relict [widow] of the late President, died at East Pascagoula, on Saturday night."[8] Margaret was buried beside her husband in the Taylor family plot in Louisville, Kentucky.

What Margaret taught me:

Margaret Taylor remains today an anonymous woman. Yet her life experience provided a valuable reinforcement for me: it is essential for each individual to make his or her own life choices. As much as Margaret wanted to prevent her daughter Knox from experiencing the harsh realities of military life, she could not prevent it from happening.

Although not mutually exclusive, loving someone does not equate to being in favor of their choices. Margaret taught me that showing love and acceptance is imperative, even when we do not endorse another's decision. Additionally, although it is impossible to replace the loss of a child, Margaret demonstrated how one can still embrace and welcome the affection of surrogate family.

14

Library Matron

ABIGAIL FILLMORE

I have spent the day at home, your society is all I have thought of.

—ABIGAIL FILLMORE, IN A LETTER TO
HER HUSBAND, MILLARD

BEST REMEMBERED for being the First Lady who established the White House Library, Abigail Fillmore was a self-made woman who helped her husband to become a self-made man. Her love of books and reading began Abigail's improbable journey from Stillwater, New York, to the executive mansion in Washington, DC. It was the love and encouragement she gave her husband that made the journey a reality.

Abigail Powers was born the youngest child of a Baptist clergyman, Reverend Lemuel Powers, who died in 1800 when she was barely two years old. Her widowed mother, Abigail Newland Powers, was then left to raise and educate two sons and two daughters alone. Abigail's mother taught her with the library of books young Abigail's father had collected and preserved. Education and religion were the values the Powers family believed in most.

Growing tall and with good posture, Abigail wore her naturally

> #13 Abigail Powers Fillmore
>
> **Born:** March 13, 1798
> **Birthplace:** Stillwater, New York
> **Married:** 1826 (Millard Fillmore)
> **Children:** 2
> **White House Years:** 1850–1853
> **Died:** March 30, 1853
> **Fact:** Established White House Library
> **Aka:** The Teacher

curly auburn hair in ringlets. Her oval face featured a prominent nose below a high forehead, light blue eyes, and a fair complexion.

If you were a woman in need of employment in the early 1800s, becoming a teacher was one of the few paid occupations open to you. Abigail's lifelong thirst for knowledge was a blessing: in order to support herself the sixteen-year-old became a schoolteacher.

Teaching fed Abigail's passion for further development and by nineteen, in addition to working at the first lending library in the county (borrowing privileges cost two dollars a year), Abigail was teaching at New Hope Academy in New York. One of her students was a young man, seventeen years old, who had never had the opportunity or money for earlier schooling.

Although he lacked confidence in himself, he had a desire to learn, and Abigail took a special interest in encouraging and supporting his growth. By the time she was twenty-one Abigail had fallen in love, and was engaged to her nineteen-year-old former student, Millard Fillmore.

Opposed to her engagement, Abigail's family considered Fillmore below her father's social status. A greater obstacle was Millard's inability to support a wife. Be that as it may, the young couple was intent on marrying. Living in an era when men were expected to be able to provide for a family before marriage, Millard began studying law. Then when prospects elsewhere seemed brighter for employment, Millard moved to Buffalo, New York, and the couple postponed their wedding. It took nearly seven years, during three of which the couple never saw one another, before they could follow through on their marriage plans.

Considering Abigail's commitment to education, it seems fitting that during this time (1821) the first college-level school for women in the United States would open in Waterford, New York.

Finally, in 1826, the same year the literary classic *The Last of the Mohicans* was published, Abigail and Millard were united by an Episcopalian priest. Settling in East Aurora, New York, Millard practiced law and built their first family home himself, while Abigail continued to teach school until her first child, a son, was born.*

Ironically, around the time Abigail stopped working, Noah Webster published the *American Dictionary of the English Language.* It was not in time to assist her with teaching, but a major asset for all future educators.

With his family now growing Millard, eager to succeed, included the state legislature in his ambitions. The family moved back to Buffalo, then a flourishing town of eight thousand people, where Abigail gave birth to a daughter, and the couple established themselves in the community. Intelligent and independent, Abigail studied French and the piano in addition to attending chamber recitals, lectures, and plays. She joined the Unitarian Church, helped to start a lending library to improve public education, and above all continued her lifelong love of reading.

Now a congressman, Millard would travel to Washington while the family remained in Buffalo. With Millard's habit of purchasing books for his wife during his frequent trips, Abigail accumulated a library similar to her father's, which eventually amounted to some four thousand books. Although Abigail was often lonely while her husband was away, she never doubted his love or commitment. One of Abigail's letters read: "I am happy and proud in the thought that your heart is firm, and that no fascinating female can induce you to forget her whose whole heart is devoted."[1]

After Millard's reelection to Congress, he brought his wife to Washington with him. Since it was a city with inferior schools and clearly not an ideal place to bring up a family, Abigail left eight-year-old Powers and four-year-old Abby with her relatives in upstate New York. She and her husband then stayed in a boardinghouse frequented by other congressmen.

For the next six years, Abigail dutifully accepted the obligations of a congressman's wife. Staying abreast of political issues, she was in a po-

---

* Millard Powers "Powers" (1828-1889); Mary Abigail "Abby" (1832-1854).

sition to make recommendations to her husband in addition to calling on other congressional wives, government officials, and foreign dignitaries. Nevertheless, she retained her penchants for listening to intellectual lectures, attending church regularly, and frequently writing to her children. Regarding other aspects of social life, Abigail once noted that she "found the society there amusing, but, it does not interest me."

Washington, DC, was notorious for nasty, harmful weather. It was not uncommon for spouses to return to their home state to recuperate from various ailments, and it was not long before Abigail's health began to deteriorate. She suffered from headaches, back and hip problems, a cough, and also turned an ankle from slipping on a sidewalk. She needed to use crutches for two years and could never again walk or stand for long periods without great pain. Abigail had chronic problems for the remainder of her life.

In 1850, the Whig presidential nominee, Zachary Taylor, asked Millard to be his vice presidential running mate. Taylor was opposing former president Martin Van Buren who was making his third attempt at getting reelected. He had already been defeated in the polls by both William Henry Harrison and James Knox Polk, two of the three presidents who succeeded him. When Van Buren was defeated in his final effort to regain the chief executive position, Abigail returned to Buffalo to pack up her home and completely relocate to Washington.

However, she remained in Buffalo, too unwell to pack or move. By this time Powers was attending Harvard and his sister, Abby, was at a finishing school. Alone and ill, Abigail was depressed during this period of isolation and experienced premonitions of an early demise.

Abigail was still in Buffalo when President Taylor died unexpectedly in July of 1850, only sixteen months into his tenure. Returning to Washington with little enthusiasm, she delegated some of her social responsibilities (not the required receptions or state dinners) to Abby, an engaging, cheerful eighteen-year-old. With Abby as part-time hostess and Powers now his father's private secretary, Abigail was happy to be living together again as a family after so many years apart.

Appalled to discover the White House devoid of any books, including a Bible, the new First Lady immediately turned her attention to the omission. With Abigail's prodding, Congress approved a two-thousand-dollar appropriations bill to purchase several hundred books for the president's home. The complete works of Dickens, Thackeray, and Irving, in addition to a supply of duplicate government documents from the Library of Congress, were added to the president's collection. It is feasible that *The Scarlet Letter* by Nathaniel Hawthorne and *Moby Dick* by Herman Melville, two widely popular books published at that time, were part of the mansion's collection.

Future presidential families, including the Lincolns, cherished the library. Ultimately secured in its present location on the ground floor of the White House, directly behind the Vermeil Room (aka the Gold Room) and next to the East Room, the presidential library is now the first room featured on White House tours. In addition to the volumes of books in the original upstairs location, today known as the Yellow Oval Room, Abigail had her personal piano and harp shipped in, creating a dual-purpose music room.

The First Lady was an accomplished pianist and Abby was proficient on the harp; they created hours of enjoyment for both formal and informal gatherings. Since that time, other White House residents have used Abigail's music room for their own private needs.

One of the many advantages available to the First Lady was the opportunity to entertain the intellectuals, authors, and artists she admired—such as Jenny Lind, Europe's "Swedish Nightingale," one of America's first popular culture icons, and Washington Irving, Charles Dickens, and William Makepeace Thackeray, two of her favorite authors.

An author's impact on the country cannot be underestimated, particularly during impassioned times. When Harriet Beecher Stowe's literary classic, *Uncle Tom's Cabin,* was published in 1852, it fueled the continually burning slavery conflict. President Fillmore, unlike his predecessor, favored the Compromise of 1850, which temporarily prevented the Union from splitting apart.

However, by signing the Fugitive Slave Act, which Abigail was opposed to and tried to influence her husband against, the president alienated many of his former supporters. The Whig Party refused to nominate Fillmore for reelection, just as they had John Tyler, eight years earlier.*

At the end of her husband's presidential term, Abigail looked forward to returning to Buffalo, a desire which would not be fulfilled. While attending the inauguration of her husband's successor, Franklin Pierce, Abigail caught a severe cold that developed into bronchial pneumonia. A few weeks later, the former First Lady's premonition became a reality. At fifty-five, Abigail died at the Willard Hotel in Washington, DC.

Millard mourned his wife's death as well as the loss of her disposition: "For twenty-seven years, my entire married life, I was always greeted with a happy smile."[2] Newly elected president Pierce ordered public offices closed and postponed his cabinet meeting, and the Senate adjourned, all in honor of the former First Lady. This was similar to the respect shown to Louisa Adams by Congress after her passing just ten months earlier.

Adding to the family's sadness, Abby, scarcely twenty-two, took ill and died suddenly the following July. In 1858, after five lonely years, the fifty-eight-year-old former president married Caroline McIntosh, a wealthy forty-four-year-old widow.†

What Abigail taught me:

Not wanting to draw attention to herself, preferring to focus instead on books and learning, Abigail Fillmore certainly accomplished her goal. Although not a much-remembered First Lady, Abigail left her imprint on the chief executive's home—the White House Library continues to be a popular visitors' attraction.

* Both Fillmore and Tyler were vice presidents who succeeded to the presidency. Neither man was their party's (Whig) first selection.
† Millard and Caroline had been married for sixteen years when the former president died. During that time, Fillmore had agreed in a marriage contract to manage his second wife's fortune without sharing it. They had no children.

Abigail believed strongly that women should devote as much effort and energy to cultivating their minds as their male counterparts did. By reading extensively, attending lectures, and taking note of political debates, she could converse with any individual, regardless of their educational background or intellect. Abigail taught me and exemplified a key element to building confidence—knowledge is empowering, and reading is the key that opens the door to knowledge.

15

The Ultimate Devastation

JANE PIERCE

I was obliged to turn and seem interested in other things.

—JANE PIERCE,
IN REGARD TO BEING FIRST LADY

JANE PIERCE is probably one of the most tragic, reluctant, and bereaved First Ladies to ever reside in the White House. Certainly not the only First Lady to dislike politics, Jane, however, despised it. The fact that she agreed to marry a politician is remarkable in itself.

When Franklin Pierce was inaugurated president in 1853, both the country and his wife were dangerously close to their breaking points and desperately needed the new chief executive's undivided attention. The emotionally and physically frail Jane

> **#14 Jane Appleton Pierce**
>
> **Born:** March 12, 1806
> **Birthplace:** Hampton, New Hampshire
> **Married:** 1834 (Franklin Pierce)
> **Children:** 3
> **White House Years:** 1853–1857
> **Died:** December 2, 1863
> **Fact:** Prayed husband would lose election
> **Aka:** Reluctant First Lady

required her husband's empathy and forbearance, but most of all she needed his attentiveness. During this time of tremendous struggle, the country needed a leader with strong character, superior moral strength, and leadership. Yet far from being his Democratic Party's major contender, Pierce, a heavy drinker, had not even been on the short list for the top job. While the nation was inching its way toward civil war his wife was about to face her own personal Armageddon.

The story of Jane's life is sadly poignant. Recounting her experiences raised thought-provoking questions, for me, that led to deep, insightful answers. Her life also says something about the impact of childhood wounds. It is best to start with her formative years, where her delicate health and fragile disposition began.

A sensitive young girl with flimsy energy, Jane Appleton was born in 1806. Plagued with poor health much of her life, it is believed she contracted tuberculosis as an adult. Sandwiched in the middle of her siblings, she was the third of six children, and found comfort in being surrounded by her family.

Her father was Reverend Jesse Appleton, a congregational minister who served as president of Bowdoin College (located in Maine) for twelve years. Reverend Appleton died when Jane was thirteen, and his death inevitability added to her innate teenage insecurities. Soon after, Jane's mother, Elizabeth Appleton, moved her four daughters and two sons into her wealthy parents' mansion in New Hampshire.

Considering her grandparents' prosperity, Jane most likely received a broad home schooling. It appeared she had a natural talent for the piano, though she never pursued music. Raised with a strong religious education, the Bible soon became her closest friend. In fact, other than reading the Bible and other religious works, she seemingly had no hobbies or interests.

Insulated within her relatives' cocoon, Jane found it very difficult to separate from her family, even as an adult. Making friends and socializing in general did not come easily for her. Later in life, intermingling and merriment did not come at all, nor did she seek them.

A very slender woman, Jane was around five foot four, and weighed no more than a hundred pounds. She had brown eyes and chestnut hair worn in ringlets. Painfully shy, Jane looked perpetually sad. Reclusive and prone to deep depressions, the Bible was her only solace. Always a religious woman, her faith was of the utmost importance to her.

When she was twenty, Jane met twenty-two-year-old Franklin Pierce, a lawyer with his eye on politics. Franklin had been a student of Jane's brother-in-law at Bowdoin College. Despite their disparate personalities—Jane spinsterish and introverted; Franklin exceptionally handsome with a magnetic personality—they began to see one another.

On the surface, it is difficult to say what attracted these two individuals to one another, since their respective natures, personal tastes, and needs all seemed to oppose each other, like repelling magnets. Franklin was born in a log cabin, had a reputation for frequenting bars, was gregarious, mixed readily, and enjoyed socializing. Jane lived in a mansion, disapproved of drinking, was very shy, and preferred a secluded life. But their greatest obstacle and the issue that would create most of their discontent was politics.

Within the first three years of their courtship, Pierce had been elected to the New Hampshire House of Representatives, notwithstanding the fact that Jane detested politics, describing it as a "dirty and an uninteresting business." Not yet dissuaded, Franklin continued to pursue his political ambitions. After eighteen months as a member of the U.S. Congress and eight years of courting, the two decided to marry.

Jane must have chosen to disregard their differences, thought she could change Franklin, or simply felt she had invested too much time in the relationship to let go. Her mother advised against the marriage, disapproving of Franklin for a variety of reasons, his stance on slavery being only one of them. Franklin opposed slavery in theory but regarded it as constitutionally protected. Consequently, he supported the South and states' rights. In addition, Mrs. Appleton was concerned about his excessive drinking, and she considered Pierce socially inferior, frowning on his manners.

It is fair to assume that at twenty-eight, Jane's decision to ignore both her mother's advice and her own misgivings might have been motivated by her fear of becoming a spinster. Openly abhorring her fiancé's profession, Jane proved to be a handicap to Franklin's career. Not to mention the inner torment it caused her.

Immediately after marrying, the couple settled into a quiet boardinghouse in Washington, DC. In a letter to her new father-in-law, Jane revealed her earnest desires for church and undisturbed evenings:

Today is so excessively windy that I am disappointed in my wish of going to church which is a deprivation to which I hope I shall not often be subjected—these high winds are common here and exceedingly disagreeable . . . We have an invitation to dinner to Gov Cass'on Wednesday which is accepted notwithstanding my predilections for a quiet dinner at home.[1]

According to a fellow occupant at the boardinghouse: "[Jane seemed] in very delicate health and wanting in cheerfulness." A common reoccurrence, as she would struggle with bouts of depression much of her life.

Another frequent theme in Jane's life was her need to lean on others; it was apparent in all her relationships. Shortly after being married one year, Jane returned to New Hampshire where her husband had purchased a home and hired a couple to run it for his frail wife. It was there that she gave birth to her first child. Her infant son, Franklin Jr., regrettably died three days later.*

Jane's acute gloominess continued to affect her health, and as her health deteriorated, so did her attitude toward politics. During one of her many attempts to persuade her husband into another career, Franklin received news of his Senate election win. At thirty-two, he was the youngest man elected to the Senate to date.

Unfortunately, Jane's life and marriage resembled that of another of her political predecessors. Louisa Adams's husband, John Quincy, was also in his thirties when he was elected to the Senate, and she too had a difficult marriage with moments of happiness and times of estrangement. Both women had lost children and both suffered immeasurable heartache with the politicians they could never detour.

Unlike Martha Washington, who believed her misery depended on her disposition and not her circumstances, Jane was miserable living in Washington, a place she hated, and equally miserable staying in New Hampshire because she and her husband were separated. "Oh,

* Franklin Jr. (1836–1836), Frank Robert (1839–1843), and Benjamin (1841–1853).

how I wish he was out of political life! How much better it would be for him on every account!"[2]

Never giving up her campaign to dissuade her husband from politics, Jane finally found an argument that convinced him. After the birth of two more sons, Frank Robert and Benjamin ("Benny"), Jane argued that the environment in Washington was too "unhealthy" to raise their boys.

In 1842, Franklin resigned his Senate seat and resumed his law practice in New Hampshire. It was a short-lived victory for Jane, because in 1843 four-year-old Frank died from typhus. Jane's agonizing pain can only be imagined. Also struggling to come to terms with his son's death, Franklin wrote: "My prevailing feeling has been that we were living for our children . . . We should have lived for God and left the dear ones to the care of Him who is alone able to take care of them and us."[3]

Three years later, feeling a sense of duty, Franklin volunteered for the Mexican War. The year her husband was away at combat, Jane wrote of her anguish: "It is truly such a state of absence and entire separation as almost amounts to widowhood—and the feeling of dependence on myself alone so different from what I have been accustomed to is excessively painful."[4]

Always the devoted mother, Jane concentrated all her energies and emotions on her surviving son. After his return, Franklin refused repeated political invitations (to be US attorney general, a senatorial appointment, and a run for governorship) to resume his law practice.

In spite of his decision, very few red-blooded politicians can resist a try at the topmost position, regardless of how remote the chances are. In 1852, no less than ten Democratic candidates for the presidency emerged. The presidential convention was deadlocked and Pierce's name eventually surfaced; he ultimately appeared as a candidate on the thirty-fifth ballot. (Talk about a dark horse contender!) On the forty-ninth ballot, Franklin Pierce, the far-flung compromise candidate, received the winning nomination. Upon hearing the news Jane fainted in shock.

Contrary to Jane's prayers, including her indoctrination of Benny—who wrote: "I hope he won't be elected, for I should not like to be at Washington and I know you would not either"[5]—Franklin miraculously won the election. With the utmost reluctance, Jane prepared to move into the White House, stating: "The expectation seems too heavy to be borne."[6]

Historians Dorothy and Carl Schneider fittingly said of Jane: "She anticipated no happiness in Washington, and consequently she found none." Surely, nothing could be worse than the fate Jane was just dealt. Or could it?

A disaster occurred just two months before Franklin's inauguration. The family was traveling on a train that derailed. Before his parents' very eyes, eleven-year-old Benny was mangled to death in the wreckage. He was the only fatality.

Jane's grief was so overwhelming that she could not travel to Washington to attend her husband's inauguration. In consideration of the first family's bereavement, the presidential inaugural ball was cancelled. When Jane finally arrived in Washington with widow Abigail Means she sequestered herself in an upstairs bedroom for two years.* Jane's faithful companion, "Aunt Abby," resided in the White House with her. Franklin immersed himself in his presidential duties while Jane, writing letters to her dead son, was immersed in profound mourning and her Bible.

On January 23, 1853 Jane wrote Benny a four page letter:

Dear, dear child – I cannot bear to think of that agonizing [sic] time, when I had just seen you all alive to what was passing around and near me, but not near enough—oh had you but been within reach of your dear father—in a moment changed my dear boy bright form into a lifeless one insensible to your parents' agony –
...Oh what anguish was mine on returning without you, and feel-

---

* Abigail Kent Means was a young and trusted friend of Jane's. Abigail went on to marry Jane's uncle, Robert Means, becoming her aunt through marriage.

ing that it must still be so, while I live - . . . to think of you kneel-
ing by me at our evening prayer tonight, dear child – has not the
Savior made you His as we so often asked. But now I must kneel
alone and beg for strength and support under this crushing sorrow, that the blessed Savior would comfort the heart of your pain
stricken Mother - and help me better to bear the burden of your
loss which has brought desolation such as I have never (with all my
former griefs) known. . . . -my dear son, how much I feel my own
faults in regard to you—I know that I did not take the right way
and should have dealt with you very gently often when I judged
hastily and spoke harshly. I can see that I was "unreasonable" and
sometimes almost wonder that you loved me at all. – Oh Benny, I
have not valued such a sweet blessing as I ought.[7]

Both the president and First Lady believed their son's death was
an act of God. The president thought it was punishment for his weaknesses, while Jane believed Benny's death was a sacrifice taken by God
for her husband's election to the presidency. The wretchedness of her
despair was enough to topple any woman's reasoning. She wrote: "God
decided to take our precious little boy, so that you [Franklin] will have
no distractions as you set out to effect reconciliation between sec-
tions of our nation." Her comments regarding sacrificing their son for
his political ambition crushed Franklin. To add insult to injury, Jane
insisted that her husband had actively sought and was truly eager to
become president.

The First Lady was so absorbed in her grief that she was perceived
as being deliberately withdrawn from her spouse, giving him little support or reassurance and making no effort to lighten his burden. The
one area Jane did seem to make an impression on was Franklin's
soberness, at least while he was in her presence.

Gradually and cautiously, avoiding public events, Jane bravely
began to attend private dinners and receptions in the White House.
Eventually, although her heart was never in it, she stood alongside the
president and publicly received guests. A contemporary wrote of the

president's wife: "Traces of bereavement were legibly written [upon her face] . . . too ingenuous for concealment."[8]

Predictably, considering the circumstances at the beginning of the Pierce administration (Benny's death followed by that of the former First Lady), the White House took on an air of melancholy and disappointment. Sadly, the atmosphere never improved. The only shadow Jane cast was that of gloom. At the same time, Franklin was so overworked in the presidency that it became evident neither his wife nor the country would benefit from his judgment. Undoubtedly, both occupants were deprived of the mutual support each so desperately needed.

It was President Pierce's intention to keep peace between the North and the South. Yet maintaining his position on states' rights, he supported the controversial Kansas-Nebraska Act of 1854. That decision proved destructive and politically fatal. The act allowed settlers residing in the territories of Kansas and Nebraska to decide for themselves whether or not to allow slavery. In protest of the act, the Republican Party was formed that same year.

After four years in office, President Pierce sought but did not win his party's nomination for reelection. He is the only elected president with that distinction.* Furthermore, historians unanimously place Franklin Pierce at the very bottom of presidential rankings.

The following summer was darkened by yet another death. Jane's companion, Abby Means, passed away. Franklin took Jane on an extended vacation abroad to tour Europe for two years. Everywhere she went from then on, Jane carried a small box containing locks of hair from her precious dead family members. Nothing ever again seemed to comfort her physically or emotionally.

After living a sad, isolated, and depressed life, Jane died at fifty-seven, six years before her husband. She succumbed to "consumption," a term commonly used for tuberculosis. Jane was buried beside

---

* John Tyler and Millard Fillmore succeeded to the presidency upon the death of a president and were also denied their party's renomination.

her children and will forever be remembered, if remembered at all, for her massive, tragic grief. Mourning his wife's death, Franklin fought loneliness and alcoholism for the last half dozen years of his life.

What Jane taught me:

An old adage I ardently agree with is "If everyone put all their troubles into a hat, you would invariably favor picking out your own." Heaven knows, considering Jane Pierce's plight, that viewpoint could not be more accurate.

Still, her life demonstrated for me why a house of cards should not be built on an unrealistic foundation. Jane had a strong distaste for politics, yet she married an ambitious politician. Her marriage is a testimonial to the fact that you cannot change another individual. Jane taught me that relationships do not survive, let alone thrive, on insecurity, fear, or the impracticable belief that you are going to "convert" someone.

16

Presidential Niece, Fill-in Hostess

HARRIET LANE

Pleasant but dreadfully troublesome.

HARRIET LANE,
IN REFERENCE TO HER NUMEROUS BEAUX

THOSE WHO ACTED solely as White House hostesses are only briefly mentioned in this book, as they were not married to the chief executive. Their duties and responsi-bilities, significant as they were, did not carry the same influence or burdens as those of the First Lady.

The only president who remained a bachelor was James Buchanan. He followed Franklin Pierce into the White House in the same year (1857) that a slave named Dred Scott sued his owner for freedom.* By then the slavery issue had been in serious de-

> #15 Harriet Lane
> (White House Hostess)
>
> **Born:** May 18, 1830
> **Birthplace:** Mercersburg, Pennsylvania
> **Married:** 1866 (Henry Elliot Johnston)
>   (After leaving the White House)
> **Children:** 2
> **White House Years:** 1857–1861
> **Died:** July 3, 1903
> **Fact:** Niece to only bachelor president
> **Aka:** Hal

bate for nearly ten years. Other important individuals during that time in history were John Brown, a radical abolitionist who was hanged after attempting to start a slave rebellion, and Frederick Douglass, a former slave and abolitionist.

President Buchanan soon became a mere spectator as events be-

* In 1857, the Supreme Court ruled that Scott was not a citizen and therefore could not file a lawsuit.

tween the heavily divided North and South spun out of control around him. The only glimmer of light shinning from within the sullen White House windows was Harriett Lane. She was the president's twenty-six-year-old unmarried niece who resided in the White House with him. Buchanan had become Harriet's guardian when she was orphaned at the age of ten. The young girl grew up calling her favorite uncle "Nunc" and he called her "Hal."

A refreshing change from Jane Pierce, Washington society eagerly welcomed the rather tall, educated, and accomplished blond hostess. With enthusiasm and social grace, Harriet brought a flicker of gaiety to the despondent occupants of the mansion for the first time in several years. Filling the hollow rooms with flowers and taking special care to diplomatically work out seating arrangements for her weekly formal dinner parties, Harriet won national popularity.

However, with the growing national hostility, including within her uncle's administration, no amount of effort could prevent the inevitable. Seven Southern states had seceded (South Carolina, Mississippi, Florida, Alabama, Georgia, Louisiana, and Texas) after futile compromise attempts were made to save the Union. The state of Georgia went so far as to pass a law forbidding owners from "freeing their slaves in wills" upon their owner's demise.

Upon leaving the White House, President Buchanan's now famous comment to incoming president Abraham Lincoln described his emotions best: "If you are as happy, my dear sir, on entering [the White House] as I am in leaving, you are the happiest man in the country!"

Within six weeks of the first elected Republican president's inauguration, an attack occurred at Fort Sumter, South Carolina. The country's bloodiest civil war had commenced.

It was not until after the Civil War ended that Harriet Lane married. Nearly thirty-six, she wed Henry Elliot Johnston, a wealthy banker.

After eighteen years of marriage Harriet was widowed. During that time she also lost two teenage sons, James Buchanan Johnston and Henry Elliott Johnston Jr., as well as her favorite uncle, Nunc.

When Harriet Lane Johnston died in 1903, she dedicated $400,000 to the Johns Hopkins hospital for invalid children as a memorial to her two sons. In addition, her rather sizable art collection was bequeathed to the Smithsonian Institution. She is sometimes referred to as the First Lady of the National Collection of Fine Arts.

PART FIVE

WOMEN OF THE CIVIL WAR

THE CIVIL WAR was the greatest war in American history. Americans were fighting each other, brother against brother, on United States soil. Approximately 3 million men fought; over 51,000 died during the three-day Battle of Gettysburg. The number most often quoted as the full death toll is 620,000 lives. These casualties exceed the nation's loss in all other wars, from the American Revolution to Vietnam.

The bloodiest, most devastating battle in US military history was Antietam, near Sharpsburg, Maryland, on September 17, 1862. When it was over 23,000 men were dead, wounded or missing. Fifty-thousand survivors returned home as amputees.

In January 1863 the war was costing $2.5 million daily. A final official estimate in 1879 put the total cost of the war at $6,190,000,000.[1]

Providing precious aid to sick and wounded soldiers, approximately two thousand women, from both the North and South, served as volunteer nurses in military hospitals. These compassionate, heroic women witnessed firsthand mutilated bodies, disease, and death.

Every man, woman, and child living in America during that period was adversely affected by the war in one way or another. The experiences of Mary Todd Lincoln, Eliza Johnson, Julia Grant, Lucy Hayes, Lucretia Garfield, and Ellen Arthur are only six of the stories. Three of these six women had close family and relatives fighting for the Confederacy; all six of them were married to men committed to the Union.

This well-known phrase (origin unknown) says it best: "If not for the brave, there would be no land of the free."

17

Controversial and Unstable

MARY TODD LINCOLN

Oh it is no use to make any defense; all such efforts would only make me a target for new attacks. I seem to be the scapegoat for both the North and the South!

—MARY TODD LINCOLN

THE CIVIL WAR is often referred to as the war between the North and South. With dramatic, diametrically opposed philosophies and principles existing in the country, it is fair to say that deep-seated hatred existed among many individuals who lived in the United States during the middle of the nineteenth century.

The farmers and plantation owners in the South were dependent upon slave labor. In the North where larger metropolitan cities existed, individuals opposed slavery. While legislatures made several futile attempts to negotiate the issue, they ultimately learned that slavery holds no compromises.

> **#16 Mary Todd Lincoln**
>
> **Born:** December 13, 1818
> **Birthplace:** Lexington, Kentucky
> **Married:** 1842 (Abraham Lincoln)
> **Children:** 4
> **White House Years:** 1861–1865
> **Died:** July 16, 1882
> **Fact:** 1st First Lady whose husband was assassinated; institutionalized for mental incompetency
> **Aka:** The Traitor

Localized animosity and bitterness only increased over the years, ultimately encompassing the entire nation. Hostility grew so pervasive that the survival of the Union was now at stake.

It was easy for those living in the North to point their fingers at those in the South, and vice versa. About the only thing the two areas agreed on was their animosity toward Mary Todd Lincoln, the country's sixteenth First Lady.

Because Mary had been born and grew up in Lexington, Kentucky, many Northerners believed the First Lady was a spy who supported the Confederacy. On the surface one could make that conclusion: her paternal grandfather had been one of the founders of Lexington, and her father, Robert Todd, was a wealthy banker and cotton manufacturer as well as a slave owner.

To add insult to injury, Mary's younger brother was a surgeon for the Confederate army, and three of her half-brothers—Mary's father remarried and had another family—died fighting for the Confederacy. However, the First Lady sincerely supported the survival of the Union and freedom for all people.

Upon hearing that one of her brothers had been killed in the war, Mary pragmatically responded: "Of course, it is but natural that I should feel for one so nearly related to me, but not to the extent that you suppose. He made his choice long ago. He decided against my husband and through him against me. He has been fighting against us; and since he chose to be our deadly enemy, I see no special reason why I should bitterly mourn his death."[1]

With constant negative news reports from what Mary called "the vampire press," she found herself in a no-win situation. Neither her work for the Contraband Society, an organization created to help displaced African-Americans, nor her many visits to the hospitalized was reported.

If the First Lady carried on customary White House social receptions and balls, she was called callous or coldhearted toward those fighting. But when she cancelled a levee,* she was contributing to the somberness or mournful atmosphere of the war.

On one rare occasion Mary was initially praised for her efforts to refurbish the desperately dilapidated public rooms in the executive mansion. Paint and wallpaper were literally peeling off the walls, and

---

* Word often used to describe a presidential reception.

the carpets were tattered and stained. A refined, well-bred woman, the First Lady showed good taste in her selection of furnishings.

Her choices were also expensive. First-of-its-kind wall-to-wall carpeting was installed, along with beautiful new lace curtains beneath heavier gold-fringed drapes. Furniture was either reupholstered or refinished, and the East Room walls were covered with gold velvet wallpaper. The First Lady went on to redecorate the Green Room, the Red Room, and the State Bedroom in addition to the private resident's quarters.

Congress had appropriated twenty thousand dollars for the job. When Mary went over budget by sixty-five hundred dollars, praise soon turned into harsh criticism. The First Lady was genuinely embarrassed and her husband was furious. President Lincoln had not been aware of the overruns until the bills started flowing in.

Upset as he was, Lincoln was willing to pay the difference out of his own pocket and refused to ask Congress for more money. Adamant, the president said: "It never can have my approval . . . It would stink in the nostrils of the American people . . . flub dubs for this damned old house, when the soldiers cannot have blankets." Fortunately for Mary, the commissioner of public buildings convinced the merchants to reduce their inflated bills.

In all fairness to her detractors, Mary's personality did contribute to some of the negativity directed toward her. Although she was known for being a warm and gracious hostess, the First Lady also had a quick temper, a sharp tongue, and was very impulsive. Purportedly, she once purchased three hundred pairs of gloves in less than a year.

The distaste society had for the new First Lady began immediately after her husband's presidential victory, before they were even acquainted with her. Margaret Taylor, a former First Lady, had been subjected to the same preconceived notions. Women from the frontier, which included Mary's home state of Kentucky, were considered unsocialized hicks who lacked sophistication. The elite who had long lived within the capital city's close-knit high society tended to snub outsiders, particularly those considered Yankees.

The reality was that Mary was a very intelligent woman who had received far more education than the average female of her era. She surely read more, and was always interested in literature and politics. After completing her basic schooling at Shelby Female Academy, she went on to attend finishing school at Madame Mentelle's Boarding School. Mary was also an accomplished dancer and spoke fluent French.

Yet prior to her husband's inauguration, local socialites refused to call on the First Lady–elect and went so far as to boycott the president's inaugural ball. Mary received hate mail and was accused of accepting bribes for cabinet appointments, to support her reckless shopping habits. It is true that the president enjoyed talking politics with his well-informed wife, and often asked her opinion, albeit he took her advice far less frequently.

An emotional woman, Mary was aware of the cruel rebuffs directed toward her; she initially made several attempts to impress her critics and prove them wrong. But regardless of her approach, she never received a favorable response. Personal insecurities, jealousy, and her shopaholic tendencies would then rear their ugly heads and often get her into further trouble.

Those insecurities had already been aggravated when a plot to kidnap the newly elected president was uncovered. On their first train trip to Washington, the president-elect was separated from his family and arrived alone in an unscheduled, unmarked train.

Terror over her husband's safety never left Mary's consciousness. In fact, it was not the first time she had had fears of losing her spouse or other close family members. Considering her background, the First Lady's fears were reasonable.

Anxiety was evident throughout Mary's entire life—not only after her husband had become a powerful political leader, but also in her early married years, during their courtship, and going all the way back to her childhood when she lost her mother at the age of six.

Mary's mother, Eliza Parker Todd, died just days after giving birth to her seventh child. Mary was the third of four girls and three boys.

Less than a year and a half later, her idolized father remarried and went on to have eight more children.

Lost in a large family with a stepmother she disliked and found unsympathetic, Mary referred to her childhood as "desolate." Lavish spending was common in the distinguished and affluent families both her parents came from; shopping was an effortless and convenient escape.

In another attempt to flee her unhappiness, at eighteen Mary left her stepmother's home to live with her older married sister, Elizabeth, in Springfield, Illinois. Betsey, as she was known, regularly invited eligible doctors, lawyers, and businessmen to her parlor for discussions on important topics of the day. Along with the exchange of ideas, matchmaking proved to be an added bonus.

Opinionated, intelligent, and witty, Mary was an outspoken and ambitious young woman. Often the life of the party, Mary's brother-in-law once said of her: "[She] could make a bishop forget his prayers."[2] With always something to add to the conversation, politics was very important to her, and Mary never hid the fact that one day she wanted to reside in the White House.

Although Mary had several suitors, none had stolen her heart. Then again, she had not yet met Abraham Lincoln, a junior partner in her cousin's law firm. Betsey found Lincoln rough around the edges, so to speak, and considered him a country bumpkin beneath her sister's status. He was therefore not included in her coterie.

Returning to Lexington, Mary continued her education—something highly unusual for the times—and studied intensely for two more years. Eventually finding her way back to Springfield, now the state capital, Mary's romantic life was about to turn into an emotional roller-coaster ride.

At a ball, a gangly six-foot-tall, rather homely looking man with a long narrow face approached Mary, saying: "Miss Todd, I want to dance with you in the worst way." After accepting the gentleman's invitation, Mary confessed he had in fact "danced in the worst way."

The couple made an odd-looking pair. Compared to Lincoln's lean and lanky frame, buxom Mary stood at five feet two inches; she had bright blue eyes, a round, dimpled face, and dark chestnut hair. Considering their personalities and backgrounds, a meaningful relationship between Mary and Abraham seemed dubious.

Very close to ten years her senior, Lincoln had been raised, in hardship and poverty, in a log cabin in the backwoods of Kentucky. Self-educated, he had a mild temperament, was an outstanding storyteller, was quite magnanimous, and made friends with all types of people.

Mary, on the other hand, came from a distinguished, prosperous family. She was raised in a sophisticated city, had slaves who were responsible for all the domestic housework, and received an exceptional formal education. In addition to her hot temperament, Mary was self-centered and could unkindly mimic individuals, which made her many enemies.

This sounds somewhat like the upbringing and behavioral disparities Jane and Franklin Pierce experienced with one another. But Mary and Abe did enjoy important similarities as well: the two were highly intelligent, loved literature, were ambitious, and politics was important to both of them.

At twenty-two, Mary was already a politically astute woman who joined the Whig Party and campaigned for her neighbor Henry Clay, a man both she and Abe admired greatly.*

Another common factor, and probably the most essential, was the insecurities they both lived with throughout their lives. As time went on, they understood one another more and more, respected, supported, and in the end deeply loved each other.

Initially, Lincoln was indecisive about their relationship. Not only did he lack a high opinion of himself, he did not believe he could support a wife or make one happy. In addition to Lincoln's hesitation, Mary herself was not yet persuaded that she wanted to wed. So an extended visit to another relative's home sounded like a good alternative to her. After spending several months with an uncle, a judge who lived

---

* Clay, a prominent politician and family friend, unsuccessfully ran for the presidency three times.

in Missouri, and scouting eligible bachelors there, Mary returned to Betsey's home in Springfield more and more convinced of Lincoln's merits.

In addition to Lincoln, another politician named Stephen A. Douglas began to court Mary. But Mary was far more convinced of Abe's potential. When her sister realized just how close Mary and Abe had become, she immediately tried to convince Mary that her emotions were misguided. Betsey's negative opinion of Lincoln had not changed; she believed he would never measure up to her sister's status.

The strong-willed Mary had already made her decision. She was in love with Lincoln and turned down Douglas's proposal. Furthermore, a premonition told her he would one day be president.

Rather than being officially engaged, Mary and Abe "reached an understanding." At some point in their courtship, Abe had second thoughts and called off the relationship. It was the first time Mary thought she might lose her beloved Mr. Lincoln, as she always referred to him, never calling her sweetheart Abe or Abraham.

Prone to depression, Lincoln was battling his own demons. During their separation Lincoln wrote to a friend: "I am now the most miserable man in the world. If what I feel were equally distributed to the whole human family, there would not be one cheerful face on the earth."[3]

Over a year and a half went by before a mutual friend prompted them to once again "be friends." It was not long before Mary announced to her sister that she and Lincoln had decided to marry immediately. It took considerable coercion to convince Betsey to host the nuptials; however, six weeks before her twenty-fourth birthday Mary Ann Todd married thirty-three-year-old Abraham Lincoln in her sister's home on November 4, 1842. The groom had three words engraved on his wife's wedding band: "Love Is Eternal."

The couple moved into a four-dollar-a-week room over the Globe Tavern; with debts yet to be paid, it was the most Lincoln could afford. Leaving Mary alone a great deal of the time, Lincoln spent months on the circuit, traveling and building his law practice. Three days shy of their nine-month wedding anniversary, Mary gave birth to her first of four sons. She named him Robert Todd after her beloved father.*

The Lincolns moved into a slightly larger residence; eventually, with financial assistance from her father, the couple purchased a larger home—with a loft they converted into extra bedrooms—for fifteen hundred dollars. Two and a half years later, son Eddie was born and like all mothers Mary became immersed in the endless household chores of cooking, cleaning, washing, and child rearing.

As a girl Mary had never learned the typical female housekeeping duties, with the exception of sewing. After a predictable learning curve, she did manage the family home efficiently, although she was never praised for being a particularly good cook.

Together, Mary and Abe—or "Father," as Mary now sometimes called her adored Mr. Lincoln—were loving and lenient parents. Family meant everything to them. Yet both parents continued to struggle with their own emotional troubles.

Lincoln's clever wit added humor and laughter to an otherwise volatile home. He was a moody man with periods of depression. Mary, with a lifelong history of migraine headaches, was known for her temper tantrums and crying spells. Yet they held one another in high regard, and each tried to bolster the other.

Quick to nag, Mary worked to convert her husband's modest and humble tastes to her own more sophisticated preferences. Meanwhile, Lincoln treated his wife with tenderness and affection, calling her "my child-wife." Historian Doris Goodwin may have said it best: "Over the years, they had supported each other, irritated each other, shared a love of family, politics, poetry, and drama."

In 1847 Lincoln was elected to the House of Representatives, the only member of the Whig Party to be elected from Illinois. Intensely proud of her husband, Mary was ready to move to the nation's capital with him.

Like many of her fellow congressional wives, Mary was incredibly disenchanted living in Washington. In addition to the unpaved streets,

---

* Robert Todd (1843–1926), Edward Baker (1846–1850), William "Willie" Wallace (1850–1862), and Thomas, aka Tad (1853–1871).

poor weather, and horrifying slave market, her husband was totally consumed with work. It soon became clear why so many wives returned to their home states while their politician husbands remained behind living in boardinghouses. Mary was no exception. After spending time introducing her children to family in Kentucky, Mary returned to live in Springfield with her boys.

Tragedy struck in 1849 when Mary's fear of losing her family became a nightmarish reality. Her father died, and before she could fully accept his death, her grandmother passed away as well. Both individuals had been strong influences on Mary, and she had loved them deeply.

An old wives' tale that eerily survives to this day asserts that deaths occur in threes. Mary was terrified, as three-year-old Eddie was suffering from diphtheria or something similar. For two drawn-out, draining, and arduous months, she never left her son's bedside. Morning, noon, and night she helplessly watched over her young boy. When he died, Mary crumbled in grief, refusing to eat. (All three deaths occurred within six months.)

It was her equally devastated husband who convinced Mary that they both needed to live for the sake of their other son, Robert. Immediately after Eddie's February funeral, the couple who dearly loved children was again expecting. Lincoln made a decision to leave politics and remain at home with his family, practicing law. In December of 1850, Mary gave birth to William, her third son, known as Willie.

A regular churchgoer all her life, Mary was now accompanied by her husband to services on a regular basis. They found joy in their two surviving sons, attended Shakespearian plays, and began to host a number of dinner parties. Some of their social events were attended by hundreds.

According to one guest, "It was the genial manner and ever kind welcome of the hostess, and the wit and humor, anecdotes and unrivaled conversation of the host which formed the chief attraction and made dinner at the Lincolns an event to be remembered."[4] Another described Mary as "amiable and accomplished, gracious, and a sparkling talker."[5]

Their fourth son, Thomas, born in 1853, was named after Lincoln's father who had died two years earlier. Lincoln nicknamed his son Tad because his unusually large head, in contrast to his tiny body, resembled a tadpole. All of Mary's pregnancies had been difficult, particularly her last; Tad was born with a cleft palate and ultimately spoke with a lisp.

Although Lincoln never lost his interest in politics, his career had stalled while he remained focused on his law practice. He had argued a case before the Illinois Supreme Court, spoken out against the Dred Scott decision, and won an acquittal in a murder trial.

Despite being disappointed and saddened when her husband lost his bid for the Illinois U.S. Senate seat in 1855 as well as the vice-presidential nomination in 1856, Mary continued to have confidence in her spouse's political career. In fact, she maintained that he should never accept anything less than the presidential position.

Both Lincolns had been lifelong supporters of the Whig Party; however, a new party, one opposed to the expansion of slavery, was now emerging. Lincoln identified with this position and became one of the original members of the Republican Party. Not a full abolitionist, he nonetheless opposed the extension of slavery into new territories.

Lincoln again ran for the U.S. Senate in 1858, this time against prior colleague (and his wife's former beau) Stephen A. Douglas. The two received national exposure during a series of eight famous debates. Douglas, nicknamed "the Little Giant," never measured up to one in Mary's eyes. She referred to him as "a very little, little giant by the side of my tall Kentuckian, and intellectually my husband towers above Douglas just as he does physically."[6]

Once again Lincoln lost; however, due to his notable debating skills, his reputation had been significantly enhanced. For the next eighteen months, Lincoln gave one remarkable speech after another, all over the country. Mary participated when she could. When the Republican Party nominated Lincoln for the presidency in 1860, Mary was his most devoted crusader.

The campaign would yet again pit Lincoln against his old rival Stephen Douglas. Only this time, with an even more important goal at stake, Lincoln came out the victor. Many thousands of well-wish-ers gathered outside the Springfield telegraph office where Lincoln went to hear the returns. They were anticipating a speech from the new president-elect, but Lincoln's only comment was: "I need to tell Mary *we* are elected."

Elated, Mary's dreams and premonition had become a reality. After all her relatives' uncertainties, the financial struggles, the uphill social climb, the political setbacks, and the grievous family losses, she was finally going to the White House as the president's wife.

With pride and delight in her heart, Mary had fought her battles, endured her trials, and now wanted to live in the glory of her triumphs. As she would soon discover, glory was not meant to be and the White House was no victory.

Before he had even arrived in Washington to take office, the conspiracy to kidnap the president-elect set the tragic tone of the Lincoln presidency. It is fair to say that Mary could never have envisioned the dreadful and destructive turn her life was about to take. Things were going to get worse; in fact, they would never improve.

A mere thirty-nine days after taking office, President Lincoln was enmeshed in the country's most devastating and awful war on U.S. soil. It is an understatement to say he was completely absorbed in work. Surrounded by a large staff of cabinet members and advisors every minute of the day, the president's time was constantly monopolized by others. Making wide-ranging, vital decisions became a daily all-consuming task.*

Mary quickly became aware of what her past White House "sorority sisters" already knew: the presidency was an all-consuming job that left little time for anything else. Many First Ladies had felt isolated and detached from their fully engaged spouses.

By heading to New York to purchase gowns, shoes, jewelry, and accessories for her new position Mary immediately offended local Washington merchants. On a positive note, or so she thought, unlimited credit was extended to her. Without having to pay for items on the

---

* Lincoln appointed Charles Francis Adams plenipotenary to England. Both his father, President John Quincy Adams, and his grandfather, President John Adams, served as ambassadors to Great Britain.

spot, it was easy to spend large sums of money without feeling the financial pinch.

Reporters followed the First Lady everywhere, and Mary, never one to know when to hold her tongue, invariably created more problems. Unable to score any positive acknowledgment for her efforts, and with her husband emotionally and physically distracted, Mary's only comfort came from her boys.

Robert, a good-looking young man with a mustache, had been accepted into Harvard after initially failing the entrance exam. Willie and Tad, now eight and eleven, were fun-loving youngsters who enjoyed playing pranks; both parents believed the boys should be allowed to enjoy their youth. The president was known to wrestle on the floor with his sons, and the boys used the White House roof as a playground for their favorite war games.

Willie for one did not relish public attention. He was once heard complaining: "I wish they wouldn't stare at us so. Wasn't there ever a President who had children?"

While the press took a gentle attitude with her sons, Mary remained a public object of condemnation. She experienced bouts of crying fits, depression, and migraine headaches accompanied by an unpredictable temper. Her mood swings and violent outbursts were rumored to be the result of mental instability. Meanwhile, newspapers were in competition to print the latest dirt on the First Lady.

Other than the president, who understood his wife's tantrums and defended her— "It does her lots of good and it doesn't hurt me a bit"[7]— Mary had only one other friend. This was Elizabeth Keckley, Mary's dressmaker and a former slave (not in the Todd family) who had purchased her freedom. Mrs. Keckley later wrote in her insightful book, *Behind the Scenes,* that she hoped "the world to judge her [Mrs. Lincoln] as she is, free from the exaggeration of praise or scandal."

By February 1862, the country's civil war was in full force. Daily, more and more mothers were burying their beloved sons as news from the war front brought only sadness and heartache. The First Lady understood such despair; it was the twelfth anniversary of Eddie's death, and no amount of time could fade her misery. But this

February, Mary had additional burdens to bear. The political congressional season had begun and it was customary for the White House to host a series of state dinners.

Mary knew the dinners would result in much criticism, so she suggested substituting smaller and fewer receptions as an alternative. Either way it did not matter, as she received protests proclaiming: "Don't Mr. and Mrs. Lincoln know there is a civil war!"

As Mary planned for the first reception, both Tad and Willie developed fevers. She wanted to cancel the function, but the boys' doctor assured her that things would be fine. Tad recuperated, but Mary remained preoccupied with Willie, who was still ill.

On the evening of the reception, Mary was visibly troubled, and left several times to check on her boy. His condition grew more grave with every passing hour. By the following afternoon her twelve-year-year-old son was dead.

Elizabeth Keckley, who assisted in the washing and dressing of the deceased boy, recounted the dramatic scene. Referring to the president, she wrote: "I never saw a man so bowed down with grief." Lincoln then murmured: "My poor boy, he was too good for this earth. God has called him home. I know that he is much better off in heaven, but then we loved him so. It is hard, hard to have him die!"

Mrs. Keckley went on to write: "Great sobs choked his utterance. He buried his head in his hands, and his tall frame was convulsed with emotion. His grief unnerved him, I shall never forget those solemn moments—genius and greatness weeping over love's idol lost."[8]

Devastated, Mary remained in dark seclusion, sobbing hysterically. For months, inconsolable in her grief, she was powerless to function and unable to enter Willie's bedroom let alone attend his funeral. She gave away, destroyed, or avoided anything that reminded her of the second child she had lost. Mary mourned as none but a mother could.

Somehow the president found the strength to carry on: "Mother, [as he called his wife after the children were born] do you see that large white building on the hill yonder? Try and control your grief, or it will drive you mad, and we may have to send you there."[9]

Mary remained in formal mourning for a year, and like Sara Polk before her, she chose to wear only black for the remainder of her life. All White House receptions and dinners were cancelled, yet no public sympathy was forthcoming.

The First Lady could not help but feel abandoned while the president was forced to focus intensely on the war and his presidential responsibilities. Her depression added immeasurably to her husband's already horrific burdens and finally Mary felt compelled to adapt. She wrote: "If I had not felt the spur of necessity urging me to cheer Mr. Lincoln, whose grief was as great as my own . . . I would never have smiled again."

Functioning the only way she knew how, Mary sought out the help of mediums to communicate with her dead sons whom she saw at the foot of her bed at night. She also indulged in irrational shopping sprees, accumulating more and more debt.

In January 1863, the president issued his Emancipation Proclamation. The proclamation, not yet law, was a war measure; although it did not free all slaves, it did alter the nature of the war by committing the Union to ending slavery. As federal troops successfully advanced forward, freedom advanced with them. Slavery was legally abolished in the United States when the Thirteenth Amendment to the Constitution was ratified in 1865.

Mary continued her unannounced and therefore ignored frequent visits to military hospitals. Her personal financial donations to both the military and the Contraband Society also went unnoticed.

That summer, Mary took a dreadful fall from a carriage, hitting her head causing a concussion. Her health remained considerably poor after that incident, fueling doubts about her mental stability.

The Union army defeated Confederate soldiers in the decisive Battle of Gettysburg that July; four months later, the president gave the most quoted speech in U.S. history. Lincoln's 269-word Gettysburg Address—beginning with "Fourscore and seven years ago our fathers brought forth on this continent a new nation"—delivered in just over two minutes, redefined the Civil War as the country's "new birth of freedom."

By early 1865, Robert decided to leave Harvard Law School to enlist in the Union army. For some time he had pleaded with his parents for permission to join, and predictably his mother rigorously objected. The president finally had his eldest son assigned to General Grant's staff.

The presidential campaign was approaching, and Lincoln's reelection was not a foregone conclusion. In order to secure Southern votes, the Republican president asked Southern Democrat Andrew Johnson to be his vice-presidential running mate. When the nonconformist ticket won him reelection, President Lincoln's inaugural address personified his attitude of forgiveness, stating in part: "With malice toward none, with charity for all."

It was the first presidential inauguration in which black Americans participated, and the superbly proud First Lady reportedly chose to wear a two-thousand-dollar ensemble to her husband's second inaugural ball. The greater celebration occurred, however, five weeks later, when Confederate general Robert E. Lee surrendered to Union general Ulysses S. Grant in the presence of Robert Lincoln.

With the Civil War finally over, President Lincoln looked forward to a happier future. "We must be cheerful; between the war and the loss of our darling Willie we have both been very miserable," he told his wife. They hoped to travel and visit locations Lincoln had always dreamed of seeing, such as Jerusalem and Europe.

In the meantime, it had been several months since the presidential couple attended the theater, and they made arrangements to see the comedic play *Our American Cousin*. Holding hands and sitting in the presidential box at Ford's Theater, the unthinkable occurred. The president was abruptly and brutally shot in the back of the head by assassin John Wilkes Booth.*

Crying uncontrollably throughout the night and pleading with her dying husband to speak to her, then begging him "not to die or take her with him in death," Mary was once again inconsolable.

---

* Actor and Southern sympathizer John Wilkes Booth was hunted down and shot to death on April 26, 1865.

The following morning, April 15, 1865, President Lincoln died. To quote Mrs. Keckley: "No common mortal had died. The Moses of my people had fallen in the hour of his triumph." Regarding the president's widow, she continued: "I shall never forget the scene—the wails of a broken heart, the unearthly shrieks, the terrible convulsions, the wild, tempestuous outbursts of grief from the soul."[10]

Robert accompanied his mother back to the White House where the First Lady remained secluded in her bedroom throughout the entire funeral and beyond. Ten thousand individuals came to the Washington train station to pay their respects and say goodbye to the fallen president. His body was then carried in a twelve-day train procession that made several stops prior to Lincoln's Springfield burial.*

Five weeks passed before the deeply traumatized First Lady could bring herself to leave her executive mansion bed and depart Washington. When Mary finally left the capital city accompanied by her two sons, only Mrs. Keckley and the former president's physician were there to see the despondent widow off.

Unable to bear the thought of returning to Springfield and its memories without her spouse, Mary relocated to Chicago, Illinois, where she initially lived in hotels with Robert and Tad. Creditors soon began to aggressively pressure Mary for the debts she had secretly accumulated. They had to wait: her husband's estate, estimated at anywhere from $85,000 to $160,000, split three ways to include her sons, took two and one half years to settle.

Deeper in debt, with Tad now enrolled in private school, Mary begged and pleaded with Congress for an annual pension plus the hundred-thousand-dollar salary her husband would have received had he lived to the end of his four-year term. Instead, she was awarded a one-time grant of twenty-five thousand dollars, her husband's annual salary, which she used to purchase a home and pay off a portion of her debts.

Nearly penniless, depressed and lonely, not even Mary's sisters came

---

* Lincoln was the first president of the United States to be assassinated and the first to lie in state in the US Capitol rotunda.

to console her. Letters during that time described her life as a complete misery. In an attempt to raise money, she agreed to sell her old clothing through a commissioned agent who assured her of a large profit.

Mary not only made no money from the arrangement, she received more bad press and lost additional funds in the process. She was eventually forced to rent out her home, sell her furniture, and move into a boardinghouse with Tad; her physical illnesses, headaches, and depression were increasing.

When Mary thought matters could not get any worse, Lincoln's former law partner, William H. Herndon, wrote an appalling biography, *Herndon's Lincoln: The True Story of a Great Life*, of Lincoln. In addition to other things, he made one particularly hurtful and despicable accusation. He asserted that Lincoln's only true love had been Ann Rutledge, a young woman who died in her early twenties.

There is no way to know the truth or depth of Lincoln's feelings toward Miss Rutledge. At the time of their friendship Ann was engaged to another man, and any suggestion of a profound love on Lincoln's part or "with all his soul, mind and strength," as Herndon maintained, was simply conjecture. Although Mary never believed the rumor, that did not erase the cruel hurt it caused her. On the contrary, it only fueled the disparaging and injurious press.

When her dear friend Elizabeth Keckley published *Behind the Scenes*, it was the straw that broke the camel's back. Keckley wrote: "Everything I have written is strictly true; much has been omitted, but nothing has been exaggerated. . . . Had Mrs. Lincoln's acts never become public property, I should not have published to the world the secret chapters of her life. . . . I have written with the utmost frankness in regard to her—have exposed her faults as well as given her credit for honest motives. I wish the world to judge her as she is, free from the exaggeration of praise or scandal." [38]

With Robert now married to the daughter of a senator, in 1868 Mary and Tad moved to Frankfurt, Germany, in hope of finding a better life. But after living there for three years, Mary was still a lonely, grieving widow whose failing health had not improved. Then a smidgen of good fortune came Mary's way. Congress finally approved a three-thousand-dollar annual pension for the widow of their slain president, later increased to five thousand dollars. Furthermore, Robert and his wife made Mary a grandmother. One small rainbow's ray began to glimmer.

Like many rainbows, its beauty was short-lived. Mary had already formed the belief that every victory in her life would be immediately followed by a crushing defeat. Devastatingly, this time was no exception. Having recently turned eighteen, Tad, like his younger brother Willie, died from a fever.

Mary's despair could not be reversed. Like Jane Pierce before her, her sons' deaths were beyond consolation. Frantic with worry that Robert would also die an early death, Mary experienced bouts of hysteria; her obsession with shopping became more irrational than ever, and her fear of becoming destitute intensified. Unable to even find joy in her three grandchildren, and more forlorn and isolated than before, Mary observed the anniversary of Lincoln and Tad's deaths each month.

Convinced his mother was unable to manage her finances, let alone her life, Robert had Mary committed to Bellevue Place, a private sanitarium outside of Chicago. There was no question that Mary was far from conventional, and many believed her to be irrational, yet neither was there evidence that she was suicidal or dangerous. Nevertheless, it took only ten minutes for an all-male jury to declare her legally incompetent.

Needless to say, the wedge in Mary's already distant relationship with her son widened. It took four months, with her sister Betsey's help, for Mary to persuade the courts to release her into Betsey's care. Returning to live in her sister's Springfield home, after a period of time Mary was officially found "restored to reason."

Once again in charge of her life and hoping to find some form of peace, or maybe in fear that Robert would try to have her recommitted, Mary moved to France. Fluent in French, she was able to live in cheap Paris hotels, like a disturbed bag lady, for four years. With her health deteriorating and presumably homesick, she returned yet again to live with her older sister.

Now nearly blind (she believed it was from crying daily), Mary reconciled with Robert, who had become secretary of war in the Garfield administration.* Old and weary at only sixty-three, Mary died on July 16, 1882. She was buried beside her husband in Springfield's Oak Ridge Cemetery.

What Mary taught me:

Mary Todd Lincoln undeniably experienced and lived with the deepest possible grief. Yet, bits and pieces of her life consisted of remarkable gifts. Born into privilege, she received valuable educational opportunities, and was bestowed with highly regarded abilities.

Admired for attributes defined as "accomplished, gracious, sparkling" and as one who "could make a bishop forget his prayers," Mary was genuinely blessed. Lest we forget, she lived out her life's dream, with "no common mortal, but rather a genius with greatness."

But she did lack something extremely critical—she lost her purpose in life.

To quote Dr. Wayne Dyer: "You are not what you got." When buying and collecting objects becomes your only pleasure in life, something is seriously amiss. Mary taught me the importance of having a life purpose and living it. A purpose that is greater than ourselves and most certainly something greater than material items.

* Astonishingly, Robert Lincoln was at the scene of three presidential assassinations. Seventeen years after his father was fatally shot, Robert went to meet President Garfield at the train station; by the time he arrived, Garfield had been shot. Thirty-seven years after the first presidential assassination, President McKinley invited Robert to meet him in New York; the president was mortally wounded just prior to Robert's arrival.

18

Plain Mountain Woman of Tennessee

ELIZA JOHNSON

> It is all very well for those who like it, but I don't like this public life at all. I often wish the time would come when we could return to where I feel we best belong.

—ELIZA JOHNSON, IN REFERENCE TO THE WHITE HOUSE

Most assuredly, Eliza McCardle Johnson's preference was not to live in the executive mansion as the country's seventeenth First Lady. Nonetheless, like her predecessors Margaret Taylor and Jane Pierce, Eliza's dislike of public life did not negate the reality of her life. An actuality she could never have imagined in her youth.

Eliza McCardle was a child born into poverty in the mountains of Tennessee in 1810. She lost her father before her sixteenth birthday and lived alone with her widowed mother; they made quilts and hand-woven sandals to support themselves.

> #17 Eliza McCardle Johnson
>
> **Born:** October 4, 1810
> **Birthplace:** Leesburg, Tennessee
> **Married:** 1817 (Andrew Johnson)
> **Children:** 5
> **White House Years:** 1865–1869
> **Died:** January 15, 1876
> **Fact:** Taught husband how to form alphabet letters
> **Aka:** The Tailor's Wife

While still an adolescent, Eliza married a dirt-poor, uneducated young man—also in his teens—whose only skill was tailoring. Because he had lacked the opportunity for instruction, it was Eliza who taught her illiterate husband how to write his alphabet letters.

Thirty-eight years later, the two hard-working, committed former teenagers were residing in the White House as the president and his wife. Believing that hard work and education were the way to succeed, Eliza McCardle Johnson went from living in poverty to residing in the most respected mansion in the country. But although you can take people out of their environment you cannot always wash away their early persuasions.

Legend has it that Eliza McCardle was the first person young Andrew Johnson spoke to on ariving in Greeneville, Tennessee, from Raleigh, North Carolina; he was seeking a job as a tailor. Riding a two-wheeled cart on a dusty dirt road, Andrew was in need of directions when he stopped to speak to the tall young girl with hazel eyes, a strong nose, and brown curly hair parted in the middle.

The tale continues that Eliza said to her friends after that first meeting: "I'm going to marry him someday." Whether she actually said that or not, sixteen-year-old Eliza and eighteen-year-old Andrew were married some seven months later by Mordecai Lincoln (believed to be Abraham Lincoln's cousin), a local justice of the peace.

Renting a two-room house, the teenage couple lived in the rear while Andrew ran his hand-tailoring business in the front. The skilled craftsman was ambitious but lacked education, and Eliza is often credited with being Andrew's teacher. Eliza was skilled in reading and writing as well as proficient in mathematics. Known to have read aloud to her husband at length while he sewed clothing, Eliza gave all credit for learning to Andrew: "I taught him to form the letters, but he was an apt scholar and acquired all the rest of it himself."

Andrew may have been a scholar in his wife's eyes, but he was deeply insecure. His lack of confidence was so profound that Eliza became his constant cheerleader. Mentally and emotionally she supported her husband and his career. To further Andrew's development, Eliza encouraged her husband to join the local debating team, believing it would improve his confidence and oratorical skills.

Always quiet and reserved, Eliza's greatest influence on her husband, whom she called Andy, was her ability to soothe his temper and strengthen his weaknesses. Andrew proved to be an ambitious man who became a prosperous tailor before going into politics. He hired several employees for his business and owned as many as nine slaves at one time.

Soon Andrew was serving three terms as mayor of Greeneville while Eliza gave birth to four children, all two years apart, by the age of twenty-four.* Like many successful couples in the early 1800s, the Johnsons established a supportive marital arrangement, which suited them well throughout their forty-eight years of wedlock.

Eliza oversaw all family responsibilities, their property, farming, household, and finances. Andrew supported the family and lived wherever his career and country needed him. Often that meant Andrew had to leave the family for either the capital city of Nashville or Washington, DC.

At forty-two, after nearly twenty-six years of marriage, Eliza gave birth to her fifth and final child. By the following year, Eliza was already very ill with tuberculosis and remained an invalid for the balance of her life. Meanwhile, the modest close-knit Johnson clan grew as the children married and had offspring.

Andrew, now a senator from the South, was the only Democrat to remain loyal to the Union when the Civil War broke out. His pro-Union stand was so unpopular that he received death threats. Yet both he and Eliza remained steadfast in their anti-secession policy. The entire family proudly supported the Union. Sons Charles, now a doctor, and Robert joined the Union military, as did younger daughter Mary's husband, Daniel Stover. Eldest daughter Martha's husband, David Patterson, was imprisoned by the Confederate States of America (CSA).

When the Confederate forces took over Greeneville, they commandeered Eliza's home. Since illness had confined her to bed, she

---

* Martha (1828–1902), Charles (1830–1863), Mary (1832–1883), Robert (1834–1869), Andrew Jr. aka Frank (1852–1879).

was able to postpone leaving for a few months; during this time she and her family were verbally abused as "Unionists." Then, suddenly ordered to leave the Confederate area within thirty-six hours, Eliza managed to move her children and grandchildren through enemy lines to Nashville.

The dangerous and difficult trip took one month to navigate; obtaining food and shelter was problematic, as were the Confederate authorities who confronted them from time to time. According to one source, at least once they were forced to camp along a railroad track in the cold night. Another time, dinner for the grandchildren consisted of food Eliza had saved from her lunch earlier that day. Always maintaining her matriarchal role despite her poor health, Eliza managed to keep her family focused on their ultimate destination.

When his family finally arrived safely in Nashville thirty days after being chased from their home, Andrew wept with relief. It was seven years before Eliza returned home. By then the Confederate troops had used it for barracks, confiscated her slaves, and completely vandalized the house before moving on.

During the fighting of the Civil War, eldest son Charles was thrown from a horse (some say in a drunken stupor) and died from his injuries. Two years later in 1865, Andrew was elected vice president of the United States under Abraham Lincoln. Lincoln was a Northern Republican, while Johnson was a Southern Democrat. Not a typical presidential ticket, but Lincoln needed the balance to win his reelection.

Immediately following the election, Eliza's son-in-law Daniel Stover died of tuberculosis, leaving younger daughter Mary a widow with two children. Eliza's concern for her family continued, as Robert had become an alcoholic, and youngest son, Frank, like his mother, was now showing signs of tuberculosis.

The news of President Lincoln's assassination, only six weeks into her husband's vice-presidential tenure, horrified Eliza on many levels. Eldest sibling Martha wrote to her father: "[Mother] is almost deranged fearing that you will be assassinated."[1] Public life and politics were her husband's dream, not Eliza's. She had been a semi-invalid for almost thirteen years now, and like her predecessor Letitia Tyler, family and home were the only things in which she ever showed any interest. Longing for the simpler days when her husband was still a tailor, it took Eliza a few months to get her weak and compromised body to Washington.

For the first time a president moved his entire extended family, twelve in all, into the White House with him for the full length of his term. The Johnsons brought some cows with them to produce fresh milk and other dairy products. Occupied with family and happy to be seeing her five grandchildren daily, Eliza established herself in the upstairs private quarters where she primarily remained throughout her years in the White House.

Although Eliza would occasionally join private gatherings, she made only two public appearances—at a birthday party for her husband and a reception for Queen Emma of the Sandwich Islands (now Hawaii)—during her husband's tenure. This was partly due to poor health coupled with her aversion of public life—and, not often mentioned, to some extent because of the excessive criticism her immediate predecessor, Mary Lincoln, had received. The new First Lady was quick to recognize that scandalous gossip would sell quicker than lackluster realism.

Eldest daughter Martha disarmed critics shortly after arriving in the executive mansion by asserting: "We are plain people from the mountains of Tennessee, called here for a short time by a national calamity. We trust too much will not be expected of us." She proved to be a competent, unpretentious White House hostess in her mother's absence.

Martha had some familiarity with Washington, DC, and coincidentally the White House as well, from her school days. While her father was a congressman, Martha had attended school in the capital and been invited to spend holidays at the executive mansion with First Lady Sarah Polk. In addition, Martha was friendly with White House hostess Harriet Lane, a fellow classmate of hers at the Georgetown Catholic Female Seminary.

After years of war and a stampede of visitors paying respects to the slain president, the White House had fallen into a state of dilapidation. According to historian Bill Harris, the East Room was infested with lice and the State Dining Room filled with mold.[2] Unlike Mary Lincoln, the mansion's former hostess, Martha stayed within the thirty-thousand-dollar budget Congress approved for repairs of the torn rugs, drapes, stained walls, and floors.

Because of her interest in and respect for history, Martha also placed on public view portraits of former First Ladies and White House hostesses. Even though Eliza never learned to enjoy the executive mansion, she was proud of her family and their accomplishments.

When Eliza did appear downstairs, it was necessary for her to remain seated most of the time. Always gracious and forever the tailor's wife, Eliza was complimented for her decorum and her taste in the beautiful, plush fabrics she wore. Her successor, Julia Grant, wrote: "She always came into the drawing room after the long state dinners to take coffee and receive the greetings of her husband's guests . . . dressed elegantly and appropriately."[3]

Eliza spent the majority of her time in a room directly across the hall from her husband's office. Maintaining involvement in his life, Eliza was an important political advisor to Johnson. An avid reader of national newspapers and political journals, every day she clipped articles for her husband to read.

Eliza would show Andrew the "good news" in the evening and save the "bad news" for after breakfast the next morning. In addition to assisting the president with his speeches, the First Lady would walk across the hall to calm her husband down whenever it became necessary.

In spite of Eliza's frail health, unlike her predecessor Jane Pierce, she was rather strong in the face of adversity. Never wavering in her support for her husband despite political pressures, Eliza encouraged him to stand by his principles.

Political pressure on the president was coming from the radical Republicans in Congress who opposed him. Johnson was trying to enact former president Lincoln's "leniency reconstruction" for the South, but resentful radicals refused to yield. Sadly, we will never know if Lincoln's superior leadership abilities would or could have improved Reconstruction.

Tensions escalated after the president vetoed several major Reconstruction laws. In defiance, Johnson suspended the radical Republican secretary of war, Edwin Stanton, and appointed General Ulysses S. Grant in his place. Believing the president could not remove a cabinet member without Senate approval, Congress retaliated and began impeachment proceedings against the president, the first step toward possible removal from office.*

The nightmarish impeachment ordeal weighed heavily on Eliza. She told a visitor: "But for the humiliation and Mr. Johnson's feelings, I wish they would send us back to Tennessee—if it were possible, give us our poverty and peace again, so that we might learn how to live for our children and ourselves."[4]

The impeachment proceedings lasted over two months, with Johnson finally being acquitted by one vote. Upon the president's acquittal, the devoted First Lady commented: "I knew he'd be acquitted; I knew it!"

When the Johnson family left the White House nearly ten months later, they were praised for their conduct. "Seldom has the White House had such harmonious and well-behaved tenants" and "Highminded and honorable people" were quotes from a Washington newspaper. That was all true—as was their son Robert's alcoholism. He committed suicide at the age of thirty-five, just one month after his parents departed the executive mansion.

In addition to the sorrow of Robert's death, the family was distraught over the fact that their widowed daughter Mary's second mar-

* Like an indictment, impeachment is a formal statement of charges leading to possible conviction via legislative vote. When a majority of the House of Representatives passes "articles of impeachment" against a high official of government, the individual has been formally "impeached." Then a two-thirds majority of the Senate is required for conviction, prior to removal from office.

riage, to William Brown in 1869, was an unhappy union. Having grown up in a different era, her dutiful father wrote to Mary's husband: "Rather than have anything like [separation] happen in my family, I would sooner have everything I have sunk in the depths of Hell."[5] Mary and William Brown did hold their marriage together, but only temporarily. Out of respect for her father, Mary waited until after both her parents had died before filing for divorce.

In concert with their dispositions, Eliza longed to return home and Andrew yearned for politics. In 1874, five years after departing Washington, Andrew returned as the elected senator from Tennessee.* He believed the Senate election was his career vindication. The following July, Johnson went to visit Eliza, who was staying with their daughter Mary.

Senator Johnson remained at Mary's home after suffering a series of strokes, and died in 1875. His family and the entire town were present at the former president's funeral. That is to say everyone with the exception of his loyal, loving, supportive wife, who was too weak to attend. Six months later, also in Mary's home, Eliza died and was buried alongside her husband in the Andrew Johnson National Cemetery in Greeneville, Tennessee. Eliza's home, the one she so longed to return to during the Civil War, became a national monument in 1942.

What Eliza taught me:

Eliza Johnson, if remembered at all, will be recalled as the invalid wife of the first U.S. president to be impeached though not convicted. However, she was so much more. As an amiable, proper, and support-

---

* Johnson became one of seventy-four senators, fourteen of whom had taken part in his impeachment trial. Of the fourteen, two had voted him not guilty and twelve guilty of the charges against him.

ive wife devoted to her family, Eliza's beliefs in hard work, commitment, and schooling speak volumes. Eliza reinforced for me that regardless of one's humble beginnings, the way to succeed in life is through education and dedicated work.

19

Undeterred Devotee

JULIA GRANT

My life at the White House, was like a bright and beautiful dream and we were immeasurable happy. It was quite the happiest period of my life . . . the White House was a garden spot of orchids, and I wish it might have continued forever, except that it would have deterred others from enjoying the same privilege.

—JULIA GRANT

AFTER SO MUCH carnage from war—and four of the five preceding First Ladies (the exception being Mary Todd Lincoln) desperately not wanting to live in the White House— Julia Grant provided an invigorating change. The first First Lady to occupy the executive mansion for a full eight years since Elizabeth Monroe had departed in 1825, Julia brought back memories of Dolley Madison.

Both women loved being center stage, and each had great esteem for every aspect of the president's home, lifestyle, and hospitality.

> **#18 Julia Dent Grant**
>
> **Born:** January 26, 1826
> **Birthplace:** St. Louis, Missouri
> **Married:** 1848 (Ulysses Simpson Grant)
> **Children:** 4
> **White House Years:** 1869–1877
> **Died:** December 14, 1902
> **Fact:** Was cross-eyed
> **Aka:** The General's Wife

Julia's version of Dolley's dining abundance was serving twenty-course meals with constantly flowing wine. Dolley hosted the first White House wedding, for her sister Lucy Washington, and Julia hosted possibly the most lavish White House wedding, for her daughter Nellie Grant. Befriending several other First Ladies of both political parties, Julia and Dolley returned to Washington as widows, assuming the role of "grande dame." Jointly, they will be remembered for their charm and warmth.

Yet with all of their similarities, the two women grew up with very dissimilar families and backgrounds. Unlike Dolley's, the next story is about a woman who was born into wealth, lived financially bankrupt the majority of her married life, then moved into a garden spot of orchids and sobbed like a child when it came time to leave the executive mansion.

Julia Boggs Dent was born on the western frontier in 1826. She was the eldest daughter in her family, the fifth of eight children and the favorite child of her slaveholding prosperous father, Colonel Frederick Dent. Colonel Dent made his fortune in the fur trade, allowing Julia to grow up enjoying wealth and cultural benefits. Educated at a local school, she also spent seven years at Mauro Boarding School in St. Louis; she excelled at horseback riding and dancing.

Short and stocky, barely five feet tall, with dark, thick hair and crossed brown eyes, Julia acknowledged: "I was the shyest of little girls, and if I had any admirers, I am sure I did not know it."[1] Often referred to as plain, Julia's attractiveness came from her quick, winning smile and sparkling charm.

When she was eighteen Julia met Ulysses S. Grant,* a West Point classmate of her older brother, Frederick Jr. Fond of the outdoors, they both enjoyed riding horses through the countryside, and although Ulysses did not dance, he escorted Julia to many.

Both Julia and her mother, Ellen Wrenshall Dent, were convinced Ulysses was destined for great things. Colonel Dent, on the other hand, was not as impressed with the young soldier's future prospects, disagreed with Grant's politics, and opposed a marriage.

---

* Ulysses' given name was Hiram Ulysses Grant. Not liking the acronym HUG, he changed it to Ulysses Hiram. The West Point military academy mistakenly registered Grant as Ulysses Simpson Grant, and he never chose to change it. Simpson was his mother's maiden name.

Secretly engaged, Ulysses went off to fight in the Mexican War, serving under General Zachary Taylor; he wrote to Julia faithfully. Four years passed and purportedly Julia saw her beloved only once during that time. When Ulysses returned, Colonel Dent reluctantly consented to their wedding in his St. Louis home.

Julia first met the parents of "Ulyss," as she called her sweetheart, on her honeymoon. The Grants so disapproved of their son marrying into a Southern slaveholding family that they refused to attend the wedding. Jesse Grant, Ulysses's father, later objected to Julia's spending habits and overindulgence of her children. So much so, that he repeatedly made attempts to separate Ulysses from his bride.

Despite continued opposition from both fathers, Julia and Ulysses had a loving, supportive marriage with four children who grew up in a happy home.* Like Margaret Taylor before her, Julia was the ideal army wife. She was adaptable, had a good disposition, and was able to make their surroundings into a warm home away from the pressures of the military.

Julia took responsibility for her children's early education, encouraged their independence, and tolerated their mischievousness. The only thing that seemed to bother Julia was the necessary separations she suffered due to her husband's military assignments.

After being promoted to captain in 1854, Ulysses resigned from the army, saying: "I have the dearest little wife in the world . . . and I want to live with my family." Unsubstantiated rumors, which haunted Ulysses throughout his life, circulated saying that he resigned to avoid a court-martial for drunkenness.

Historians all seem to agree that Ulysses S. Grant was an alcoholic. Nevertheless, he did not drink, or at least not often, around his wife as she had a calming effect on him. This appears to be a reoccurring attribute of many presidential wives. His sister-in-law later wrote: "If General Grant was ever a victim of the liquor habit, it was a condition

---

* Frederick Dent (1850–1912), Ulysses "Buck" Simpson (1852–1929), Ellen, aka Nellie (1855–1922), Jesse Root (1858–1934).

which he happily concealed from those nearest his heart, closest in their association with him, and who loved him best." A colleague said of Grant: "He was never under [alcohol's] sway to the direct or indirect detriment of the service for a single moment."[2]

Now a civilian with a growing family to support, Ulysses failed in one job or business adventure after another. Although the Grants were seemingly dependent on both their families and constantly needed to borrow money, Julia never lost faith in her husband. She maintained: "[Ulysses] was made for great things, not for little things."

During this time, Ulysses built the family a log cabin on a plot of farming land Colonel Dent had given his daughter. Ulysses called it "Hardscrabble," and true to its name, the farming venture failed. Ulysses tried his hand in vain at real estate management before moving his family to Illinois. There they shared living accommodations with Ulysses' brother while he worked in his family's leather business. Despite several years of financial embarrassment the couple's secure and blissful family life was not affected.

When the Civil War broke out, an even greater wedge divided the Grant and Dent families. Colonel Dent was a passionate Confederate, and even some members of the Grant family urged Ulysses to fight for the Confederacy when he reentered the army. Once a Democrat like her father, Julia was now a Republican like her husband; to her father's displeasure, the couple was pro-Union.

After Ulysses was commissioned a brigadier general in the US Army, Julia made repeated wartime trips, living wherever she could on the way, to visit her spouse. She refused to settle in Detroit, where Ulysses believed she and the family would be safe. Not feeling welcome herself, she would periodically send the children, now three to eleven years old, to stay with their paternal grandparents.

Like so many other military wives, Julia was left alone to deal with family crises; she once narrowly escaped Confederate capture. When confronted by women loyal to the Confederacy, she told them: "I did not know a thing about this dreadful Constitution . . . I would not know where to look for it even if I wished to read it . . . I really was much grieved at my ignorance of these matters, but since then I have learned that even the Chief Justice is sometimes puzzled over the interpretation of this same Constitution."[3]

Victory in the Civil War as supreme commander of the Union forces catapulted General Grant into celebrity status. With her husband becoming the great man Julia always knew he was, she and her children were now in the public eye as well. Conducting herself with dignity and sense, Julia entered the world of politics and society, intermingling with the wealthy. It was a far cry, and undoubtedly a considerable step up from her life at Hardscrabble.

Around this time, Julia considered having an operation to correct her crossed eyes, confiding in a friend that her eyes "always made her feel ugly." Ulysses interfered, saying: "Did I not see you and fall in love with you with these same eyes? I like them just as they are." Many years later Julia would say that she "rested and was warmed in the sunlight of his loyal love and great fame."[4]

In April of 1865, the Grants were invited to join President Lincoln and the First Lady at Ford's Theater for a performance of *Our American Cousin*. Reportedly, the messenger delivering the invitation told Julia that the general had already accepted. However, Julia dreamt of tragedy that night and declined the request.

Family folklore had it that Julia's mother was psychic, and Julia believed she had inherited this gift from her mother. Whether you believe in Julia's supernatural ability, or assume she was merely irritated by Mary Lincoln's embarrassing displays of jealousy (recalling a particular occasion directed toward her), it is not unreasonable to suppose that Grant's life was spared by Julia's decision not to join the president at Ford's Theatre. Undoubtedly, the same individuals who assassinated President Lincoln that evening would also have targeted General Grant.

Now living in Washington where he advised President Lincoln's successor, Andrew Johnson, the general was frequently honored. Julia earned the reputation of being "a sensible, plain, good woman." She sincerely enjoyed entertaining and was praised for her sociability. After her husband, the fifth nationally known war hero—following George Washington, Andrew Jackson, William Henry Harrison, and

Zachary Taylor—was elected president in 1869, Washington society added "unaffected First Lady" to Julia's attributes.

The Grant White House was homey and welcoming, with moderate elegance. It was a warmhearted home where various friends and relatives spent frequent, lengthy visits. The family worshiped at the Methodist church and shared private dinners. The First Lady's brother Fred, Grant's former schoolmate, served as the president's secretary.

While older sons Frederick and Buck were studying at West Point and Harvard, the two younger children—Nellie, fourteen, and Jesse, eleven—along with their now widowed maternal grandfather, resided in the president's home full time. Even after occupying the executive mansion, Colonel Dent forever remained unimpressed with his presidential son-in-law. He was not the last in-law to have the same sentiment.

Julia had been accustomed to owning slaves prior to the Emancipation Proclamation, and she relied heavily on domestic help. She hired a new housekeeper and an Italian steward who made the multicourse meals at the White House famous. The First Lady was notorious for serving up to twenty courses on hand-painted French china, with six wineglasses and flowers at each place setting. It was the period in American history known as the gilded age when homes were overdecorated and most things generally overdone.

Like her predecessor Mary Todd Lincoln, Julia could be lavish in her spending, but unlike Mrs. Lincoln, Julia was not criticized for it. The *New York Tribune* spoke for the public when it described the First Lady as "a sunny, sweet woman; too unassuming to be a mark of criticism, too simple and kindly to make the mistakes which invite it."[5] Moreover, the country was no longer fighting a civil war, another important factor for the change in public attitude.

When President Grant ran for reelection in 1872, he was the first man to run against a female presidential candidate. The Equal Rights Party ticket consisted of Victoria Woodhull and Frederick Douglass, the first black vice-presidential candidate. The prominent leader of women's rights at the time was Susan B. Anthony, a good friend of

Julia's. Miss Anthony chose to support President Grant, proving once again that a First Lady's influence cannot be ignored. Women's rights would be contested for many years to come, and another forty-seven years would pass before women won the right to vote.

The same year the president won reelection, Julia's unabashed Confederate father passed away. His funeral was held in the Blue Room of the White House.

The following year, 1874, perhaps one of the most elaborate of all White House weddings took place. A far cry from the wedding of Elizabeth Monroe's daughter, fifty-four years earlier, eighteen-year-old Nellie Grant married Englishman Algernon Sartoris. Although Julia had misgivings about her future son-in-law, she did not object to the marriage.

The East Room was decorated in white blossoms, including a wedding bell of white roses. The bride wore a white satin gown with a two-thousand-dollar rose-point veil ordered from Brussels.[6] Inundated with wedding presents, the couple also received a house in London, a gift from Nellie's father-in-law.

According to reports, the president and First Lady gave their daughter a diamond necklace, diamond earrings, and a ten-thousand-dollar check. After marrying, Nellie divided her time between her English and American families; however, Julia's doubts about the success of her daughter's marriage were valid. Nellie eventually divorced her husband, and returned to the United States with her three children.

It was no secret that Julia loved living in the White House and hoped for a third term. The president, knowing his wife, did not tell Julia of the letter he personally mailed to the Republican State Convention. The message, with copies to the press, announced that he would not seek a third term. When Julia protested after belatedly learning the news, the president replied: "I know you too well. It would never have gone if [you] had read it."[7] Julia cried upon leaving the White House.

For the next two years Julia and the former president toured the world, were received as dignitaries, and greeted by cheering crowds. Always perfectly composed, Julia's engaging personality and warmth were forever evident.

After returning home, the family finally entered private life. With loans from millionaire friends like William Vanderbilt, Ulysses once again went into business. The venture was a partnership in a brokerage firm with Ferdinand Ward (Grant & Ward), a friend of their son Buck. As he had in all his other business ventures, the former president went bankrupt.

In addition to being humiliated, Ulysses was acutely worried about Julia's welfare. The Grants sold much of their personal property and belongings, including prized swords from the Civil War, to meet their financial obligations of around $150,000.

When creditor friends insisted Julia keep her personal mementos from her White House years, she amiably gave them instead to the Smithsonian Institution. Struggling to support his family, the former president wrote magazine articles about the war. In the midst of financial ruin, Ulysses was diagnosed with inoperable throat cancer, presumably caused by smoking twenty cigars a day during the war.

Another woman might have collapsed under the pressure, but not Julia. With genuine courage, she continued to do what she had always done—she maintained a warm, cozy, and cheerful home, and devoted herself to her husband's care. Ulysses then began to write his memoirs in hopes of supporting his wife after his death. Good friend Mark Twain persuaded a publisher to purchase them.

Julia was devastated when her husband died in 1885 after nearly thirty-seven years of marriage. In the end, Ulysses did manage to provide comfortably for his bride by completing his *Personal Memoirs of Ulysses S. Grant* just days before his death. Not only highly regarded, but also a bestseller of its time, *Personal Memoirs* remains popular to this day. Royalties estimated at $500,000 made Julia's seventeen years of widowhood comfortable. But I am convinced that Julia would have preferred to live in poverty with the general than to be wealthy without him.

After refocusing her interests on her children, their families, and her twelve grandchildren, Julia eventually moved back to Washington, DC. There she cultivated friendships with her successors Frances Cleveland, Caroline Harrison, and Edith Roosevelt, before her death in 1902 at seventy-six. Both General Grant and Julia are entombed in the Grant Memorial in New York City.

What Julia taught me:

Julia Grant is a prime example of the philosophy "beauty is only skin deep." True beauty resonates from within. Julia taught me that warmth, poise, cheerfulness, and self-confidence will always trump aloofness, tactlessness, melancholy, and insecurity. Julia not only loved her husband, she also took care of him. Ulysses not only "saw" his wife's beauty, he was able to "feel" it as well—an exceptionally far greater quality to possess.

20

Lemonade Lucy

LUCY WEBB HAYES

If a contraband [runaway slave] is in Camp, don't let the 23rd
Regiment [of which her husband was a colonel] be disgraced
by returning [him or her] or anything of the kind.

—LUCY HAYES

WITH THE CIVIL WAR over, Reconstruction struggled to resolve
the Southern states' secession issues, and the gilded age of unprecedented economic, industrial, and pop-
ulation expansion had begun.

It appeared the nation had taken
notice of a momentous moral message: the first black man was elected
to the US Senate. Also, the US Justice
Department was created, and the Fif-
teenth Amendment to the Constitution—which affirmed the right to vote
and forbade states to deny that right
based on race, color, or "previous condition of servitude"—was ratified.

> **#19 Lucy Webb Hayes**
>
> **Born:** August 28, 1831
> **Birthplace:** Chillicothe, Ohio
> **Married:** 1852 (Rutherford Birchard
> Hayes)
> **Children:** 8
> **White House Years:** 1877–1881
> **Died:** June 25, 1889
> **Fact:** 1st First Lady to graduate college
> **Aka:** Lemonade Lucy

The importance of education was recognized, and more states
began to institute compulsory school attendance laws; the first free
schools for poor students were opened.

Women were also beginning to break out of the mold. Between
1870 and 1877, the first woman would graduate from law school, an-

other was admitted to the Massachusetts Institute of Technology, earning a bachelor's degree and became a professional chemist, and a third earned a PhD.

The nation was evolving and education was improving, yet segregation, prejudice, and injustice would continue for another century and beyond. It appears that generations of Americans would be taught discrimination in tandem with justice and righteousness.

Lucy Webb Hayes was opposed to slavery long before her husband fought in the Civil War. This ingrained conviction began in early childhood, passed down from her Southern physician father and equally moral and principled mother.

Lucy's father, Dr. James Webb, served in the War of 1812 and thereafter made a career in medicine. When Dr. Webb inherited over a dozen slaves from a deceased aunt in 1833, he traveled to Kentucky from his home in Ohio to free them. While still in Kentucky, a sweeping cholera epidemic hit the region. Dr. Webb worked long and hard to save the victims, all the while losing his own brother and parents to the disease. Dr. Webb himself became infected and passed away before his wife could reach him.

Now a widow facing poverty with three small children (two-year-old Lucy, born in Ohio in 1831, was her youngest), Maria Webb was asked why she did not sell her husband's slaves. Maria's reply made a deep and lasting impression on her only daughter: "I will take in washing to support my family before I would take money for the sale of a human being."[1] Maria did in fact take in boarders and cleaned other people's homes to support her family. Years after Lucy married; she employed some of her father's family's former slaves and encouraged them to get an education.

In addition to opposing slavery and supporting temperance, the Webbs emphasized Methodist morality and education for all their children. While her two older brothers went on to become doctors like their father, Lucy herself was a conscientious student with proficient reasoning abilities. In addition to her studies, she played piano and guitar.

Considered pretty and petite, Lucy had wide-set dark, shining eyes beneath gently sloping eyebrows set in an almost heart-shaped face. She wore her dark hair parted in the middle, held together with a comb high on the back of her head. Outgoing and always in good spirits, Lucy had a rather angelic smile, and was often described as kindhearted.

At fifteen, she met twenty-four-year-old Rutherford Hayes, a promising lawyer. Young, and with her college education ahead of her, Lucy enrolled in Cincinnati Wesleyan Female College with approximately four hundred other female students. She did well in school, liked to read, excelled at public speaking, and graduated with honors four years later in 1850, delivering a dissertation entitled "The Influence of Christianity on National Prosperity."

Just prior to graduation, Lucy became reacquainted with the skilled attorney she had met years earlier. As it turned out, Lucy's and the gentleman's mother were good friends. Recognizing a good match, the women secretly hoped their children would grow fond of each other. With a little motherly endorsement they did, and after a year and a half of courting, twenty-one-year-old Lucy Ware Webb married thirty-year-old Rutherford Birchard Hayes.

Mother's intuition being what it is—you will recall Abigail Adams's advice to her son, and Jane Pierce's mother's attitude toward her beau—Lucy and Rutherford had a happy, affectionate marriage. In addition to a close relationship with her spouse, Lucy maintained a loving bond with both her and Rutherford's family. Together, the extended families visited frequently, cared for one another's children, and helped each other often. In fact, Rutherford's closest sister, Fanny, became Lucy's dearest friend.

It was Fanny who introduced Lucy to the women's rights movement that was taking hold and supported her active interest in it. Fanny would take Lucy with her to lectures and, in addition to friendship, they both shared a strong interest in public affairs. When Fanny died during childbirth, Lucy not only lost a valued friend and family member, she also lost the one ardent and influential female voice regarding women's rights in the family.

With her own family beginning to multiply and Fanny's voice silenced, Lucy's involvement in the women's movement waned. Lucy was a traditional woman and remained so; she had married a traditional man of his times, and he spoke for the family.

Lucy's child rearing, which began before the Civil War, continued to increase after the war. Of the eight children she bore five lived to adulthood.* The family circle included Lucy's mother and one bachelor brother who also lived with them. While Lucy was busy with child rearing and household responsibilities, Rutherford was building his law practice with partner John Herron (Herron was the father of Helen Herron, later Mrs. William Howard Taft) and attending political meetings. It was Lucy who urged her husband to defend fugitive slaves in court and encouraged his political career—a career she referred to as "ours."

The Civil War disrupted their nine years of pleasant married life. Like countless other wives, a valiant, pregnant Lucy supported her husband's decision to volunteer for this "holy and just cause," as she called it. Six months later, Lucy gave birth to her fourth son. Home now with three active boys and a colicky baby, Lucy wrote to her husband: "Drilling a regiment would be play." Any mother could appreciate her situation; still, there was nothing playful about the Civil War.

For the next four years, Rutherford saw active duty and was wounded several times, most seriously in 1862 while Lucy was still breastfeeding their youngest. After receiving a telegram regarding her husband's injury, Lucy left the children with her mother, who then had to seek a wet nurse for the baby, and began a prolonged search that led her to several locations before locating her injured husband in Maryland. Many years later after being elected president, Ruther-

* Birchard Austin (1853–1926), James Webb Cook (1856–1934), Rutherford Platt (1858–1927), Joseph Thompson (1861–1863), George Crook (1864–1866), Fanny (1867–1950), Scott Russell (1871–1923), Manning Force (1873–1874).

ford would joke "Here's my wife who visits Washington and Baltimore before she visits her wounded husband!" Despite her good nature, Lucy never saw the humor in his comment.

It was Lucy's older brother Joe who treated Rutherford's shattered left elbow and managed to save his arm. In addition to nursing her husband, Lucy would also care for other wounded soldiers and "come back in tears," according to her spouse. She developed a compassionate and sympathetic concern for her husband's comrades that lasted throughout the war and beyond. Lucy spent so much time in camp with Rutherford and his men of the 23rd Ohio Volunteer Infantry that they nicknamed her "mother of the regiment."

The following year, Lucy rented out her home so that she and her sons could join her husband, now a colonel. The family's happy reunion was saddened by the death of their youngest boy, Joseph, just eighteen months old. Remaining with her husband, Lucy stoically sent her baby's body home for burial.

Pregnant once again with another boy, George, Lucy continued to care for the sick and mother the young enlisted men (including future president Lieutenant William McKinley), all the while waiting for her husband and his regiment to return from battle. She herself suffered from rheumatism and chronic "sick headaches."

Nominated for Congress and promoted to brigadier general of the Ohio Volunteers in 1865, Hayes refused to leave his military duties to campaign. Even after being elected, he did not leave the army until the fighting ended. Ecstatic that the war was at last over, Lucy still held some bitter feelings. She wrote: "I am sick of the endless talk of Forgiveness—taking them back like brothers . . . Justice and Mercy should go together."[2] Lucy grieved for all the men, particularly those she had known who would never return home, as well as for their families.

With her husband now in Congress, and fascinated with politics, Lucy would attend congressional debates while visiting her husband in Washington. However, after her return home from one such visit in 1866, Lucy described the year as her "worst." All of her children were afflicted with scarlet fever and, nearly three years after losing her son Joseph, Lucy lost baby son George, not yet two years old.

In addition to that tragedy, Lucy also lost her mother and mother-in-law that same year, both of whom she nursed. Prior to her passing, Rutherford's mother, Sophia Hayes, complimented her daughter-in-law's "tender regard for the elderly a rare and excellent trait of character."[3]

Away from home more than he wanted to be, Rutherford began to feel isolated from his family and wrote to his wife: "There is nothing in the small ambition of Congressional life . . . to compensate for separation from you [Lucy]."[4] Wanting to remain in politics yet not wanting to be away from family, Rutherford returned home and sought the governorship.

The following year, Lucy became the proud mother of her only daughter, Fanny (named after her departed sister-in-law), as well as the wife of the governor of Ohio. Now that she was the First Lady of the state, there were those who looked to Lucy for a supportive feminine voice.

Although a firm believer in higher education for women, Lucy refused to speak out publicly for women's suffrage or female business enterprises. A passionate and fervent supporter of orphanages, she presented herself as a traditional woman as opposed to the "new woman" struggling to emerge.

Lucy's delivery in 1871 of an eleven-pound son, Scott, took a heavy toll on her health. Nevertheless, she gave birth to one last child, Manning, who died a year later on Lucy's forty-third birthday. Years afterward, reflecting on her life and the loss of three children, Lucy remained grateful; in a letter to a son she wrote: "With all our changes and sorrows, a happy and blessed family we have been and are."[5]

One of the county's most heavily contested and intensely partisan presidential contest took place in 1876 between Rutherford B. Hayes and Samuel J. Tilden. During this most passionate campaign, many feared bodily harm for both candidates. Not an unreasonable fear considering that a bullet came through the Hayes' dining room window while the family was having supper one evening. Yet Lucy continued her unfaltering support of Rutherford as he went on campaigning.

Though Tilden won the popular vote, both parties were in dispute over the electoral votes necessary for a win. History was repeating itself fifty-two years after Andrew Jackson won the popular vote yet lacked the electoral votes he needed against John Quincy Adams in the 1824 election. Republicans controlled the Senate, but Democrats controlled the House. A bipartisan commission of seven Republicans, seven Democrats, and one Independent was established to determine the election.

When the Independent Politician, a Supreme Court justice, unexpectedly retired from office, he was replaced with a Republican and the vote went strictly along partisan lines. The election results remained in doubt for months, being decided only three days before the inauguration. As in so many other grueling and difficult times in her life, Lucy demonstrated enormous strength of character.

The Hayes waited until March 1, 1877, before boarding a train to Washington, not knowing if they would be returning home in a few days.* Finally, they received a telegram en route notifying them of Rutherford's win. Because the outcome of the 1877 election was uncertain for so long, no preparations for the customary parade and inaugural ball were ever made.

This was the first time in history that a president-elect took the oath of office in the White House. Retiring President Grant insisted on a private swearing-in ceremony due to all the controversy surrounding the election. Additionally, the inauguration was put off from Sunday, March 4 to Monday, March 5, creating a one-day gap between the outgoing and incoming president.

The Hayeses moved into the White House with three of their five surviving children. Birchard was away at Harvard Law School and Rutherford Platt was attending Cornell. Eldest son James (referred to

* In October 1933 the Twentieth Amendment (aka the Lame Duck Amendment) was ratified, ending the president's and vice president's terms of office on January 20; all prior administrations had ended on March 4.

by his middle name Webb), who had already graduated from Cornell, became his father's confidential secretary and general aide. The two younger children, Scott and Fanny, were only five and nine years old when their father was elected president.

Although in the past the term "First Lady" had been periodically used in reference to the president's wife, it was not until Lucy resided in the White House that it became common usage. In 1877, an article in the *Independent* officially designated Lucy Webb Hayes as the "First Lady."

In 1880, Lucy crisscrossed the country with the president, from Washington to San Francisco, earning the name "First Lady of the Land." Years later, when the popular play *Dolley Madison or The First Lady in the Land* by Charles Nirdlinger was staged (the titled referred to President Taylor's eulogy of Dolley Madison) it became even more popular and has been used ever since.

However, because all alcohol was banned from the Hayes White House, the one title Lucy will be remembered by is "Lemonade Lucy." Because she strongly supported the temperance movement, the public believed it was Lucy who insisted on the ban. In reality, it was the president who instituted it, continuing the family's practice of serving no liquor in their home. Jokes like "water flowed like wine in the Hayes White House" were often repeated.

Although she received political support from the temperance movement, Lucy did not advocate Prohibition. She believed people should set individual practices within their own homes. When asked to forbid the use of wine in the White House by a minister's wife, Lucy replied: "Madame, it is my husband, not myself, who is President. I think that a man who is capable of filling so important a position, as I believe my husband to be, is quite competent to establish such rules as will obtain in his house . . . without any interference of others, directly or through his wife."[6]

Reminiscent of her immediate predecessor, Lucy entertained extensively, though dancing and card playing were banned on principle. According to her husband's diary, Lucy "hated" state dinners and felt inadequate to Julia Grant's elaborate formal affairs. Her preference was casual, relaxed social programs like the annual Easter Egg Roll she instituted on the White House Lawn in 1878.

The First Lady's "madonna-like" appearance, college degree, and modesty were written about often. A religious woman, Lucy prayed with the president and her family after breakfast each morning, and played the piano in church on Sundays.

Lucy embodied Christian morality and was known for her genuine interest in human welfare. She continued to extend charity to those in need, as she had done all her life, and particularly provided for Civil War veterans and their families. She was known for her generosity toward the homeless, feeding and often giving them money. In addition to visiting prisons and reform schools, providing improved care in mental health asylums became a priority for Lucy.

According to written accounts of the time, Lucy was universally admired as First Lady, although criticized for not supporting women's suffrage. Her reasoning was straightforward: first, her husband did not support it; second, illiteracy was still high among women. If a woman was denied an education and considered incapable of reasoning, what good would giving her the vote do? She later wrote to a son: "Without intending to be public I find myself for a quiet mind-her-own-business woman rather notorious."[7]

Congress was also concerned with education and now required states, in their constitutions, "to guarantee" free nonsectarian education to all children. A nation once so completely divided was trying to become whole again, with seceding states gradually rejoining the Union. The South, so financially devastated by the Civil War, had little money for extravagances like schooling. In spite of that, by 1877 more than 500,000 black children were attending school.

While the country was slowly moving toward better education, the issues of voting and abstinence from intoxicating drinks were being debated. Medicine was also advancing, but unfortunately not in sufficient time to save the thirteen thousand people who died during the last great yellow fever epidemic in Mississippi.

The following year, in 1879, Alexander Graham Bell installed and demonstrated the first White House telephone (the phone number was 1)[8], and Thomas Edison introduced the First Lady to the phonograph. The Hayeses also installed running water and plumbing in the White House bathrooms.

In addition to these advancements, it only seems appropriate that women lawyers were now permitted to practice before the Supreme Court at the same time that the first First Lady to earn a college degree was residing in the executive mansion.

By 1880, the census recorded the US population at 50.1 million, including about 2.8 million immigrants. Lucy felt it was time to recognize all former presidents whose pictures were not in the White House. She commissioned an Ohio artist to paint those portraits, as well as a full-length portrait of Martha Washington to accompany her husband's.

One of Lucy's happiest memories in the executive mansion was her twenty-fifth, silver wedding anniversary celebration. She wore her wedding dress (with the seams taken out a bit) and she and Rutherford stood in the Blue Room and reenacted their vows before the minister who had married them so many years ago.

Like James K. Polk, true to his resolution, President Hayes did not run for another term. Considering what he wrote to a former classmate in January 1881—"Nobody ever left the Presidency with less regret, less disappointment, fewer heart-burnings, or more general content with the result of his term (in his own heart, I mean) than I do"[9]— the President sounded more than content to leave the executive mansion.

The White House doorman said that never before or since had a First Lady's departure caused so many tears to flow. Loved by the entire White House staff, every year Lucy gave Christmas gifts to each employee. All were remembered by name as her young children distributed the items. Being the committed advocate she was to education, the First Lady even allowed the staff time off to pursue their studies.

The Christian Temperance Union commissioned a portrait of

Lucy to hang in the White House. Furthermore, an Illinois women's organization presented her with a set of six leather-bound volumes of praise, including hundreds of autographs from prominent men and women, some offering their own words of respect.

During retirement, Lucy was happy in her last years, spending time with family. She became the first president of the Woman's Home Missionary Society of the Methodist Episcopal Church. She did not participate publicly with the temperance organizations, remaining true to her principles and policies.

Eventually, the former First Lady's health began to deteriorate. At the age of fifty-eight, Lucy had a paralyzing stroke that left her unable to speak. She died four days later in her husband's arms. The former president wrote in his diary: "I consider the single most interesting fact in my life is my marriage to Lucy Ware Webb. She was the Golden Rule Incarnate."

What Lucy taught me:

Lucy Hayes personified her moral philosophy, yet at the same time did not believe in imposing her beliefs on others: A good example of this was her position on Prohibition. She had a very strong viewpoint regarding alcohol, yet her position remained within her household. Lucy taught me to live and support one's values without radicalism. Additionally, her commitment to the importance of education, a re-occurring theme among our first ladies, emphasized the need and significance of continual learning in life.

21

First Betrayed, Then Widowed

LUCRETIA GARFIELD

> Very many men may be loved devotedly by wives who know them to be worthless. But I think when a man has a wife who holds him in large esteem, who knows that in him there is no pretense, nothing but the genuine then he has reason to believe in his own worth.

—LUCRETIA GARFIELD, IN LETTER TO HER HUSBAND

HISTORIAN Margaret Bassett said: "It is a pity that James Garfield had so little time in the presidency, if only for the sake of this interesting woman [Lucretia Garfield], now largely lost to history." A highly intelligent woman with an independent mind, Lucretia had a strong work ethic and high moral values. She was also born into a man's world that held limited opportunities for women and maintained narrow, prudish Victorian attitudes toward sexuality. Like her fellow sorority sisters Abigail Adams and Sarah Polk before her, this is the story of another woman's remarkable struggle to reconcile her life within the values of the times she lived in.

> **#20 Lucretia Rudolph Garfield**
>
> **Born:** April 19, 1832
> **Birthplace:** Hiram, Ohio
> **Married:** 1858 (James Abram Garfield)
> **Children:** 7
> **White House Years:** 1881
> **Died:** March 14, 1918
> **Fact:** 2nd First Lady whose husband was assassinated
> **Aka:** Crete

The eldest of four children, Lucretia Rudolph was born in Ohio in 1832 and named after her maternal grandmother. Lucretia had a happy, although ailing, childhood and was close to her two younger brothers and sister. Her family, particularly Lucretia's father, the very core of the Disciples of Christ in their village, believed strongly in education. Zebulon Rudolph was a religious leader and farmer who co-founded the Eclectic Institute (later Hiram College) in Ohio.

Sickly as a young girl, Lucretia was educated at home and also attended Garrettsville Public Grammar School until her early teens. She loved to read and did so extensively, as her health prevented many outdoor activities. A small, thin girl of medium height, Lucretia had delicate features, with high cheekbones, dark brown hair, and brown eyes.

By the age of fifteen, Lucretia was a boarding student at Geauga Seminary, where in addition to algebra, science, and geography, her studies focused on Greek and Latin. It was there that she met fellow student James Garfield, an ardent convert to the Disciples church. He wrote that she had "good, practical, sound common sense" and "a well balanced mind . . . logical and precise."

Both students went on to the Eclectic Institute where Lucretia continued her original course of study in addition to French, classical literature, music, and art. When James began to teach Greek at the institute, Lucretia became his student for a brief period of time.

James had a commanding, magnetic presence. He was handsome and charismatic, with a magical voice; yet in his youth he was almost unaware of his charm. Someone you might call a heartbreaker—and many girls' hearts were broken when James moved on. He departed for Massachusetts to earn his bachelor's degree from Williams College.

With a shared foundation of beliefs and dreams for the future, the two then began a courtship by letter. They confided in and revealed themselves to one another, and their letters developed an intimacy that Lucretia, a shy, reserved woman, would not ordinarily have been able to express.

When James was able to visit home, his outgoing, tactile nature was deflected by Lucretia's timid bashfulness and modesty. It almost appeared that their awkward personal contact disturbed the closeness they had developed in their correspondence. In the meantime, James continued his studies while Lucretia was growing into a respected teacher of Latin, French, and algebra in the communities of northern Ohio. Their relationship continued through correspondence.

In 1854, James and "Crete" as he called her, came to an "understanding," or engagement of sorts. Recalling Mary and Abe Lincoln's understanding, it appears that couples who were not ready for a public announcement would make private agreements between themselves.

Lucretia loved James profoundly, but her reserved upbringing prevented her from expressing her love easily and warmly. James demonstrated and required more passion, and as a result their courtship was an on-again, off-again roller-coaster ride.

While away at college, James made other female friends. Later he admitted to carrying on a romance with college friend Rebecca Selleck. When it came time to graduate, he invited both Rebecca and Lucretia to his graduation, and both women attended.

James was forced to grapple with his conflicting amorous emotions; ultimately he returned to Hiram to teach, later becoming president of the Eclectic Institute. Lucretia offered to release him from their "engagement," but James declined. "I can't lose you," he told her, "but give me time."

Although Crete was patient, as time went on she finally decided to take a teaching job in Cleveland rather than remain humiliated and single in Hiram.

In order to truly appreciate and possibly better understand Lucretia, it is helpful to have a more comprehensive picture of the man she loved. James was an intelligent, complex individual. He walked at nine months old, began to read at age three. Having grown up in poverty, he always believed that being poor had held him back. A religious man, he was a lay preacher in college and considered entering the ministry before becoming a college professor who taught Latin, Greek, higher mathematics, history, philosophy, and English literature. James could write Greek with his right hand, Latin with his left, and speak German, all at the same time! Yet he was a human being subject to prolonged periods of mental depression who struggled with fears, frailties and faults. Extremely tactile, he was known to hug and stroke his friends, both male and female. James was convinced he was a child of destiny marked for some special purpose.

After a great deal of soul-searching on his part, twenty-seven-year-old James married twenty-six-year-old Lucretia at her parent's home, on November 11, 1858. Their first few years of marriage were most trying. To begin with, Lucretia lived with the insecurity that James still cared deeply for Rebecca, his friend from college. Then, there were long periods of separation between the two. James had become a member of the Ohio State Senate, and his congressional duties, coupled with his preaching obligations, took him away from home a great deal of the time. In addition to his work obligations, Garfield's volunteer service in the Civil War created additional lonely absences for both of them.

Although James and Lucretia were pacifists, they so fiercely opposed slavery that James joined the Union forces. In addition, he convinced many of his former students to volunteer with him, creating the 42nd Ohio Volunteer Infantry, which fought in at least eleven battles. James returned home in 1862 depressed, emaciated, and sick with dysentery. Lucretia hoped he would remain home on sick leave; however, he returned to war to serve as chief of staff.

When his dysentery became chronic, James came home to stay, at least part of the time. Elected to Congress while still in military service, one month later he was off to Washington as a member of the U.S. House of Representatives from Ohio.

In just under five years of marriage, Lucretia calculated that she and James had lived together for only twenty weeks. According to Garfield's biographer Margaret Leech, he was unfaithful throughout the earliest years of their marriage. However, by now his family had begun to grow, and it is extremely doubtful that divorce was ever discussed.*

The letters Lucretia and James exchanged best tell their story of mutual anguish and heartache.

---

* Eliza Arabella (1860–1863), Harry Augustus (1863–1942), James Rudolph (1865–1950), Mary aka Molly (1867–1947), Irvin McDowell (1870–1951), Abram (1872–1958), Edward (1874–1876)

There are hours when my heart almost breaks with the cruel thought that our marriage is based upon the cold stern word *duty*. . . I hope time may teach me to be satisfied with the love you will teach your heart to give. [Crete]

I hope we may be able to get along as pleasantly and happily as is possible [given] the chances and changes of life. [James]

It seems to me sometimes that you do not care very much whether we are ever any nearer and dearer to each other; but I do not believe this. I know that you desire to become the true husband and to see me the wife who can fill up the whole measure of your happiness. [Crete]

[I] felt it was probably a great mistake that [we] had ever tried married life. [James] [1]

Daughter Eliza brought the couple a desired and welcomed sunshine they had not previously experienced. Their mutual joy in the birth of their second child, Harry, was soon crushed when Eliza died from diphtheria only two months after Harry's arrival.

It is not unusual that individuals grieve in their own diverse ways, and the Garfields were no exception. Lucretia's preference was to remain at home with their infant son and adjust to the tragedy, while James returned to Washington and Congress. Miserably lonely, James lived in a boardinghouse for the winter. Isolated from one another, both parents privately suffered dreadful heartache and sorrow.

The following spring, Lucretia joined her husband in the capital. She found him depressed and considering the notion of returning to the army. After some time had passed, James finally confessed that he had fallen in love with a twenty-year-old widow. Regardless of everything else, it was apparent that James never wanted to lose his wife, the one woman who had developed so much insight and empathy for him.

James promised to end the affair; Crete, who had waited nearly eight years for her husband's marriage proposal, found the internal fortitude to forgive him. James was obviously still struggling with his own inner turmoil; after returning home Crete received a letter from her spouse that read:

> I still believe that I am worthy to be loved after all the books are balanced. Still, I do not know what I shall be after I have fathomed the deep waters of the gulf through which I shall try as bravely as I can to wade . . . I ought to have a great deal more head, or a great deal less heart.[2]

Garfield decided to firmly commit himself to the marriage, and having done so their love had the opportunity to deepen and flourish. Lucretia began to spend the winters with her husband, living in Washington's boardinghouses, and he would return to their home in Ohio for the summers. Their mutual love of literature influenced them to join the Burns Literary Society on Capitol Hill.

As a family, they grew closer together. More children followed; by the birth of their fifth child, the couple had built a home in Washington so they could comfortably live together both there and in Ohio.

When Lucretia and James needed to be separated periodically during this time in their lives, their letters grew more devout and committed. Each reassured the other that their "dark days" were behind them. With patience, tolerance, and undeniable love, Lucretia was building the marriage she had always envisioned.

James's desire for a large family was well known, and two more children followed. At one point, Crete conveyed her feelings to her husband by pen, as she had done so eloquently in the past: "If your jewels [children] cost you what they do me, you would not sigh for more, I am sure."

Though domestic chores were not as appealing to Lucretia as cultural and literary affairs, she centered her life on domesticity, believing it the proper conduct for a woman. In her determination to overcome her dislike for domestic duties, Lucretia decided to take a very special interest in them. When she made that mind shift, she confirmed: "The whole of life became brighter . . . and this truth, as old as creation—

that I need not be the shrinking slave of toil, but its regal master."[3]

Over the years, it was obvious Lucretia struggled with the conventional attitudes that dictated a woman's position in the world. Her dilemma was that of an educated woman confined by society to child rearing and housekeeping. Lucretia kept a journal of her feelings both before and after marriage:

> Woman's province is her home, and if she is not fitted to make it a place around which warmest affections cluster, and on whose hearthstone attractions center, she is not prepared to act her part in life.
>
> It is horrible to be a man but the grinding misery of being a woman between the upper and nether millstone of household cares and training children is almost as bad. To be half civilized with some aspirations for enlightenment, and obliged to spend the largest part of the time the victim of young barbarians keeps one in a perpetual ferment!
>
> . . . [thinking] all we are made for is work, and as for accomplishments, it is a sin even to think of them. What an idea of life! Bake bread, wash dishes, scub, iron and mend. . . . True, these things must all be attended to, . . . but to make their thorough performances the end and aim of life, and the only object to receive any attention is most intolerable.
>
> . . . it has become almost a proverb that when a lady is married, she may as well lay aside her books, still I do not believe it contains very much wisdom after all.
>
> The wrongly educated woman thinks her duties a disgrace and either frets under them or shirks them if she can. She sees man triumphantly pursuing his vocations, and thinks it is the kind of work he does which makes him so grand and regnant, whereas it is not the kind of work at all, but the way in which, and the spirit with which he does it [4]

The kind of work Lucretia would have pursued, had she not been born female, is not clear. Yet she was a woman and clearly her family was her life; being a housekeeper, mother, and supportive wife became her full-time occupation.

When Lucretia was forty-four years old, her youngest child, as her eldest had, died in childhood. Yet despite the inevitable sense of mourning she felt for her lost children, it appeared Lucretia finally attained the marital bliss and love she had fought so hard to secure.

Continually supportive of her husband's life choices, Lucretia's correspondence once again communicated her innermost emotions. Early in her husband's career, she wrote to James saying: "I want you to be so great and good. So worthy of the highest respect and love of all. So unimpeachable in every relation that your bitterest enemy can find no just cause for accusation."

With each passing year, she remained ever more convinced of her husband's worthiness. After he had served in Congress for seventeen years, Lucretia wholeheartedly supported his decision to run for the country's top executive position. Regarding the presidency, she was confident in her husband's "true manliness and statesmanship although a terrible responsibility . . . to him and to me." On the other hand, Lucretia did not support woman's suffrage on the grounds that it would disturb domestic peace, a position to which she obviously had given serious and exhaustive thought.

In March of 1881, just six weeks prior to her forty-ninth birthday, the former shy, lovesick, teenage student stepped into the role of First Lady with dignity and tact. Married for over twenty-two years to a man she had never stopped loving and admiring, Lucretia was now the cherished wife and mother of his five surviving children. Patiently, painfully, and profoundly, Lucretia Garfield had earned her position alongside her "destiny's child."

With Lucretia's awe-inspiring devotion and protective wisdom, James understood better than ever before how much he depended on his wife. Respecting her judgment, he solicited her advice, beginning with his political appointments. James Blaine, newly appointed secretary of state, wrote: "I wish you would say to Mrs. Garfield that the knowledge that she desires me in your Cabinet is more valuable to me than even the desire of the President-elect himself."

Always the scholar, Lucretia immediately began a serious study of the White House. It was her desire to restore the president's home in a historically documented style. After lobbying Congress for money to refurbish it, the First Lady spent much of her time at the Library of Congress studying the mansion's history and authenticity. She commented: "These little scraps of reminiscence [of previous first ladies] that I gather up now and then lend this old place a weird charm.[5] She was one of the earliest First Ladies who sought to accurately restore the mansion's character.

Less than three months into her tenure, Lucretia came down with a critical case of malaria that lasted four weeks. The president, terrified for his wife's well-being, could barely leave her bedside. Initially horrified she might die, when Lucretia began to recuperate in June James moved her, along with the family, to New Jersey to convalesce. He planned to join her shortly—but on July 2, 1881, he was struck by an assassin's bullet.*

The wounded president's first thoughts were of his wife: "Tell her I am seriously hurt, how seriously I cannot yet say. I am myself, and hope she will come to me soon. I send my love to her." Returning immediately to the White House fatigued and frail, Lucretia assumed command.

Never again leaving her husband's side, she even prepared his meals. The president lingered for more than two months before he died of blood poisoning with his wife and teenage daughter at his bedside. In shock and dismay, Lucretia cried out: "Oh why am I made to suffer this cruel wrong!"

Molly, fifteen at the time of her father's death, was most expressive in her comments: "After suffering with all the tortures that any human could possibly do, he died . . . Dear little Mamma bore up with heroic courage and bravery until the very last, and then she was completely broken hearted for about an hour, after which she calmed herself."

During the presidential funeral and burial, Lucretia impressed the country with her dignity and self-control. Within one week of her hus-

---

* In 1882, six months after assassin Charles Julius Guiteau was tried, he was hanged at a Washington, DC jail.

band's death, she and her family were headed home to Ohio to a private, modest life outside of the public eye.

Dedicated to only two things now, Lucretia's attention turned to protecting her husband's memory and her family's privacy. Whenever possible, she reviewed all books and articles published about her spouse. Lucretia built a library on the second floor of her home to maintain all his public and private papers, including books, thus creating the first "presidential library." She also preserved the twelve hundred personal letters they had exchanged over the years.*

Appalled when rumors circulated in the press that she would marry again, Lucretia categorically enforced her position saying: "[I feel] humiliation that anyone could believe me capable of ever forgetting that I am the wife of General Garfield."[6]

Mercifully, Lucretia was able to raise and educate her children, then nine to eighteen years old, with over $300,000 collected from public funds, a $50,000 grant from Congress, and a $5,000 annual congressional pension. Insisting on absolute privacy, she declined interviews and all editors' requests to write about her children. After the devastating murder of their father, Lucretia sought a life of normalcy for her children and achieved it for the next thirty-six years.

Always well read on a wide range of subjects, during the course of building a new home Lucretia took special interest in the design and construction of a well, and a water tower with a large windmill that pumped water into a storage tank. The former First Lady was said to have a full understanding of the complicated hydraulic engineering involved in the construction.

Lucretia wrote essays for a book club, addressed women's groups on literature, and maintained a correspondence with former White House residents Julia Tyler and Harriet Lane. Additionally, Lucretia

---

* The Garfield family home is now an Historic Site. Prior to Garfield, presidential papers and records had been lost, destroyed, sold, or simply damaged beyond repair. Years later, President Franklin D. Roosevelt began a tradition of raising private funds to construct a library to house his documents. Today, the National Archives and Records Administration maintains twelve presidential libraries, from presidents Hoover to Clinton.

was a frequent guest of subsequent First Ladies Frances Cleveland and Ida McKinley.

Waiting until 1912, Lucretia assisted historian Theodore Clarke Smith from Williams College in writing the first official biography of President Garfield. Her interest in politics continued, and she even voted for a Democrat, Woodrow Wilson, a friend of her son Harry. She spent the winters with her family in south Pasadena, California, and volunteered for the Red Cross during World War I.

With pride and great gratification, she watched sons Harry, James, and Irvin all become lawyers. Harry went on to become president of Williams College and James became secretary of the interior under President Theodore Roosevelt. Youngest son Abram became an architect after receiving his bachelor of arts from the Massachusetts Institute of Technology.

Just five weeks shy of her eighty-sixth birthday, Lucretia died of pneumonia in Pasadena, California. The former First Lady was buried next to her slain, essentially forgotten, presidential husband in Cleveland, Ohio.

What Lucretia taught me:

There is no doubt in my mind that Lucretia Garfield fought an intense and complicated internal battle. She was a strong, independent, highly intelligent woman born into an era that compartmentalized females. The expectations and demands placed on women—to become mothers, housekeepers, and caretakers—was the blueprint chosen for her at birth.

I believe Lucretia found her designated position in life both stifling and oppressive, yet she learned how to triumph. Lucretia taught me the importance and value of embracing the "toil" in life. As she discovered, "the truth as old as creation" is a choice. I can be a "shrinking slave" to drudgery and difficult tasks, or choose to be their "regal master."

Never Forgotten Wife

ELLEN ARTHUR

Honors to me now are not what they once were.

CHESTER ARTHUR,
AFTER HIS WIFE'S DEATH

ELLEN ARTHUR is linked in history with Martha Jefferson and Hannah Van Buren. They are two women Ellen never met, probably never heard of, yet all three shared some rare experiences. They all married ambitious lawyers who went into politics and ultimately became president of the United States. All three died in the prime of their lives before ever knowing of their husband's immense political success. From all outside appearances, they shared happy marriages, and gave birth to children with loving, devoted spouses who never remarried.

> **#21 Ellen Herndon Arthur**
>
> **Born:** August 30, 1837
> **Birthplace:** Culpeper County, Virginia
> **Married:** 1859 (Chester Alan Arthur)
> **Children:** 3
> **White House Years:** 1881–1885
> **Died:** January 1, 1880
> **Fact:** Died before husband became president
> **Aka:** Little Rebel Wife

More is known of Ellen's distinguished family than of herself. (No documentation of her words survives.) Ellen's mother, Frances Hansbrough Herndon, reportedly came from a wealthy Southern heritage. Her father's family had ancestors in Virginia dating back to 1674, while her father was the distinguished Captain William Lewis Herndon.

Captain Herndon had attained fame in his early forties when he charted the exploration of the Amazon River by order of President Millard Fillmore. He was last seen in 1857 in full uniform, standing at the helm of his sinking ship, the SS *Central America*. The *Central America* had been caught in a hurricane for three days and three nights; Herndon managed to evacuate 153 individuals, most of them women and children. He was hailed a hero after he, with over four hundred men and thirty thousand pounds of gold still on board, went down with his ship in true naval tradition.

The Herndons were a close-knit family who lavished much attention on their only child, Ellen (nicknamed Nelly), born in Virginia on August 30, 1837. The family moved to Washington, DC, when Ellen was still a small girl. Growing up and attending school in the capital city, Ellen had a rich and cultured childhood.

Described as very attractive, Ellen had a delicate appearance, a fair complexion, and beautiful dark eyes set above strong cheekbones. She was slender, of medium height, with brown hair severely parted in the middle and worn in braids woven together at the back of her neck.

Considered sweet and lovable by those who knew her, Ellen was best known for her gifted soprano voice. She sang in the choir while attending Saint John's Episcopal Church on Lafayette Square, and continued to sing for charity events throughout her life.

While visiting New York, a cousin of hers introduced her to his friend Chester A. Arthur, a handsome, influential lawyer seven years her senior. Chester was one of nine children, a true Northerner whose father, a committed abolitionist, was a Baptist preacher. Although their backgrounds could not have been more different, everything else in their relationship seemed to be a perfect match.

Courting only a brief time, it was apparent to both Ellen and Chester that they had each found their life partner. It was very shortly thereafter that Ellen's father was lost at sea. Twenty-year-old Ellen had idolized her father and was devastated when he died. Chester readily stepped in to assist Frances Herndon with her legal and financial affairs.

Two years passed and on October 25, 1859, Ellen and Chester were married in the bride's Calvary Episcopal church. It was her father's birthday. The couple initially lived with Ellen's mother in Manhattan, in the home given to Mrs. Herndon by a group of New York citizens as a tribute to her heroic husband.

When the Civil War erupted, less than two years into their marriage, Chester found himself at odds with his wife's Southern family. All of Ellen's male relatives fought for the Confederacy while Chester became a brigadier general on active duty for the Union. His mother-in-law in particular was openly hostile to the Union, so much so that Mrs. Herndon left for Europe and lived there the rest of her life. Because she remained a confederate at heart, Chester jokingly called Ellen his "little rebel wife."

The Civil War was difficult for everyone. Men were dying daily and the stress of opposing family loyalties, like those that Ellen (and Mary Todd Lincoln and Julia Grant) experienced, only added an additional burden. When Arthur resigned from the army in the middle of the war, it was anyone's guess whether the strain of divided loyalties had influenced his decision. What was evident was Chester's frustration with the war's prolonged duration and his desire to earn more money.

Ellen's first child, a son, was named after her father. Her notable elation lasted only two years, until baby William suddenly died. Ellen was understandably distraught, and Chester wrote to his brother: "Nell is broken hearted. I fear much for her health. You know how her heart was wrapped up in her dear boy."[1] One year to the month after William's death, son Chester (aka Alan) was born. Seven years later, daughter Ellen Herndon followed.*

By now the couple was enjoying wealth and an active social life. With a taste for luxury, Ellen and her husband enjoyed top-quality clothing, exceptional furnishings, elegant dining, and basically overall fine living. Their parties soon became legendary.

The Arthurs (now living in a Manhattan townhouse on Lexington

---

* William Lewis Herndon (1860–1863), Chester Alan II (1864–1973), Ellen Herndon (1871–1915).

Avenue) were climbing the New York social ladder, and many of their friends were well-connected Republicans. Ellen seemed to approve of her husband's political ambitions. Her only conflict appeared to be in her desire to have her husband at home, whereas his political advancement required him to be absent much of the time.

Despite the fact that Ellen's mother was now living in France, Ellen remained very close to her only surviving parent. When her mother took ill, Ellen went to her only to return home with Mrs. Herndon's body for burial. Like the other losses in her life, Ellen took her mother's death very hard. It appeared the emotional toll affected her physically as well.

Less than two years later, after attending an operatic recital Ellen caught a severe cold while waiting for her carriage in the icy rain. Away on political business, Chester was notified by telegram that his wife had developed pneumonia. He raced home to be with his ill bride, but when he got there Ellen had already lapsed into a coma. She died the next day at forty-two, leaving behind an eight-year-old daughter and fifteen-year-old son.

Long after Ellen's death, historians were told stories of her unhappiness with regard to the long hours her husband spent away from home. Some believe she was considering a separation, while others go so far as to say the couple was actually in the process of separating when she died.

Whether or not Arthur felt any guilt regarding his family life is unknown. However, history does record that he never got over his wife's passing.

The following year, Ellen's husband was elected vice president of the United States under President James Garfield. Six short months later, Chester A. Arthur was president.* Like his widowed predecessor, President Andrew Jackson, Chester was still mourning his wife's

---

* This was the second time in history that there were three presidents in one year: President Hayes concluded his four-year term in March of 1881; President Garfield was inaugurated and assassinated the same year; and President Hayes was then inaugurated in September of 1881.

death when he entered the White House. Each man enshrined his dead wife and kept a picture of her next to his bed.

President Arthur went a step further. He ordered fresh flowers be maintained beside his wife's picture daily. Additionally, he dedicated a stained-glass window for her in Saint John's Church where she had sung as a young girl. The inscription on the window read: "To the Glory of God and in memory of Ellen Lewis Herndon Arthur entered into life January 12, 1880." His only request was that the window be situated on the south side of the church so he that could see it from the White House.

Mary Arthur McElroy, the president's married sister, was invited to live in the executive mansion with her family during President Arthur's administration. Mrs. McElroy assisted with White House entertaining, but it was the president who acted as the official host. His extravagant tastes set the lavish tone for his formal entertaining.

Arthur, like vice presidents John Tyler and Millard Fillmore before him, succeeded to the presidency upon a sitting president's death. None of the three won his party's nomination for reelection. Six years after his beloved spouse's death, the fifty-four-year-old former president died from Bright's disease. He was buried beside his "First and Only Lady" in a family cemetery in New York.

It should also be noted that Arthur renovated the White House to his personal taste before ever moving in. The president described the mansion as "a badly kept barracks"[2] that was "unfit to live in."[3] The public was then invited to a once-in-a-lifetime auction. Heaps of "junk," including items from the Lincoln, Grant, and Hayes administrations, plus scores of old furniture, was put up for sale. Some eighty years later, First Lady Jacqueline Kennedy headed up a campaign to retrieve taken or sold White House possessions.

What Ellen taught me:

Because so very little is known of Ellen Arthur's life, it is difficult to glean any understanding of her character. Nevertheless, historians all seem to agree that Ellen dedicated her musical talent to charity, which in itself says a great deal. She taught me that gifted talents are meant to be shared.

PART SIX

WOMEN OF ACKNOWLEDGMENT

BY 1865 THE COUNTRY had survived civil war, albeit with severe consequences. The number of fatalities for both the North and the South was massive and an immense number of individuals had had limbs amputated. Countless citizens suffered grave emotional trauma, the destruction of their property, and financial ruin.

After the South was defeated, although the Union and its government remained, President Abraham Lincoln's position of "with malice toward none, with charity for all," as he so eloquently stated in his second inaugural address, was not universally accepted. Rejecting the lenient Reconstruction measures initiated by President Lincoln, over President Johnson's veto, the Radical Republicans in Congress passed the punitive Military Reconstruction Act of 1867, establishing military rule in the former Confederate states. The Thirteenth Amendment to the Constitution, abolishing slavery, was ratified, as was the Fourteenth Amendment, decreeing citizenship and the protection of civil liberties.

In 1869, during President Grant's administration, the Union Pacific Railroad was finally able to deliver transcontinental service. Congress had failed to approve prior proposals because of the disputes over slavery and the South's discussion of secession. It now took only eight days to travel from coast to coast, as opposed to months of tedious wagon train transportation.

When Democrat Samuel Tilden lost the strictly partisan 1877 presidential election to Republican Rutherford B. Hayes—thereafter known as "His Fraudulency" or "Rutherfraud B."—outraged Southern Democrats threatened once again to secede. Their acceptance of Hayes was contingent on the new president's removal of federal troops from the South. Hayes agreed and Reconstruction ended. Segregation did not.

The country soon returned its attention and resources to continuing its modernization, including the women's rights issue. Slowly but surely, women emerged from behind kitchen and parlor doors. As early as 1866, the first woman ever to graduate an American dental school did so from the Ohio College of Dental Surgery. Twenty-four years later, the University of Michigan Dental School awarded a DDS degree to the first black female dentist. That same year, Nelly Bly, a young journalist and author in her early twenties, convinced her editor at the *New York World* to send her on a trip around the globe, imitating the novel *Around the World in Eighty Days*. She departed Hoboken, New Jersey, and arrived in New York just seventy-two days later.

Josephine Cochrane received a patent for a stove with a separate "air chamber" for baking, while a prominent socialite patented her design for a dishwashing machine after servants continually broke her fine china. Initially it was a big sensation with her wealthy friends. After the design won the highest award from a World Exposition, hotels and restaurants became interested. She started a company and went into production, which eventually became the Kitchen Aid Company.

Another woman, Clara Barton, dubbed the "Angel of the Battlefield," founded the American Association of the Red Cross, and not long thereafter, The *Ladies' Home Journal* was established, followed by *Cosmopolitan* Magazine. Vassar College created the first women's baseball team, and before the turn of the century, the first symphony composed by a woman was performed in the United States.

It was in the late 1880s that two presidential spouses publicly, albeit gingerly, endorsed working women.

Frances Cleveland and Caroline Harrison entered the White House at very different times in their lives. One was a youthful newlywed while the other was a more than middle-aged grandmother. Both were married to traditional men (both born in the 1830s) of their era. Although not yet the turn of the twentieth century, both women in their own whispered tones spoke up for their gender.

The lives of these two First Ladies—one was the first president general of the National Society of the Daughters of the American Revolution and the other a sitting member on the Wells College Board for over fifty years—are indeed fascinating stories.

23

White House Bride

FRANCES CLEVELAND

> I have not had my life yet. It is all before me.
>
> —FRANCES CLEVELAND

FRANCES CLARA FOLSOM had just turned ten years old in 1874 when her attorney father, Oscar Folsom, died in a horse and buggy accident. Concerned for his family's welfare, Mr. Folsom had asked his good friend and business law partner to watch over his wife and only child in the event Folsom could no longer care for them. Folsom knew his partner, an honorable man, took his responsibilities seriously.

Both Frances's parents came from protective, caring, well-to-do families. Her mother, Emma Harmon Folsom, was a member of the prestigious Harmon family, early benefactors of the University of Rochester in New York.

#22, #24 Frances Folsom Cleveland
Born: July 21, 1864
Birthplace: Folsomville, New York
Married: 1886 (Grover Cleveland) Died 1913 (Thomas Preston)
Children: 5 with Cleveland
White House Years: 1885–1889 and 1893–1897
Died: October 29, 1947
Fact: Youngest and only First Lady to marry in the White House
Aka: Frank or Frankie

When Folsom unexpectedly passed away, his business partner, as promised, made a point of remaining a vital part of Frances and Emma Folsom's lives. Growing up, Frances became quite fond of her unofficial guardian, whom she called Uncle Cleve, and he remained devoted

to the well-being of the child he called Frank. Uncle Cleve adminis-
trated the Folsom estate, helped plan Frank's education, and sent flowers to her on special occasions such as her sixteenth birthday.

A popular and serious student, it is not unreasonable to think that
in school Frances read the popular masterpiece *Little Women* by
Louisa May Alcott. In addition to enjoying reading and education,
Frances played the piano, spoke French, German, and read Latin.

Although physicians of the era continued to warn against the dire
effects of "too much study on women,"[1] claiming it impaired a
woman's ability to have children, Frances entered Wells College in Aurora, New York, in 1882 at the age of eighteen.

Throughout the years, Uncle Cleve was a reassuring and supportive influence. Once a sheriff, who personally carried out the hanging of
two men, Uncle Cleve found his passion in politics. Elected the mayor
of Buffalo, he went on to become the governor of New York. Status
aside, he still required permission from both Emma Folsom and the
principal of the college to continue his correspondence with Frank.

While at college Frances had grown into a tall, poised young
woman with blue eyes and chestnut hair who maintained a popular
social life. She even became briefly engaged. However, Frances broke
off her engagement and wrote her to mother: "When I marry it must
be someone more than a year older than I am, someone I can look up
to and respect."[2] It soon became apparent that the person Frances
looked up to and respected most was her Uncle Cleve.

It is unclear exactly when Uncle Cleve's and Frank's friendship
turned romantic; however, Emma approved of her daughter's relationship with the honorable man who had known Frances from the day
she was born. Not uncommon for the times, Mrs. Folsom chaperoned
the two when Governor Cleve and Frances were together.

While still governor of New York, Uncle Cleve became the Democratic nominee for the presidency, and in March of 1885 Grover
Cleveland was elected president of the United States. Although Frank
was invited to the inauguration, final college exams prevented her and
Emma from attending.

President Cleveland's sister, Rose, accompanied the bachelor to the White House and acted as hostess of the executive mansion. When Rose questioned her brother on matrimony, inquiring why he had never married, he simply replied: "I'm waiting for my wife to grow up."

During spring break of the same year, Frances and Emma did visit the White House for ten days, only now it was under the disguise of visiting Rose Cleveland. By the fall, and secretly engaged, Frank was preparing for graduation. Following her college commencement, President Cleveland was adamant that Frances tour Europe for several months. So once again, accompanied by her mother, the final touches to Frank's unfolding maturity were being applied. Not to mention the purchase of a Parisian trousseau.

With the rumor mill grinding away, reporters pursued the two women wherever they went, although most still believed that Emma was the object of the president's friendliness. It did not stop the aggressive press from questioning Frances on the issues that had plagued the president's campaign: questions about her opinion of the president's out-of-wedlock child, his hanging of criminals, and hiring a substitute to fight for him in the Civil War.

Regarding the hiring of a Civil War substitute, it was legal to do so until 1864 when Congress repealed the law. You could pay a substitute a hundred and fifty dollars to take your place in the Union army, which Cleveland did, or pay three hundred dollars to buy your way out of fighting. Not only was Grover an antiwar Democrat, at the time he was also the principle means of support for his widowed mother and four younger siblings. Believing slavery was wrong, he chose to hire a substitute rather than simply purchase his way out of the war; by doing so he was able to continue supporting his family.

Concerning the hangings, Frances understood Grover's anguish regarding the taking of another man's life. She said she respected him for personally accepting the responsibility rather than making his subordinates carry out the daunting and punishing task.

As for as the president's illegitimate child, Frances had questioned her mother when political opponents ran a cartoon prior to the election inquiring "Ma, Ma, where's my Pa?" implying that Cleveland was the father. She learned that many years earlier Cleveland had been seeing a woman named Maria Halpin; at the same time, at least two other men, both married, were also seeing her.

No one will ever know if Cleveland was in fact the boy's biological father. Nonetheless, being the only bachelor involved, Grover accepted paternity, sent five dollars monthly for financial support, and just as admirably never denied the rumors. The child's mother had named her son Oscar Folsom Cleveland, and many believed Grover was covering for his good friend and former partner.

Frances politely replied to the rude question, saying she had decided not to concern herself with something that happened so long ago. The Democratic Party, on the other hand, replied to the question "Ma, Ma, where's my Pa?" with a more patronizing response: "Went to the White House, Ha, Ha, Ha!"

While Frances was in Europe getting a taste of what was to come, Grover was planning their very private, simple ten-minute wedding ceremony for the evening of June 2, 1886. It was less than two months shy of the bride's twenty-second birthday and just over two months past the groom's forty-ninth. Cleveland personally hand wrote the approximately thirty-five invitations to the close relatives, personal friends, and cabinet members invited.

The president's clergyman brother and a Presbyterian minister were to perform the ceremony. In addition to all the other preparations, Cleveland had altered the bride's vows, omitting the word "obey" and substituting "keep." It was planned that Frances's grandfather would give her away, but on the her return trip home from Europe the elderly gentleman died unexpectedly.

While throngs of people crowded on the lawn of the executive mansion, President Cleveland, the only president to be married in the White House, escorted his bride-to-be down the grand staircase into the Blue Room where the ceremony took place. The bride wore a Parisian ivory satin wedding gown edged with orange blossoms, a lace veil, and a fifteen-foot train. The Marine Band played the "Wedding

March." Outside there was a twenty-one-gun salute while church bells rang throughout Washington. After a champagne dinner in the East Room, each guest received a slice of wedding cake in a white satin box with a card autographed by the bride and groom.[3]

Unlike her predecessors who had moved into the White House quietly with their husbands, with the exception of Julia Tyler, Frances Cleveland walked in as the star of a romantic theater production, with a deafening roar. At twenty-one, her surprise wedding to the sitting president, kept secret until the last minute, was a stage show the country could not resist. Yet it was not a play or performance at all. It was true love and real life for young Frances Folsom Cleveland, our nation's youngest First Lady.

The president planned a ten-day honeymoon in a remote cottage in Deer Park, a resort in the Blue Ridge Mountains of Maryland. Naively, he believed the remoteness would guarantee privacy. The reality was that reporters had already camped out around the cottage and set up lines of communication with observation posts (some in the trees with binoculars) to report on the couple's every move, menu details, and anything else they could find out.

Newspaper reporters were called "keyhole journalists" while the president referred to them as "those ghouls of the press." Outraged at the reporters' "colossal impertinence," the president and First Lady returned to the White House earlier than planned, seeking a little privacy.

Determined to keep the press at bay and have some marital normalcy, Cleveland broke the custom of presidential families residing only in the executive mansion. There were crowds in such enormous numbers wanting to see the new First Lady that the multitude of people on the White House grounds verged on threatening.

Cleveland purchased a small farmhouse on the outskirts of the capital so the couple could live in their own home and still work in the executive mansion. Except during the official season when both resided in the White House, the president would commute the three-mile distance daily.

Ike Hoover, chief White House usher, noted in his book *Forty-Two Years in the White House* that the Clevelands spent less time physically in the White House than any other administration.[4] He also called Frances a "brilliant and affable lady" as well as an "affectionate and tender mother." In regard to her relationship with the president, years later Mr. Hoover said she was "solicitous" and "would watch over him as through he were one of the children." Rose Cleveland thought her sister-in-law was "a woman capable of great development; a much stronger character than appears on the surface."

Energetic, healthy, and excited about life, Frances was admired for her grace and adored for her genuineness and warmth. The new First Lady embraced the Needlework Guild, a charity that made clothes for the poor; when she was unsuccessful in organizing a charity for poor and orphaned black children, she joined the Colored Christmas Club, personally distributing gifts.

Frances also scheduled receptions on Saturday afternoons so that working women could attend. When an official complained, asking how long the receptions would continue, the First Lady answered that they would last "so long as there were any store clerks, or other self-supporting women and girls who wished to come to the White House." In other words, nothing was to conflict with her Saturday receptions.

What Frances did not do was challenge the tradition of women. Instead she met the standard of a good wife described by her spouse: "A woman who loves her husband and her country with no desire to run either."

The First Lady refused to lend her name to women's suffrage, but being herself a teetotaler, she sent money privately to the Women's Christian Temperance Union, which enthusiastically endorsed women's suffrage. Like her predecessor Lucy Hayes, she believed education was a means for women to achieve equality. Frances also accepted a seat on the board of her alma mater, Wells College, a position she maintained for over fifty years.

Now becoming the latest darling of the press, "Frankie" as they sometimes called her, began to set fashion trends. "Frankie" clubs began to spring up across the country. Her hairstyle was copied, and when she stopped wearing the bustle dress it soon became fashion history.

Manufacturers also took advantage of the First Lady's enormous popularity and would use her picture and her name without her consent. She felt powerless to stop them as Congress would not pass a bill making such false claims a crime.

Her popularity with the press did not prevent them from printing anything they felt would sell. During the 1888 presidential campaign, ugly charges appeared, accusing the president of abusing, and even beating his wife that had no basis or foundation. The First Lady wrote an open letter to the public stating: "[They are] wicked heartless lies. I can wish the women of our country no greater blessing than that their homes and lives may be as happy, and their husbands as kind, attentive, considerate and affectionate as mine."[5]

When Cleveland lost his reelection bid to Republican candidate Benjamin Harrison, a disappointed Frances told the White House staff that she would return.

Her story continues in Chapter 25, Act II: Wife and Mother: Frances Cleveland, after Caroline Harrison's biography.

24

Mother to the White House China

CAROLINE HARRISON

We have within ourselves the only element of destruction; our foes are from within, not without.

—CAROLINE HARRISON

COMPREHENSION of one's capabilities, particularly regarding elements of destruction, is an insightful observation from a female advocate who believed strongly in women's education and professional opportunities. Caroline Lavinia Scott came by her advocacy naturally as the daughter of Presbyterian minister and professor John Scott. Dr. Scott founded the girls' school in Cincinnati, Ohio, where Caroline was originally educated, and later established the Oxford Female Institute. Caroline's mother, Mary Neal Scott, was also

> **#23 Caroline Scott Harrison**
>
> **Born:** October 1, 1832
> **Birthplace:** Oxford, Ohio
> **Married:** 1853 (Benjamin Harrison)
> **Children:** 2
> **White House Years:** 1889–1893
> **Died:** October 25, 1892
> **Fact:** First Lady who established White House china; 1st President General of DAR
> **Aka:** Carrie

well educated and highly cultured. Growing up in a scholarly home filled with literature, books, and music, Caroline was supported and encouraged to grow from within.

Born to the Scotts in 1832, Caroline was one of five children. Fun-loving, with a keen sense of humor—although her photographs do not hint at this—Caroline was genuinely joyful and "loved a good time." She was a serious student, yet active and carefree as a young girl. Dr. Scott once wrote to his wife about her: "Tell Caroline she must try and act the lady now, and leave off her romping and venturesomeness."[1] As an adult she told reporters that she remembered a happy childhood and enjoyed a close relationship with her parents and siblings.

She was slightly plump for her five-foot-one frame and had thick, wavy brown hair and soft brown eyes. At fifteen, she met fourteen-year-old Benjamin Harrison,* a mathematics and physics student of her father's at Farmers College. Ben visited the Scott family home frequently under the pretense of seeing his professor. However, a young teenage boy's intentions were not so easily camouflaged.

A few years later, Dr. Scott moved his family from Cincinnati to Oxford, approximately forty miles away, where seventeen-year-old Caroline enrolled as a student at Oxford Female Institute. This was the school her father had established and was principal of; her mother functioned as the head of home economics. In order to remain near Caroline, Ben followed, transferring to Miami University, also in Oxford.†

Throughout college, Caroline and Ben often spent evenings together on buggy or sleigh rides. She persuaded him to take her to dancing parties where Ben would sit solemnly and watch Caroline dance with other boys. (Somewhat reminiscent of the courtship Julia and Ulysses Grant shared.) During the day, Caroline studied English literature and developed a lifelong love of art, painting, and music.

Inheriting her talent for art and music from her mother, who had taught Caroline the piano, she also loved painting, watercolors, and china decoration. Caroline's youthful artistic ability is preserved in an unpublished book, dated 1847, that contains favorite poetry

---

* Benjamin was the son of Congressman John Scott Harrison and grandson of former president William Henry Harrison.
† Dr. Scott was once affiliated with Miami University; however, he broke with the campus over the issue of abolition. He opposed slavery and was once suspected of harboring runaway slaves.

accompanied by her illustrations; it is still preserved at the Harrison Home.*

An accomplished musician by nineteen, Caroline graduated from Oxford in 1853 with a degree in music. She went on to teach music, home economics, and painting while Benjamin, an honors student, was still in school.

Secretly engaged, Carrie, as her family called her, went to teach at a girl's school in Kentucky while Ben returned to Cincinnati to study law. He calculated that his studies would take another two years before he would be admitted to the bar. Ben then planned to start a law practice, which would enable him to support a wife.

However, within the year he was asking Dr. Scott for Carrie's hand in marriage. Although Ben could barely support himself let alone a wife, he believed Carrie was working to exhaustion—in addition to teaching, Carrie was nursing a dying patient. His argument was that a long engagement would be difficult on Carrie; he believed she would be better off with him than without him.

Ben went on to say that after he was admitted to the bar he would devote himself to making Carrie happy and comfortable. As historian Margaret Basset put it: "In other words, love had made young Harrison ardent, impractical, and human." Years later, Ben was quoted as saying: "If Carrie and I were not married now, this fall, we would never be as I would never live another year."

Dr. Scott consented to the immediate marriage of his twenty-one-year-old daughter and the twenty-year-old former student, personally officiating their vows in the living room of his home. It was a morning wedding attended by only immediate family and a few close friends. After breakfast, the newlyweds headed for Ben's father's (John Harrison) farmhouse, where they initially planned to live. Mr. Harrison was quite accustomed to large families. He was one of ten children born to Anna and former president William Henry Harrison, and had thirteen of his own children by two wives.

After Ben was admitted to the bar in 1854, Carrie and Ben shipped all their personal belongings in one large box to Indianapolis, where

* Open to the public, the Harrison Home is located in Indianapolis, Indiana.

Ben planned to pursue his law career. Being a young, unknown and untried lawyer, he hunted in vain for clients and supplemented his income by two dollars and fifty cents a day as crier of the federal court. Financially, times were very tight for the young Harrisons, which made it necessary to frequently borrow money from both their families.

Meanwhile, the couple was active in the First Presbyterian Church, where Caroline played the organ and taught children's classes. Pregnant with her first child, she delivered son Russell just eight days before his father's twenty-first birthday. Four years later, daughter Mary was born.*

Ben made good on his promise to his father-in-law, working day and night to provide for his family. As his courtroom cases began to increase, Caroline, a happy housewife with children, church work, and other charities to attend to, would eventually be the one to financially assist other family members.

At the outbreak of the Civil War, Caroline bore a baby girl who died at birth. Ben soon left the family to become a colonel in the Volunteer 70th Indiana Infantry, leaving his wife to raise their children alone. In support of her husband and the country, Caroline's interest in civic affairs increased. She served on the board of managers of the Indianapolis Orphans' Asylum, a position she held until the end of her life, and became a leader in the Ladies Sanitary Committee and the Ladies Patriotic Association.

Away at war and now a brigadier general, Ben wrote to his wife: "No object of ambition or gin could ever lead me away from the side of my dear wife and children"; he hoped "that by mutual help and by God's help, we may live the residue of our lives without having our hearts' sunshine clouded by a single shade of mistrust or anger."[2]

For the Harrisons, prosperity followed the traumatic Civil War years, and by 1875 Ben's income had increased to ten thousand dollars a year. He was able to build a spacious sixteen-room house for his family. Caroline established a daily schedule of domestic responsibil-

---

* Russell Benjamin (1854–1936), Mary "Mamie" Scott (1858–1930), a baby girl (1861–1861).

ities balanced with charitable activities and church work. She used a space on the second floor as an art studio where she produced watercolors and painted china that she exhibited regularly. Meals were served at set hours, with prayers always following breakfast; the Sabbath was strictly observed.

Although Ben was an unsuccessful candidate for governor, he was establishing himself in the Republican Party. At the same time, the family was becoming prominent in Indianapolis social, charity, and church circles. In 1879, Caroline hosted a memorial lawn party for President and Mrs. Rutherford B. Hayes.

Within two years, Benjamin had become a senator and Caroline had started to battle several unspecified health issues. These began after she took a severe fall on icy pavement resulting in a concussion; after that her health seemed to slowly deteriorate. In 1883, she was hospitalized for surgery, and a lengthy recuperation period followed. Seriously ill again the following year, Caroline was unable to attend her son's wedding. Thankfully, by the end of that year she was well enough to supervise her daughter Mary's elaborate nuptials.

Politicians began speaking of Harrison for the 1888 Republican convention. Common for the times, "front-porch campaigning" was a typical form of politicking. For Caroline, like Lucretia Garfield before her and Ida McKinley after her, campaigning meant an endless stream of visitors to her home, many of whom would spend the evening.

Ben made numerous speeches from the front porch while Carrie provided refreshments for all who came. Both her home and personal possessions were now subject to damage or theft. As she watched her carpets wear thin, furniture break, their fence knocked down, and not a single blade of grass survive, Caroline remarked tolerantly: "Well, it's either the White House or the poor house with us now."

Harrison lost the popular vote but won the electoral college, wresting the presidential election from sitting President Grover Cleveland.*

---

* Predecessors John Q. Adams and Rutherford Hayes also lost the popular vote. Several other presidents were elected without receiving the majority of the popular vote.

One hundred years having passed since George Washington was elected first president, Harrison now became the country's centennial president.

After all the crowds and fanfare subsided, the new First Lady elect commented: "I don't propose to be made a circus of forever! If there's any privacy to be found in the White House, I propose to find it and preserve it."[3]

Caroline immediately began the task of integrating her large family into the White House. Moving in with her were her ninety-year-old father, Dr. Scott, and daughter Mary with her husband, James McKee, and their children, two-year-old Benjamin ("Baby McKee") and infant Mary Dodge. Later, Caroline's niece, Mary Lord Dimmick, also came to live in the White House. Son Russell, with his wife Mary ("Mae") and their daughter Marthena, would visit often for extended periods of time.

Horrified at the condition of the executive mansion, which was infested with rats—not to mention the inadequacy of its one bathroom in the private quarters—Caroline believed it to be on the verge of collapse. She noted in her diary: "The rats have nearly taken the building so it has become necessary to get a man with ferrets. They have become so numerous and bold they get up on the table in the Upper Hall and one got up on Mr. Halford's [the president's private secretary] bed."[4]

Caroline made it her business to campaign for a new White House, and obtained public support by personally conducting tours. She said: "I am very anxious to see the family of the President provided for properly, and while I am here I hope to get the present building put into good condition."

Three plans were drawn up: one for a completely new building; a second for changes to the existing building; and a third, Caroline's favorite, for preserving the existing building and adding two new wings—a west wing devoted to offices and an east wing for an art gallery, with an enlarged botanical conservatory connecting the two.

In the meantime, the First Lady supervised the cleaning of the entire mansion from basement to attic. Coming close to what she wanted in the end, Caroline had to settle for the thirty-five thousand dollars allocated to renovate the existing building. Construction went on for two years, at the end of which the White House had its first electric lights, installed with a call bell system; a completely remodeled kitchen; a new heating system; new concrete flooring downstairs; additional bathrooms; and new furniture, curtains, and upholstery. A bargain even at five times today's prices!

The first family was so afraid to use the innovative electrical lights for fear of getting shocked that the White House usher, Ike Hoover, was made responsible for turning them on and off. If Mr. Hoover was off for the day or left early, the lights remained on all night.

During this time of modernization, Caroline's family lived the well-organized life she had created for them in the past. They rose early and had breakfast, followed by family prayers with the president before nine a.m. In addition to her full schedule of official entertaining, the First Lady helped found the Daughters of the American Revolution (DAR), becoming its first Regent.

As a result of her leadership in the DAR, Caroline was the first First Lady to compose and deliver a speech publicly. She said: "Since this society had been organized and so much thought and reading directed to the early struggles of this country, it has been made plain that much of its success was due to . . . women of that era. The unselfish part they acted constantly commends itself to our admiration and example."

In addition, Caroline continued her work on the board of a local hospital and served as director of the Washington City Orphan Asylum. Creating an art studio from a room in the attic, she contributed her hand-painted china for bazaars. With the First Lady's name recognition, and accomplished talent, Caroline was able to generate greater profits for charity.

With regard to White House entertaining, dancing became a popular part of her public receptions. Although Sarah Polk and Lucy Hayes may not have approved, Caroline was delighted: "One feature of entertainment which I was very pleased with—that was the lack of stiffness which generally characterized all such dinners and I believe all felt at ease and at home." The *Washington Post* wrote: "Mrs. Harrison has mastered the art of entertaining . . . She has a friendliness of manner that is proof against criticism."

Well not entirely, as every First Lady had discovered. Caroline was criticized for accepting a twenty-room seaside cottage in New Jersey. Reporters called it a political bribe and the public was so outraged that the president eventually paid ten thousand dollars for it.

The First Lady was also denounced for being overly domestic. Some believed cleaning the White House was not an appropriate duty for the First Lady. However, it was during that cleaning overhaul that Caroline discovered a surprising assortment of surplus presidential china. With this original china she began the mansion's most valuable and engaging collection. Also during her tenure the first decorated Christmas tree was set up in the White House for her grandchildren, now an annual tradition.

The most hurtful aspect of public life, however, was the attention directed at Caroline's grandchildren in the national newspapers, which ignored her requests for privacy. Baby McKee, President Benjamin Harrison's grandson, became the new favorite of the press, arguably the most photographed child ever to live in the White House. Author and newspaper contributor William Allen White noted that Baby McKee was "forever crawling over the front page of the newspaper."

Concerning her family's privacy, in frustration the First Lady confided to a friend: "I have about come to the conclusion that political life is not the happiest—you are [so] *battered* aound in it, that life seems hardly worth living."

In addition to being the devoted wife and grandmother that she was, Caroline had developed a sophisticated political acumen. The president respected her opinion and sought it often. She would advise him on major issues and encouraged him to hire the first woman stenographer, family friend Alice Sanger, for his staff.

Besides all her other charity work, Caroline helped raise money for the Johns Hopkins University Medical School on the condition that it would admit women on the same terms as men. Just as her parents devoted their lives to educating young women, the First Lady continued to carry the educational torch for her gender.

Unlike her immediate predecessors, Frances Cleveland and Lucy Hayes, both younger when they stepped into the White House, Caroline was an experienced and courageous woman who dared to act on her beliefs. Lucretia Garfield was also younger; however, her tenure was too short to appraise. Caroline also publicly supported organized labor.

Frequently ill with bronchial infections and other sicknesses, Caroline invited her widowed niece, Mary Dimmick, to reside at the White House and assist her with secretarial duties. As Caroline's health declined, Mary came to her aunt Carrie's aid more and more. On occasion, she was Uncle Ben's walking companion.

By the winter of 1891, Caroline's bronchial problems had increased in both frequency and severity. She developed pneumonia and later lung hemorrhaging. By the middle of the following year, her health was so critical that surgery was twice necessary to drain fluid from her lungs. Once Congress recessed, the president assisted with his wife's care and was at her bedside continuously.

It was also an election year, and the man President Harrison defeated was once again running against him. Former president Grover Cleveland wanted his old job back, and their second go-round was the most civil of all presidential campaigns. Neither opponent actively campaigned, out of respect for the First Lady's declining health.

Caroline died during the same month she turned sixty, just two weeks before her husband lost his presidential reelection bid.* The president acknowledged: "After the heavy blow of the death of my wife, I do not think that I could have stood re-election." It is probably

* Caroline Harrison is the only First Lady with the distinction of being preceded and succeeded by the same woman.

just as well, considering Harrison's opinion of the presidency. He declared: "I have often thought that the life of the president is like that of the policeman in the opera, not a happy one." She was the second First Lady to pass away in the White House.* During her East Room funeral, the *New York Tribune* reported that her elderly father stood with a "symmetrical and strong frame."[5] Overwhelmed with grief, the following month Dr. Scott passed away as well.

Benjamin Harrison had lost his teenage sweetheart. After forty-five years of irrefutable love and thirty-nine years of a committed marriage, his grief was undeniable. Apparently, it seemed only natural for him to turn to another family member for comfort over their mutual loss. Four years after his wife's death, sixty-two-year-old former president Harrison married thirty-seven-year-old Mary Dimmick, his wife's niece.

Harrison's adult children were so stunned and revolted that they refused to attend their father's wedding, beginning an estrangement that lasted the remaining five years of Harrison's life. The following year, at the age of sixty-three, Ben once again became a father, to daughter Elizabeth (1897–1955). She was younger than his four grandchildren and had just turned four years old when her father died of pneumonia.

What Caroline taught me:

Caroline Harrison remained devoted to her family and religious beliefs. Respected for her intelligence, warmth, and artistic talent, she provided evidence for me that a life can be full as well as balanced. A skillful organizer, Caroline proved to be a competent homemaker and mother, active charity worker, and devout churchgoer. By establishing daily schedules she managed to find time to incorporate all of her re-

---

* Letitia Tyler passed away in the executive mansion in 1842.

sponsibilities plus enjoy personal interests in her life. It appeared nothing was omitted from her busy life, including time for her family and grandchildren. By learning to manage her time effectively, Caroline was able to achieve productive, creative, and rewarding results in many areas.

Making time for all aspects of one's life is imperative. No one lives in a vacuum, and sacrificing a happy home life for a career, or giving up charitable endeavors to spend more time on self-indulgence, does not make one's life complete or entirely satisfying.

25

Act II, Wife and Mother

FRANCES CLEVELAND

I want you to take good care of everything in this house . . . we are coming back just four years from today.

—FRANCES CLEVELAND, TO WHITE HOUSE STAFF, 1889

IN THE SAME YEAR that the World's Columbian Exposition celebrated the four-hundredth anniversary of the discovery of America, Frances Cleveland's prediction did in fact become a reality. Four years after leaving the White House, the only First Lady to serve two nonconsecutive terms returned in 1893.

Frances began her second tenure with her sweet two-year-old daughter, Ruth, and pregnant with her second child, Esther, the first presidential child to be born in the White House.* Expressing great pleasure in being a mother as well as a dedicated wife, Frances was delighted to be living once again in the executive mansion.

> **#22, #24 Frances Folsom Cleveland**
>
> **Born:** July 21, 1864
> **Birthplace:** Folsomville, New York
> **Married:** 1886 (Grover Cleveland) Died
>   1913 (Thomas Preston)
> **Children:** 5 with Cleveland
> **White House Years:** 1885–1889 and
>   1893–1897
> **Died:** October 29, 1947
> **Fact:** Youngest and only First Lady to
>   marry in the White House
> **Aka:** Frank or Frankie

"Baby Ruth," now the newest darling of the press, became so pop-

---

* Ruth (1891–1904), Esther (1893–1980), Marion (1895–1977), Richard Folsom (1897–1974), Francis Grover (1903–1995).

ular that a candy bar was named after her. Ruth's fame and status caused her concerned parents to close the White House grounds to the public. This highly criticized action prompted false rumors that the child was somehow deficient or impaired.

The truth is that Frances was terrified when she saw her daughter being passed from one admiring tourist to another. Once again, the family resorted to living in a private home, Gray Gables, as much as duty permitted. Third daughter Marion was born two years later, but not in the White House although her father was still president of the United States.

In the summer of 1893, the president discovered he had cancer of the mouth, necessitating the removal of his upper left jaw. Like former president Grant, he too smoked cigars. To avoid alarming the public further—the failure of two railroads had already caused the Panic of 1893—the president decided to have the surgery performed on a friend's yacht.

A second "secret" operation was scheduled to fit the president with an artificial rubber jaw. The surgeries were successful, and Frances proved adept at deflecting suspicion. The White House categorically denied the president was seriously ill, and the truth was not disclosed until 1917.

In addition to evading the curious press and performing the customary White House hosting, the First Lady's second term was primarily spent being a mother to three very young daughters.

Before the end of Frances's tenure, the American public was introduced to the first use of X-rays for diagnosing breast cancer, and the first comic strip, "The Yellow Kid," appeared in Hearst's *New York World*.

Seemingly making progress on the racial front, Lucy Terry Prince, a former slave, was the first woman to address the Supreme Court of the United States, successfully defending a land claim. But a setback occurred the following year when the Supreme Court ruled that "separate but equal" facilities for whites and blacks were constitutional. It was the beginning of legalized segregation.

Around the same time, composer John Philip Sousa wrote "The Stars and Stripes Forever," Oscar Wilde wrote *The Importance of Being Earnest*, and Fanny Farmer published the *Fanny Farmer Cookbook*, which introduced cooking instructions and precise measurements, becoming a favored reference work throughout the twentieth century.

When Frances left the White House for the second time, Ike Hoover recounted that many of the staff and particularly the First Lady "wept as if her heart would break." She had always taken a personal interest in the employees' lives, remembering their birthdays and giving Christmas gifts to all, like Lucy Hayes before her and many First Ladies after her.

She explained her tears were not caused by the end of her husband's presidency, but rather by "leaving the surrounding to which she had come practically a girl, and now leaving a mature woman." During the same period of time, Frances also said: "I have not had my life yet. It is all before me."

The Clevelands decided to relocate to Princeton, New Jersey, and the college town proved to be an excellent choice for them. The former president became a trustee of Princeton University, and two more children were born, both boys. Frances enjoyed the peacefulness of the countryside, the intellectual stimulation, and the close devotion of her family.

Tragedy struck in 1903 when daughter Ruth, a young adolescent of thirteen, died of diphtheria. The next five years were trying for Frances. She could no longer return to their summer home on Cape Cod because of all her memories there with Ruth. The aging former president suffered minor ailments and would periodically write magazine articles. His view on women's suffrage never changed. In the July 1905 issue of the *Ladies' Home Journal*, Cleveland wrote: "Sensible and responsible women do not want to vote. The relative positions to be assumed by man and woman in the working out of our civilization were assigned long ago by a higher intelligence." Soon after, Frances's husband became chronically ill, requiring attention as a semi-invalid.

Cleveland undoubtedly recognized that one day he would be leaving the family he had waited so long and patiently to have. After twenty-two years of marital happiness, Frances laid her loving and devoted husband—her Uncle Cleve—to rest in June of 1908. Widowed at forty-three, Frances had four surviving children between the ages of four and fourteen to raise. Fortunately, Grover left his wife an estate worth a quarter of a million dollars; Frances admirably never accepted the five-thousand-dollar annual pension due to presidential widows.

Greatly saddened by her husband's death, Frances dressed in mourning for four years. Five years would pass before the former First Lady would remarry. Then in February 1913, Frances wed Thomas Preston Jr., a Princeton professor of archaeology. Remaining active, Frances Preston continued her charitable work, raised money for Wells College, and was involved in the Women's University Club.

During World War I, Frances gave speeches—something she had believed improper for women to do when she was First Lady—promoting the war effort for the National Security League. When cataracts threatened blindness, Frances learned Braille and made transcripts for blind students on a Braille typewriter. She continued doing so even after her cataracts were successfully removed. Always remaining close with her children, the family vacationed together every summer, and life went on as it always does.

When presidential daughter Margaret Truman first met Mrs. Preston, then eighty-two years old, she described the former First Lady as "gracious and self-assured." Also attending the same event was General Dwight D. Eisenhower. Margaret described the encounter between Mrs. Preston and the general in her book *First Ladies, An Intimate Group Portrait of White House Wives*: Eisenhower asked Mrs. Preston: "Where did you live in Washington madam?" "The same place Margaret is living now," [1] Frances replied sweetly to the embarrassed general. He obviously had no idea who the former First Lady was.

Frances Cleveland Preston died in her sleep in 1947 at the age of eighty-three, at the Baltimore home of her older son Richard. She was buried beside former president Grover Cleveland in Princeton, New Jersey.

What Frances taught me:

Long after Frances Cleveland departed the White House for the second time, her image could still be seen on ads, posters, and newsprint. Known nationally, Frances was loved as much as Dolley Madison.

Even in the face of cruel falsehoods, she sustained her genuineness and warmth. In addition to the various "firsts" that history attributes to Frances, her good common sense and gracious charm remain lasting and memorable. I learned from her that truth is permanent; falsehoods and trumped-up stories are simply fictional gossip to be ignored.

PART SEVEN

WOMEN OF THE TURN
OF THE CENTURY

⊰❈⊱

BY THE TURN of the twentieth century, the United States had experienced astonishing expansion and development. The country was no longer a cluster of individual territories but rather a whole and complete nation.

The populace, originally located exclusively on the eastern seaboard, now stretched from coast to coast. The Battle of Wounded Knee in December 1890 had ended the Indian wars. It was the last military encounter between American Indians and white soldiers. Once uncharted, unfarmed, and sparsely occupied land was now heartily populated.

Most of the free land was gone, and all but three of the contiguous states—Arizona, New Mexico, and Oklahoma—were now part of the forty-eight states in the Union. The population had swollen to nearly 76 million. In order to process the multitudes seeking a better life in the New World—3.6 million people in the last decade alone had migrated to the United States—the government opened Ellis Island in Upper New York Bay, the first federal immigration station.

At the beginning of the preceding century, no railroads, telegraphs, steamboats, electricity, telephones, plumbing, or photography existed. At the turn of the new century, Americans could travel eighty-seven thousand miles in a nationwide rail system, and enjoy gas, electricity, running water, and sewer systems in their homes. However, only the wealthy could afford indoor plumbing. Outhouses plus bathing tubs heated with water warmed on the stove were the norm for most people.

Procter and Gamble had begun to make Ivory Soap, and the consumer now had access to products through catalogs from Sears, Roebuck and Co. and Montgomery Ward and Co., two large mail order houses. Coca-Cola was first introduced as a "brain and nerve" tonic sold in pharmacies, and drugs could be freely purchased. Heroin, for example, was sold as a cough medicine, and its abuse was not uncommon. More conventional forms of entertainment such as roller-skating, baseball, and golf were enjoyed. With prosperity increasing, American Express first began to offer traveler's checks for the increased number of Americans now traveling abroad.

By all accounts, only nineteen millionaires resided in the United States in 1850. Within thirty-five years the nation saw its first skyscraper—a ten-story building built in Chicago. Sixteen years after it was first proposed the Brooklyn Bridge, the longest suspension bridge in the world, had opened. By the end of the century, the number of millionaires had increased to over four thousand individuals. Many of them earned their wealth from the numerous creations that were being designed and manufactured.

Inventions such as the zipper, adding machine, and electric stove were in common usage. Thomas Edison filed patents for the motion picture machine camera and the first incandescent electric lamp. Because innovative concepts and discoveries were so diverse and numerous, Charles Duell, commissioner of the US Patent Office in 1899, declared: "Everything that can be invented has been invented." Well, as we all know, not entirely.

The first Ford automobile was completed in 1896, and by the end of the decade eight thousand automobiles registered—with only ten miles of paved roads in the country. Horses and mules were tallied at eighteen million and bicycles numbered in the millions.

Educating the masses was important. The number of public high schools continued to increase, from one hundred schools in 1860 to six thousand by the end of the century. Illiteracy declined to reportedly 13.3 percent of the population and 75 percent of all teachers were women.

America had become a primary player on the world stage. A news story was published reporting: "American industry becomes the most productive in the world, including steel, cotton, meat packing, electric power, steam turbines and electric motors."

The age of giant corporations had arrived. American Tobacco, the American Sugar Refining Company, and General Electric had all been established. Labor unions were formed, such as the United Mine Workers and the American Railway Union.

The country had indeed evolved and become urbanized. Yet, insightfully, the *Washington Post* admonished: "[Despite] all our progress of luxury and knowledge . . . we have not been lifted by so much as a fraction of an inch above the level of the darkest ages . . . We enter a new century equipped with every wonderful device of science and art . . . [but] the pirate, the savage, and the tyrant still survives."[1]

The role of the First Lady was also evolving; there was now more focus on her opinions regarding fundamental issues beyond matters of social entertaining. With coverage in magazines such as *Harper's Bazaar, McClure's,* and *Ladies' Home Journal* she was also receiving more public attention. With a few exceptions, the turn of the century began to witness stronger, more influential presidential wives.

The first, Ida McKinley, was a delicate invalid with a devoted and sympathetic husband. In her own unusual manner, Ida held considerable power over her accommodating spouse. Edith Roosevelt and Helen Taft followed. Both women set the stage for expressing their own opinions. One did so with notable visibility while the other was enormously private. Each influenced her spouse more than any of her immediate predecessors.

Still traditional nineteenth-century women, all three were born in the mid-1800s, between 1847 and 1861. They possessed greater educations and better senses of identity than most of their predecessors, and their opinions—although not yet encompassing topics such as women's suffrage or temperance—were heard and acknowledged.

26

Dearly Loved Epileptic

IDA MCKINLEY

I am more lonely every day I live.

—IDA MCKINLEY,
AFTER HER HUSBAND'S ASSASSINATION

ONCE CALLED "a pathetically spoiled . . . woman," Ida McKinley had to live a tortured adult life in order to reap the benefits of excessive pampering. Born into prosperity in 1847, she was the eldest of three children born to James and Katherine Saxton. Her paternal grandfather, John Saxton, had created the Ohio Repository, while her father, a pillar of the Presbyterian church, owned the Stark County Bank. He was also said to be the second-wealthiest man in Canton, Ohio.

> **#25 Ida Saxton McKinley**
>
> **Born:** June 8, 1847
> **Birthplace:** Canton, Ohio
> **Married:** 1871 (William McKinley)
> **Children:** 2
> **White House Years:** 1897–1901
> **Died:** May 26, 1907
> **Fact:** 3rd First Lady whose husband was assassinated; an epileptic
> **Aka:** The Major's Wife

As a young girl Ida was pretty and petite, with auburn hair and blue eyes. After attending both public and private schools, she went on to the Brooke Hall Seminary, a finishing school for women. Following the completion of his daughters' educations, Mr. Saxton sent Ida and her younger sister, Mary, on an eight-month tour of Europe with a schoolteacher as chaperone. Youngest sibling George presumably was still in school. The year was 1869 and the trip was said to have cost two thousand dollars per child.

The Saxton girls visited nine countries including Germany, Scotland, and England where they had ancestral roots. Ida wrote to her family of visiting various museums and cathedrals; she also wrote of chronic headaches, later believed to be migraines, from which she suffered all her life.

After returning home from Europe, Ida began working in her father's bank. James Saxton, a most progressive man for his time, believed in business training for his girls. Beginning as a teller and bookkeeping clerk, Ida would later manage the bank during Saxton's short absences. Considered cheerful and outgoing, in addition to working she loved social gatherings, traveling, and also taught Sunday school.

Some believe Ida met Major William McKinley, a practicing attorney, while he was conducting banking transactions at the Ohio Repository. Others say their courtship began when the two would walk past one another on their way to church services—she to the Presbyterian church, he to the Methodist. Either way, the twenty-seven-year-old Civil War veteran fell deeply in love with his twenty-three-year-old belle.

On January 25, 1871, they were the first couple married in the bride's church, which Ida's father and grandfather had helped to build. The lavish ceremony was performed jointly by Presbyterian and Methodist ministers before a thousand guests.

The following Christmas Day was particularly special for the McKinleys. Not only was it the first Christmas Ida and William spent as husband and wife, it was also the day they became parents. Daughter Kate was born and named after Ida's mother.* Within six months, Ida was pregnant again, and life could not have been brighter—for the next few months anyway. Then the bottom of Ida's world dropped out from under her.

Katherine Saxton died during Ida's second pregnancy, and her mother's sudden death added to Ida's difficult labor. Her second

---

* Katherine (aka Kate 1871–1875). Some historians contend that she was born on the couple's first wedding anniversary, January 25, 1872, not on Christmas Day, December 25, 1871. Ida (1873–1873).

daughter was a frail infant who failed to thrive; she lived only five months. Ida would never again be the same.

Constantly frightened, ill tempered, and sad, Ida focused her fears on her surviving daughter Kate. Then, at four years of age, her precious daughter cruelly died of typhoid fever. What her physician described as an exceedingly "nervous disorder" plagued Ida for the rest of her life.

Often confined to her sickbed, she was diagnosed with phlebitis, migraines, stomach ailments, and epilepsy. From the age of twenty-six Ida was crippled physically, emotionally, and mentally for the remainder of her life. She became childishly dependent on her husband; throughout the rest of her marriage Ida was never again left alone, requiring a full-time attendant at all times.

Once an independent, headstrong workingwoman, Ida now suffered from seizures, depression, blackouts, crippling headaches, digestive problems, frequent colds, and premature aging. Frequently medicated into a stupor, she had become dependent and needy—a demanding wife who clung to her husband.

Ida's "Major" (as she referred to William) responded with total devotion, evoking envy from other women who believed McKinley to be a "knight in shining armor." Throughout his career—as a member of the House of Representatives, governor, and ultimately president of the United States—William was always accessible to his wife; leaving his responsibilities, he would stop and check on her, sometimes up to ten times a day during particularly stressful periods. Ida need only mention a desire and William rushed to fulfill it. He left strict instructions with whoever was taking care of her to never cross her, keep her amused, and wait on her completely.

Living the life of a semi-invalid, Ida was never very far from her husband. When not residing in their Canton home, a wedding present from her father, Ida lived in hotels where her room could be seen from William's office. Every day at the same designated time, regardless of his workload or meeting schedule, William would wave from his window, and Ida would respond by waving back with her lace handkerchief. Colleagues knew that McKinley could always be found either in his office or with his wife—period.

McKinley gave Ida a detailed itinerary of his daily schedule to help ease her anxiety. He also gave up his long walks and horseback riding so he could return to her quickly. According to historian Betty Boyd Caroli, the only pleasure William continued to enjoy was his cigar smoking—which he did away from home because Ida did not care for the odor. If the major was gone longer than expected, he would find his wife sobbing uncontrollably when he returned.

Ida spent her days sitting in a rocking chair, incessantly crocheting slippers: red for children, blue for Union veterans, and gray for former Confederate soldiers. In her lifetime Ida made over ten thousand pairs of slippers, approximately thirty-five hundred of them while she lived in the White House. Now and then she would make silk ties for her "precious William."

All was not entirely bleak. When Ida was up to it, she and her husband ("always your lover," as William would sign his letters) would attend the opera and plays, which she loved. Occasionally they would entertain colleagues and constituents. During William's tenure in Congress, sitting First Lady Lucy Rutherford became a friend, inviting Ida for private luncheons at the White House and both McKinleys for dinner.

Walking with the aid of a cane or resting on her husband's arm, Ida was determined to be a part of William's social and political life. Health permitting, she would sit beside her standing husband in reception lines, holding a bouquet of flowers, which prevented her from shaking individual hands. Often moved to tears in the presence of children, there was never a time Ida did not warmly welcome the opportunity to visit with young people.

In 1896, the same year William won the presidency, the couple celebrated their silver wedding anniversary before five hundred guests. Ida wore her original wedding dress, and one guest remarked: "She looked like a very faded souvenir."

Regarding Ida's various ailments, her diagnosis of epilepsy was never made known to the American public. At the time it was a dreaded, incurable and mysterious disease that carried social stigma. There were times when Ida's health could tolerate longer periods of activity, yet her mental fears never seemed to improve.

Too ill to accept retiring president Grover Cleveland's invitation for dinner, Ida was able to attend her husband's inauguration the following day. She was portrayed as happy, yet pale and frail-looking. Feeble and sickly would probably describe her best.

After becoming First Lady, Ida did her best to muster enough energy to function in her new role; however, the majority of the time she was a fragile participant during receptions and state affairs. In *I Would Live It Again, Memories of a Vivid Life,* Julia Foraker, a senator's wife, wrote: "Everyone was under a certain strain when the McKinleys were hosts. Mrs. McKinley, so physically unequal to the thing she bravely was attempting to do, and the President, masking his tender concern about his wife under a deferential solicitude for his guests that went to our hearts."

Seldom leaving the White House, Ida spent much of her time alone, with an aide on hand. Occasionally, she could be charming, even amusing, while at other times, probably under serious medication, she lived in her own thoughts. When possible, she would receive friends and official visitors. One such visit was recorded in *Washington Wife, Journal of Ellen Maury Slayden:*

> [Mrs. McKinley] sat propped with pillows in a high armchair with her back to the light. Her color was ghastly. . . . her poor relaxed hands, holding some pitiful knitting, rested on her lap as if too weak to lift their weight. . . . and her pretty gray hair is cut short as if she had had typhoid fever. Mrs. Maxey murmured some commonplace about her kindness in receiving us. . . . [Mrs. McKinley replied] "I've had a great deal of experience . . . , my husband was in Congress a long time, and then he was governor of the state." We all shrank from being there with a poor, suffering woman who ought to have been hidden from the gaze of the curious.

William became an expert on Ida's illness and recognized the symptoms of an approaching attack. He would gently put a handkerchief or napkin over his wife's face to hide a seizure from view. Afterward, the president would quietly remove the cover, while continuing his conversation. Breaking presidential protocol and custom, the First Lady was always seated beside her husband so he could assist when her embarrassing illness struck.

Ida's seizures did occur from time to time during White House functions, and the superb White House staff charted an escape route for such emergencies. Personnel would quickly whisk the First Lady away, as they did during the president's second inaugural ball.

Both somberness and celebration came to the White House at the turn of the century. As much as the president tried to prevent it, the United States declared war against Spain in early 1898. Eight months later, a treaty was signed and the United States was established as a world power. The same year, the First Lady's only brother, George Saxton, was murdered by his mistress. Showing remarkable strength of will, Ida refused to wear mourning clothes; she continued with as many of her official duties as she was able, and did her best to ignore the juicy gossip.

The press covered every succulent detail of the trial, with the accused woman eventually being acquitted. Suffering her most acute epileptic symptoms after the trial ended, Ida sank into a deep depression for many months. Returning to Canton, Ohio, to recuperate, she was confined to a wheelchair for a period of time.

In November of 1900 the president won reelection, and on December 12 the White House celebrated its one-hundredth birthday. According to Jane and Burt McConnell, the authors of *First Ladies: Martha Washington to Mamie Eisenhower,* Ida helped her husband plan the special occasion known as Centennial Day. Considering how far in advance White House observances were prepared, it is fair to assume everything had been done well in advance of Ida's collapse.

After the presidential inauguration the following March, the McKinley embarked on a grand tour of the country. The First Lady, who always liked to travel, wanted to be with her husband despite the inevitable exhaustion the two-month trip would cause her. Accompanied by her maid and physician, things were going well until Ida developed an infection in her finger that spread throughout her delicate body.

By the time they reached San Francisco, Ida was gravely ill and lay near death for almost a week. Crowds waiting for bulletins on the First Lady's condition gathered outside in the streets. As soon as the First Lady was able to travel again, the second half of the tour was abandoned and the president's train sped back to Washington. Somehow Ida had miraculously survived.

One of the many cancelled events was an important, long overdue speech the president was scheduled to make at a public reception at the Pan-American Exposition in Buffalo, New York. President McKinley's attendance at the exposition had already been cancelled twice before by his secretary, Mr. Cortelyou, who believed it would be impossible to protect the president's safety.

When he finally made it to the reception, on September 6, 1901, the unbelievable happened—President McKinley was shot. The wounded president's first thoughts were of his wife. "My wife—be careful, Cortelyou, how you tell her—oh, be careful."[1]

The president survived eight days during which Ida mustered her courage and rose to meet the crisis. Very similar to her predecessor Lucretia Garfield, Ida remained sitting beside her dying husband, lifting his spirits, until he succumbed to an infection from his wound.

Unlike Mary Todd Lincoln, who could not tear herself away from her White House bedroom, Ida participated in all the ceremonies of the state funeral, and then returned to Canton with the president's body for burial.

The day of the internment clouds let loose a thunderous rain. One reporter noted that the "sky openly wept with the grieving nation." A third president's life had been cut short at the hands of an assassin.*

* Anarchist Leon Czolgosz was tried in the Supreme Court of New York and electrocuted in October of 1901.

Ida, the woman who had been sheltered from responsibility and burden, was now forced to face the reality and loneliness of her life. No one could have possibly guessed that she would continue living another six years. Residing with her sister, the only time Ida left the house was to visit the graves of her beloved husband and children or to attend a small local tribute to her "dear William." It was said that she never again had a seizure, yet it is questionable whether anyone could know that for certain.

On May 26, 1907, Ida's prayers to be at her husband's side were answered. Thirteen days before her sixtieth birthday and three months before the dedication of her husband's national memorial, she died of a stroke. Ida was once again reunited with her "Major" and their two daughters, in Canton's McKinley Memorial Mausoleum.

Doubts remain as to how much of Ida's illness was due to her physical condition, her psychological status, or even her medication. Whether her dependence was completely or partially due to her illness or, for that matter, her need to keep her husband's attention, will never be known. What we do know is that Ida paid a very high price for her poor health and that it was her decision not to remain secluded away, but rather to participate in life as much as possible.

What Ida taught me:

Time and again, I have witnessed how personal tragedies can rob human beings of attaining significant accomplishments. Illness, mourning, and depression can destroy the strongest mortal among us, but it does not have to. As Ida noted in her diary on April 15, 1901: "I am feeling very miserable, headache most of the time . . . I will go out with my Dearest and enjoy it." Ida McKinley taught me to always do the best one is capable of, even when one's best is not exceptional.

Ida could have chosen not to participate at all in her husband's social life or her White House duties. Any one of her various physical limitations, her emotional disposition, or even her medications could well have sidelined Ida from participating in life. Instead, she chose to do the best she could. Not surprisingly, Ida's best sometimes fell short. On the other hand, because of her willingness to participate and her perseverance to be included, at other times her best far surpassed anything that could be imagined.

27

Second Wife, First Lady

EDITH ROOSEVELT

If I could not have both, I should choose my children's respect rather than their love.

—EDITH ROOSEVELT

FIRST AND FOREMOST, Edith Roosevelt saw herself as a mother. After all, she quickly became a mother upon marrying at the age of twenty-five, and went on to have five more children. In fact, Edith gave birth to her first child just nine months after saying "I do." By her eleventh wedding anniversary she was raising six children.

Furthermore, Edith referred to her husband, Theodore Roosevelt, as her "oldest and rather worst child." Confirming this in a letter to her husband's cousin, Franklin Roosevelt, Edith wrote: "Managed TR [a favorite nickname for her spouse] very cleverly without his being conscious of it—no slight achievement as anyone will concede."[1]

On another occasion, according to historian Betty Boyd Caroli, someone suggested that Edith wait until her husband could accompany her (and presumably the children) to their home, Sagamore Hill.

> **#26 Edith Carow Roosevelt**
>
> **Born:** August 6, 1861
> **Birthplace:** Norwich, Connecticut
> **Married:** 1886 (Theodore Roosevelt)
> **Children:** 5; plus 1 stepdaughter
> **White House Years:** 1901–1909
> **Died:** September 30, 1948
> **Fact:** Established First Lady picture gallery
> **Aka:** Edie

Edith laughed and rejected the suggestion, saying, "I already have my hands full."[2] In some respects, Theodore Roosevelt was in fact a large overgrown kid. In addition to being the man who organized the First Volunteer Cavalry, known as Roosevelt's "Rough Riders" during the Spanish-American War, Theodore loved nothing more than to rough-house and play pranks with his children. No activity was too danger-ous, too adventurous, or too audacious.

Edith's home was more like a camp, with a unique group of enthu-siastic, zealous, and mischievous campers, both male and female. A loving mother, Edith had a reputation for a casual attitude toward her children's many escapades and adventures. Never rattled by the nu-merous cuts and scrapes from her offsprings' abundant mishaps, Edith would simply remind them not to drip blood on the rugs. One son was quoted as saying: "When Mother was a little girl, she must have been a boy!"

One might think Edith was indeed a tomboy growing up, but one would be mistaken. Born into money and position, on August 6, 1861, Edith Kermit Carow lived a cultured life filled with literature, poetry, and Shakespeare. Living with only one sibling, a younger sister, Edith's favorite sport was reading.

Theodore commented that even as a young girl Edith was "the most cultivated, best-read girl" he knew. He was speaking from years of personal knowledge, given that even before they ever attended school, "Edie" and "Teedie," as the youngsters were called, both learned to read and write at the Roosevelt home, taught by the same governess. Edith's passion for reading earned her recognition as a bookworm. An avid reader himself, Theodore read a remarkable number of books, often one a day.

Both lived in the Union Square district of New York, and their re-spective families were affluent and socially well placed. Edith could trace her American ancestors all the way back to the 1630s. Her dear-est girlhood friend was Corinne Roosevelt, Theodore's kid sister.

In her biography *Edith Kermit Roosevelt: Portrait of a First Lady*, Sylvia Jukes Morris describes how nearly four-year-old Edith and not quite seven-year-old Theodore watched President Lincoln's funeral procession as it passed through New York City in 1865.

Young Edith's once-successful father, Charles Carow, was an alcoholic; it was not long before Mr. Carow's poor business sense and alcoholism negatively affected the family's finances. Edith's mother, Gertrude Tyler Carow, was described as a spendthrift hypochondriac.

Edith's formal studies at Comstock School stressed literature and languages (she became fluent in French) as opposed to sciences and higher mathematics, which were considered more appropriate for boys. Considering her love of poetry, presumably she enjoyed such classics as "The Raven" by Edgar Allan Poe, published when she was sixteen years old, and later as an adult, *Poems* by Emily Dickinson.

Standing at five foot seven, Edith weighed approximately 125 pounds and had dark brown hair and blue-gray eyes. Scholarly, dignified, and intelligent, she was reserved in her manner. Some historians have described her as being aloof.

Edith would spend summer vacations with the Roosevelts at Oyster Bay on Long Island, and visit Theodore at Harvard, with his family. In addition to being deeply in love with her closest friend's brother, Edith was an opposite and an outstanding counterpart for the energetic, exuberant Theodore Roosevelt.

Purportedly engaged at one point, a significant quarrel (its reasons unknown) in 1878 drove the couple apart. Later that year, Theodore met Alice Hathaway Lee; when he decided to marry her, Theodore confided in Edith before telling anyone in his own family. An intensely private person, no one will ever know what Edith's feelings were when she attended Theodore and Alice's wedding in 1880.

Traveling in the same social circles, Edith saw the newlyweds at various social events and was a bridesmaid at her dear friend Corinne's wedding. At twenty-two, Edith mourned her father's death, the parent she was closest to. After Charles Carow died the family's financial struggles increased considerably. Ultimately, her mother, Gertrude, moved to Europe where she could live less expensively.

During this period, Theodore both became a father and tragically lost his wife two days after she had given birth to their daughter. She had contracted Bright's disease (a kidney illness). He baptized his daughter Alice after her mother.* The tragedy was compounded when Theodore's mother died from typhoid fever on the same day in the same house as his wife. It was Valentines Day, February 14, 1884.

Although both Edith and Theodore made a conscious effort to avoid one another, it was almost inevitable that their paths would cross. When that happened in September of 1885, Theodore again began to see Edith socially. By November, the two were secretly engaged.

When Theodore's cousin James West Roosevelt learned of the engagement, he wrote to Theodore: "Now that you are to marry a girl who has been one of my best friends, a girl whose main characteristic is truth, I am very much delighted. . . . You are marrying a woman who can enter into your plans and who can appreciate your aims. . . . You are marrying one also who will love you—that is best of all."[3]

The two married in London on December 2, 1886, honeymooned in France, then spent time with Edith's mother in Italy before moving into their home, Sagamore Hill, at Oyster Bay. Edith's immediate family began with three-year-old stepdaughter Alice, whom she raised as her own. Soon Alice had four brothers and one sister.[†] Edith's life consisted of family, nonstop activity, relatives, and her never-ending passion for reading.

Thankfully, she did not inherit her father's poor business sense or her mother's spending habits. Just the opposite, Edith proved to be a better financial manager than her husband, taking frugal charge of the household's expenses. She was a practical woman with sound judgment; it was very apparent that Edith was an indispensable presence in her husband's life.

---

* Alice Lee (1884–1980).
† Theodore (1887–1944), Kermit (1889–1943), Ethel Carow (1891–1977), Archibald Bulloch (1894–1979), Quentin (1897–1918).

Being the family money manager, Edith made the decisions involving what and where to cut back, but never lost sight of their social status; living in a mansion with servants never changed. She was a skillful economizer, giving her husband an allowance that eventually came to twenty dollars a day. But I think it is fair to say that Theodore's inclinations prevailed in all other areas.

A good part of the couple's days was typically dedicated to work. Edith was involved with household necessities, while her husband pursued his writing. In order to spend quiet time together, the devoted couple would often go on a boat ride in the afternoon, an activity that provided many benefits. Theo, as his wife often called him, would row the boat, getting in some exercise, while Edie read aloud. Other times, they would go off horseback riding by themselves.

Although Roosevelt attended Columbia Law School after graduating Harvard Phi Beta Kappa and magna cum laude, he found law boring; public service was his true calling. Theodore had been in the New York State Assembly for two years and was an unsuccessful candidate for mayor of New York before President Benjamin Harrison appointed him US civil service commissioner in 1889. His personality lent itself perfectly to politics.

Public service has been known to strongly resemble public property, and Edith was far more private and reserved. Always self-controlled, she was reticent and detached, remaining somewhat mysterious her entire life. A classmate of hers confirmed this: "I believe you could live in the same house with Edith for fifty years and never really know her."[4] This became even more apparent when her husband became a public figure. To quote Edith: "One hates to feel that all one's life is public property."

Now the Roosevelts' life began to change. With her husband's rise to public prominence, the family found themselves spending winters in Washington, participating in the social season; money concerns became a recurring issue. But fortunately—as public service pay has seldom proven sufficient to finance political entertaining—Theo received an inheritance.

Theodore's political career continued to rise. He became the police commissioner of New York, then the assistant secretary of the navy—a post he resigned in order to volunteer and fight in the Spanish-American War, returning a hero—before being elected the governor of New York. Although Edith preferred a quiet family life with lots of time for reading, she proved herself a gracious, efficient, and exceedingly thrifty hostess.

Edith enjoyed living in the Governor's Mansion. Always independent minded, she began her practice of holding two bouquets of flowers, one in each hand, to prevent her from shaking the thousands of outstretched hands extended to her in reception lines (a technique Ida McKinley perfected). All around, her life was good; it consisted of a happy, boisterous family and a husband who adored her, along with new financial security from Theo's writing ventures.*

Reluctant to have her life change, and convinced her husband would never be happy in the second position, Edith discouraged Theo from accepting the vice presidential spot under William McKinley in the 1900 presidential election. Although he did initially decline, Edith sat inside the Republican Convention and watched as enthusiasm built for her husband, the hero of San Juan Hill. The party had spoken, and the McKinley-Roosevelt ticket was approved.

Roosevelt's tenure as vice president was short-lived: President McKinley was assassinated just six months after his reelection. At forty-two, Theodore Roosevelt was the youngest man in history to become president. Edith's fear for her husband's safety was understandable, when she wrote: "I suppose in a short time I shall adjust myself to this, but the horror of it hangs over me, and I am never without fear for Theodore."

A pleasant, welcome change from the sickly Ida McKinley, Edith became a role model and was considered an ideal First Lady, one who balanced official duties with family responsibilities. A close aide to

---

* Theodore Roosevelt was the most prolific presidential author, with thirty-eight published books.

the president recalled: "In all her seven years in the White House, she never made a mistake."[5]

Nonetheless, no First Lady has ever escaped criticism of some kind, and Edith took hers good naturedly. Ridiculed for spending too little on her clothes, it was reported that the First Lady dressed "on three hundred dollars a year and looks it." Edith saved the news report in her scrapbook, accepting the remark as a compliment.

Economical as well when it came to housekeeping, Edith accepted those responsibilities herself and chose not to hire a housekeeper. If the president invited last-minute guests for lunch (not uncommon for most chief executives), they often discovered the First Lady had not ordered sufficient food. Remaining true to her nature, Edith went on calmly undisturbed.

One area where Edith felt extra expenditure was justified was when it came to the annoying, persistent, insatiable press. She was the first First Lady to hire a social secretary to deal with all the information, correspondence, and photos the hungry public was constantly interested in. Wanting her children to have as normal a life as possible, Edith would provide posed photographs of the family, to satisfy curiosity and thwart photographers.

The children had no problem living in the White House, and quickly commandeered the executive mansion as their own private playground, which to some extent it was. There was not an inch of the White House they did not play in, investigate, or explore, from the basement to the rooftop. When it came to stories of the mischievous Roosevelt children—Alice, Theodore, Kermit, Ethel, Archibald, and Quentin—now ages three to seventeen, the press was well supplied with commentary.

Tales of their mini zoo were only an introduction to the many amusing news stories shared with the country. Over the years, the Roosevelt family was home to fifteen dogs, eight horses, five guinea pigs, two cats, two birds, and four exotic animals, plus a one-legged rooster, snakes, lizards, rats, raccoons, a zebra, a bear cub, and an owl.[6]

Some of the more favored pets that resided in and around the

White House were a kangaroo rat, which demonstrated his hopping ability across the dining room table; Eli Yale, a blue macaw; Josiah, a badger; Jack and Pete, both dogs; Tom Quartz, a cat; Emily Spinach, a green snake Alice named after her rather thin spinster aunt (Edith's sister); and Algonquian, a calico pony.

Algonquian made the newspapers because of Quentin's thoughtfulness. While Archie was upstairs, sick in bed with the measles, Quentin smuggled Algonquian into the White House elevator; he then pulled the pony into his brother's bedroom, in hopes of making him feel better. Rumor has it that Archie smiled when he saw the pony, as did the First Lady when she later heard the story. There was no mention of any punishment for Quentin's good-natured effort.

It was a common occurrence for all of the children (including younger daughter Ethel, known to be a tomboy) to walk through the mansion on stilts, slide down the banister, or sit on metal cooking trays while descending down the steps. Only eldest brother Ted, who was away at school, could not join in.

The youngest and by far the favorite child was Quentin. He and a group of his school friends (including Charles Taft, son of Secretary of War William Howard Taft) were called the "White House Gang." Notorious for throwing snowballs from the roof of the White House at unsuspecting Secret Service agents below, carving a baseball diamond on the White House lawn, and discharging spitballs at Andrew Jackson's presidential portrait (which the boys were disciplined for) were only a few of their many escapades.

Quentin would surprise a more refined visitor by running down the halls laughing loudly, crawling under the table during a formal dinner, or imitating a dignitary. Once when a reporter was attempting to obtain some information on his father, Quentin replied: "I see him occasionally, but I know nothing of his family life." Edith called him a "fine bad little boy."

Stories of "Princess Alice," as the elder Roosevelt daughter was dubbed, are legendary. Entire books could be written on her antics alone. To begin with, she refused to go to a school of any kind. Alice had studied the Bible as instructed, yet also refused to attend church in preparation for confirmation. Meanwhile, her pet snake, Emily Spinach, often got loose in the White House, terrorizing the servants.

When she was prohibited from smoking "under this roof," Alice climbed onto the roof of the White House, where she continued to smoke. When someone complained to President Roosevelt about his daughter's behavior, the president said: "I can run the country or control Alice, I cannot possibly do both."

The new First Lady soon found living in the White House "cramped and like living over the store." After persuading Congress of the need for an overhaul, and hiring an architectural firm in 1902, the presidential family moved out of the White House. For the next six months, the executive mansion was renovated, at a cost of $500,000. In addition to enlarging the existing structure by adding a third floor, new buildings were constructed to accommodate office space; this area is known today as the "West Wing." It is not surprising that Edith also included a tennis court, to assist her husband with his weight and accommodate his desire to exercise.

Never abandoning his exercise commitment, several times a week the president boxed with sparring partners, until one blow detached his retina, leaving him blind in his left eye. After that he took up ju-jitsu and (like former president John Adams) continued to skinny-dip in the Potomac River during the winter months. President Roosevelt is also credited with naming the president's home in 1901, when he had "The White House" printed on the official presidential stationery.

Edith considered the White House a museum, and was responsible for further contributions. She added to former First Lady Caroline Harrison's china collection, in addition to putting it on permanent display. Today's much-admired First Ladies Portrait gallery was also her idea. It is now tradition for every First Lady to have her portrait painted. The paintings are rotated within the White House, with the most recent former First Lady's portrait displayed at the gallery entrance.

Being the efficient manager she was, and determining her time could be better spent elsewhere, Edith delegated the preparation of official dinners to professional caterers, who charged seven dollars and fifty cents per person.[7]

It soon became obvious that in addition to instituting renovation improvements in the executive mansion and establishing organizational precedents for the role of First Lady, Edith was a major influence in shaping the president's outlook, as well as his actions.

Theodore admired and respected his wife's practical and prudent judgment, and sought it often. He once wrote to one of his sons: "Mother . . . when necessary, pointed out where I was thoughtless, instead of submitting to it." Edith could be more objective in her opinions than her husband and did not hesitate to set him straight. She also proved to be a better judge of men, and her political insights saved Theodore from making personal gaffs more than once. The president said: "When I went against her advice, I paid for it."[8]

During the same period, while the president was "busting trusts" (prosecuting monopolies) and initiating his innovative "conservation" projects, other exciting firsts were occurring in the nation.

Renowned educator, author, and leader Booker T. Washington became the first African American to be invited to dine at the White House. Edith then gave her stepdaughter a stately coming-out party, with guests from all over the country, when Alice turned eighteen.

In 1903, an eleven-minute film, *The Great Train Robbery*, was shown in theaters; and the Wright brothers took a twelve-second airplane flight at Kitty Hawk, North Carolina. The following year, New York passed the first speed law for automobiles: 10 mph in the cities, 20 mph in the countryside; and the Panama Canal Zone was formally acquired by the United States.

Prior to the next presidential election, on one of his many hunting trips Roosevelt, an avid hunter, refused to shoot a captured black bear. After the *Washington Post* ran a now famous cartoon depicting the incident, a clever toy maker named a stuffed bear "Teddy" after the president, and soon Teddy Bears were being sold across the entire country.

When Roosevelt won the presidential election in 1905, the entire family was exuberant. However, beyond exuberant, the president must have been temporarily out of his mind, because he made the greatest gaffe of his life. He announced to the press that he would not accept another presidential nomination after this term.

Edith knew instantly that Theodore would regret making the statement; unfortunately, he had not discussed it with her beforehand. The First Lady knew her husband better than he knew himself, and she recognized he could never be happy outside of political office. Moreover, anything less than the top position would never be acceptable. The only thing to do now was move forward.

With the sadness of President McKinley's assassination behind them, the first family and seven thousand guests enthusiastically attended Roosevelt's inaugural ball. Edith was radiant that evening. (She had the design for the exquisite gown she wore destroyed, to prevent imitations.) The First Lady began her husband's first elected term as president with tireless energy; she hit the ground running.

 On the world front, Russia and Japan had been in crisis for some time. Finally, in June of 1905, both countries formally accepted America's offer for peace talks. The following year, Roosevelt became the first American president to receive the Nobel Peace Prize for his part in the negotiations to end the Russo-Japanese War. Both the president and First Lady agreed he would contribute the forty-thousand-dollar prize money to establish an Industrial Peace Committee.

Then, on the first official trip abroad by a First Lady, Edith accompanied her husband to view the new Panama Canal. In addition to Edith's traditional role as hostess of the White House, she instituted the tradition of high cultural entertainment in the East Room with musicians such as the young Pablo Casals. The National Gallery of Art was funded under Edith's influence, giving her the distinction of being its "first patron of the arts."

If that were not enough, Edith was about to host what would be billed as the social event of the year. Following an international social extravaganza, Princess Alice, now twenty-two years old, was ready to settle down with the playboy congressman Nicholas Longworth, fifteen years her senior. Longworth shared his future father-in-law's alma mater, Harvard, as well as his political views. Regarding his future son-in-law, Roosevelt was quoted as saying: "Of course he's insane. He wants to marry Alice."

Alice had long ago established a reputation for having an acid tongue and a sharp, scathing attitude. The first daughter, who had become a recurring personality in the press because she continually pushed the envelope of proper female behavior, was now leaving the nest.

Stories of friction between Alice and her stepmother were well known. Distinguished First Lady historian Carl Sferrazza Anthony confirms that an exhausted Edith told Alice: "I want you to know that I'm glad to see you leave. You have never been anything but trouble." Many years later when a more mature, grown-up Alice was asked how Edith handled her, she replied: "With a fairness and charm and intelligence which she has to a greater degree than almost anyone I know."[9]

One thousand guests packed the East Room to its limit, including former White House bride Nellie Grant, for the high-profile, spectacular affair. Guests used three separate entrances to file into the executive mansion. Choosing not to share the spotlight with anyone else, Alice had no bridesmaids. The wedding was reported in glittering detail by the world press, and the event appeared to cement her status in Washington society for the remainder of her long life.

Alice moved out of the White House after marrying, but it was far from the last time she would be inside it. From 1909 to 1976, Mrs. Longworth (aka Mrs. L) was perhaps the most frequently invited guest to the executive mansion. She knew everyone in political Washington and had something to say about each one. Margaret Truman, another presidential daughter who knew Alice in the 1940s, recalled her as "all acid wit and sarcasm, an utterly delightful grande dame."

A few of Alice's popular quips will give you a sense of her personality:

"I have a simply philosophy. Fill what's empty. Empty what's full. And scratch where it itches."

"If you can't say anything good about someone, sit right here by me" (which Alice had embroidered on a pillow and displayed in her home).

"At a funeral father always wants to be the corpse, and at a wedding he always wants to be the bride." Roosevelt said the very same thing about Alice only he included at the end, "*and* the baby at every christening."

Just two months after the president's eldest daughter married, San Francisco, California, experienced a devastating earthquake that killed approximately five hundred people and started fires that destroyed much of the city. Two months later, Congress passed the Meat Inspection Act and the Pure Food and Drug Act, in order to correct the conditions spelled out in the book *The Jungle* by American novelist Upton Sinclair.

In 1908, Henry Ford introduced the Model T automobile, which sold for around eight hundred and fifty dollars. It could be purchased in any color, as long as the color was black. Black could very well have been the president's mood as the year was coming to a close. Profoundly regretting the comment he had made four years earlier—not to accept another presidential nomination—Roosevelt stood by his word.

Knowing he had to fill the presidential void somehow, Roosevelt decided that when his term ended he would go on safari, out of the country. Prior to leaving her tenure in the executive mansion, Edith gave younger daughter Ethel a coming-out debut, closing the White House social season.

Alice's parting exploit, just before her family moved out of the mansion, was directed at Helen Taft, her stepmother's successor. Taking an immediate dislike to the future First Lady, whom she mocked as having a "hippopotamus face" and "Cincinnasty" accent, Alice buried a voodoo doll on the lawn, "calling the gods to visit woe on the new occupants." (For those eternal skeptics, I suggest you do not skip over Helen's upcoming story.)

After returning to Sagamore Hill, Edith spent the next several months in near seclusion. Her husband and son Kermit had already left to lead a yearlong big-game hunt in Africa to collect specimens for the Smithsonian Institution.* Both a naturalist and conservationist, Theodore Roosevelt was considered the world's authority on large American mammals.

As much as Edith enjoyed basking in solitude, certainly far more than the average person, at this particular time in her life things were different. She decided to take her three younger children with her to Europe for five months.

After the entire family returned home from their separate excursions, Theodore returned to his writing and remained in the public eye by campaigning for his fellow progressive Republican candidates. As Edith predicted, nothing could stifle or equal her husband's passion for politics.

Unhappy about how his friend and hand-picked successor, William Howard Taft, was running the government, Roosevelt was ready to return and once again become head of his political party. Getting around his previous comment of not accepting another presidential nomination, Roosevelt said he meant a "consecutive" nomination.

However, things had changed politically during the four years Roosevelt was out of office, and instead of heading the Republican Party, he split it. In doing so he also lost his friendship with his former secretary of war, now the sitting president. When Taft won the Republican nomination, Roosevelt organized the Progressive Party, also known as the "Bull Moose" Party, and began running for president as their nominee.

Just prior to a campaign speech in Milwaukee, Roosevelt was hit in the chest with a would-be assassin's bullet.† Fortunately, he was car-

---

* It was a very successful expedition that included 250 porters; they collected 1,100 specimens, including 500 big game.
† The assailant, John Nepomuk Schrank, was declared insane and committed to a state hospital, where he died in 1943.

rying his rather thick speech in his breast pocket, which slowed down the bullet's impact. Insisting that it "takes more than a bullet to stop a Bull Moose," Roosevelt refused to go to the hospital until his speech was delivered. "I will deliver this speech or die, one or the other." Before a capacity crowd, in a bloodstained shirt, he began: "Friends, I shall ask you to be very quiet. . . . If you'll do that, I will do the best I can." After speaking for approximately eighty minutes, he was taken to the hospital.

Edith happened to be in a New York theater when a messenger delivered the news of the shooting. Arriving at the hospital the next day, she found her husband surrounded by a steady stream of visitors and a very unhappy doctor. The bullet, still lodged in the former president's chest, had broken a rib, and the physician was concerned his patient was not receiving sufficient bed rest. Edith obtained the room next door and immediately stopped all visits. The disobedient patient, who had been "completely out of hand," timidly began taking instruction from his spouse.

The "Big Three" election, as it was widely known, was so named because of the three leading college football powers of the day. The 1912 presidential election matched former president Theodore Roosevelt (Harvard class of 1880), sitting president William Howard Taft (Yale class of 1878), and future president Woodrow Wilson (Princeton class of 1879).

Roosevelt received a greater number of popular votes than Taft, but because of the split, Wilson won more votes than either of the other two. Perhaps Edith said it best when she wrote: "I have lived, most reluctantly, through one party split, and no good comes of it." She also advised Theo to "put it out of your mind. You will never be President again." When the Progressive Party sought his candidacy in 1916, Roosevelt declined the nomination.

Returning to their home for good, life was quieter than it had ever been before. Daughter Ethel had become a nurse, married Dr. Dick Derby, a surgeon, and moved away from home. The younger boys were involved with their studies—all four Roosevelt sons attended

Harvard; only Quentin, who was a sophomore when he volunteered for war, did not graduate—while Roosevelt continued to write and prepare for a new expedition with Kermit in Brazil.

Edith accompanied her husband and Kermit on the first part of his South American trip; then she returned home while they continued up the Amazon to find the River of Doubt. Edith had no news of them for four months. At long last, Kermit and Roosevelt emerged from the wilderness. Close to death, ill from exposure, tropical fever, and an infected gash on his leg, Roosevelt credited his son for saving his life. For his heroism and expeditionary abilities, the River of Doubt was later renamed Rio Roosevelt.*

Kermit had postponed his marriage for the Brazilian expedition; in 1914, the wedding finally took place in Europe. Edith's health prevented her from attending the ceremony with her husband. She was beginning to experience some health problems that ultimately required surgery, which some historians believe could have been a hysterectomy. Now in her mid-fifties, Edith lacked the energy she was once famous for.

When World War I broke out in Europe, Edith traveled with her husband in the United States to garner American support. When America finally entered the war, Roosevelt was the first to volunteer; however, President Wilson refused his request to take a regiment to France. Disappointed, and loathing his rival all the more, the former president continued to travel the country, recruiting; his four sons volunteered.

Edith was equally as brave as her husband, supporting their sons' involvement: "You cannot bring up boys as eagles and expect them to turn out sparrows."[10] Young Quentin went so far as to cheat on an eye exam in order to be accepted by the air force. He said: "We boys thought it was up to us to practice what Father preached."[11]

---

* Roosevelt wrote extensively about the harrowing trip in his book *Through the Brazilian Wilderness*. In it he discusses the trip's many perils and hardships, including Kermit's near death incident.

Archie was wounded in France, and received the Croix de Guerre in recognition for acts of bravery in the face of the enemy. Theodore wrote to his son that Edith sent for a bottle of Madeira and "all four of us filled the glasses and drank them off to you; then Mother, her eyes shining, her checks flushed, as pretty as a picture, and as spirited as any heroine of romance, dashed her glass on the floor, shivering it in pieces, saying, 'That glass shall never be drunk out of again.'"[12]

The sad reality of war is that many brave men will die, presidential children included. Quentin, only twenty years old, was killed: shot down in France behind enemy lines. Upon hearing the news, Theodore "paced silently, struggling to calm himself— his voice choking with emotion . . . and tears streaming down his face—but Mrs. Roosevelt!—How am I going to break it to her?"[13] Edith came close to losing control and practically collapsed. Together, both parents deeply grieved for their son.

The German military, trying to gather support for their cause, cruelly and vilely distributed pictures of Quentin's disfigured body around the world. Over two thousand Americans wrote letters or sent telegrams of condolence to the heartbroken family. Roosevelt believed that "both life and death are part of the same Great Adventure," yet inconsolable, the former president was never the same after his son's death.

Still subject to some of the same afflictions he had suffered from during his trip to the Amazon, Roosevelt's health was deteriorating quickly. During a hospitalization, Edith once again slept in the adjoining room and read to her husband during the day. Theodore returned home for Christmas and in January 1919 died from an embolism, at sixty years of age.

Only six months after the death of her youngest child, "Edie" had lost her adored "Teedie," the only person in her life whom she loved "with all the passion of a girl."[14]

The afternoon of her husband's passing, Edith shared a long walk with Corinne, her sister-in-law and lifelong friend. Archie sent his brothers a cable: "The old lion is dead." Roosevelt's own thoughts on death were that "only those are fit to live who do not fear to die; and none are fit to die who have shrunk from the joy of life."[15]

Adhering to the custom of the day, Edith did not attend her husband's funeral. In February of the same year, she left for Europe to visit Quentin's grave and see her other boys, Ted and Kermit.

When Edith returned home, she maintained her interest in reading, art, and culture. She traveled to Europe extensively and also participated in partisan politics. When Theodore's distant cousin Democrat Franklin D. Roosevelt ran for the presidency, Edith openly campaigned for his Republican opponent, Herbert Hoover. Years later, in 1935, she even spoke at the National Conference of Republican Women. (In all fairness, Eleanor Roosevelt, Franklin's wife, was said to have campaigned against Ted Jr., her first cousin and Edith's son, five years earlier, when he unsuccessfully ran for governor of New York.) Blood may be thicker than water—but in the large Roosevelt family, politics was thicker than blood, and had been for many generations.

At seventy-four, Edith broke a hip and required months of hospitalization. But even after her recuperation, Edith's pain and sorrow were not yet over. Her three remaining sons all volunteered during World War II, as well as daughter Ethel and her husband, both of whom worked at Ambulance Americaine in Paris. Archie again served with distinction (he had been severely wounded in World War I). He returned from the South Pacific a lieutenant colonel with many decorations.

While one brother was sent to the South Pacific and another to France, Kermit went off to active military duty in Alaska. (He had already received the British Military Cross for his prior service in World War I.) Edith knew that her second-eldest son had two battles to fight: Kermit was also fighting alcoholism. Inevitability, it must have brought back memories of her beloved father's struggle with alcohol. While in Alaska, Kermit committed suicide in 1943. Edith was never told the truth and believed her son died of a heart attack.

The following year, eldest son Ted Jr. (who had been wounded in 1918) was fighting at Normandy. (Ted's wife served in Paris as a volunteer for the YMCA.) After several months of horrific battle, Ted Jr. suddenly died of a heart attack. He was posthumously awarded the Medal of Honor as a World War II general.

The last years of Edith's life were not easy ones. She buried three of her four sons and a husband she had loved her entire life. Now, in her eighties, her body was failing her as well. Edith told her daughter that "Ted's death did something to me from which I shall not recover" and that she felt "too removed from life."[16]

Edith spent her last year and a half bedridden at Sagamore Hill, cared for by her daughter Ethel. Just after her eighty-seventh birthday in 1948, Edith was buried alongside her husband in Oyster Bay. "Everything she did was for the happiness of others" is how Edith said she wanted to be remembered.

What Edith taught me:

Edith Roosevelt had strict moral ethics and believed they applied to everyone. She disapproved of a double standard of morality for men and women, yet she did not believe in equality between the sexes. Edith always maintained that a woman's role was as a wife and mother. She lived her life in that role, and I do believe her demeanor and conduct were determined entirely for the happiness of her husband and family.

What I learned from Edith was how to accomplish favorable results on one's own terms, by using your intellect. A good example of this was how she provided family photos for a curious and hungry public. She was able to satisfy their need without giving up her family's privacy. Edith illustrated for me how to take charge of a situation and achieve a win-win solution.

Careful What You Wish For

HELEN TAFT

I do not like this thing of being silent, but I don't know what to do about it.

—HELEN TAFT, IN A NOTE TO HER HUSBAND

ASIDE FROM being skeptical of Alice Roosevelt's parting White House jest—the burial of a voodoo doll on the mansion's front lawn, precisely to bring woe upon the incumbent First Lady—you might consider that all wishes are not entirely in our best interest.

Helen Herron Taft's life is a good example of the old adage "Be careful what you wish for; you may just get it." No doubt, a common wish of many young girls was to one day live in the White House. Helen Herron, born just three months before the Civil War began in 1861 and known to her

> **#27 Helen Herron Taft**
>
> **Born:** January 2, 1861
> **Birthplace:** Cincinnati, Ohio
> **Married:** 1886 (William Howard Taft)
> **Children:** 3
> **White House Years:** 1909–1913
> **Died:** May 22, 1943
> **Fact:** 1st First Lady to ride alongside hus-
> band in Inaugural parade;
> established cherry blossom trees
> in capital
> **Aka:** Nellie

family and friends as Nellie, was no exception. The difference was that Helen not only yearned to live in the executive mansion, from the age of sixteen, she made it her life's ambition.

Had Helen been a boy, a career in politics would have been a logical choice, as she would have been following in the family's vocational footsteps. Helen's politically minded maternal grandfather, Eli Collins, was a congressman. Her father, John Williamson Herron, a distinguished lawyer, was a classmate of Benjamin Harrison (our twenty-third president), and the law partner and lifelong friend of Rutherford B. Hayes (our nineteenth president) before becoming a judge, then state senator. You could say politics was in her blood.

Although both her father and her mother, Harriet Collins Herron, believed in the highest quality of education for all their children, girls in the mid-nineteenth century were not afforded the same opportunities as boys. The only acceptable female career was home and family. Born the fourth of eleven siblings, Helen's brothers went to Harvard and Yale, while she studied at the prestigious Miss Nourse's private school for girls before attending Miami University in Oxford, Ohio.

An eager and excellent student, Helen stood five foot seven inches tall, had good posture, brown hair, and gray-blue eyes. Her elongated facial features kept her from being considered attractive; and her high-strung, nervous, even stubborn nature earned her the nickname "Nervous Nellie." A sadly realistic and fitting description that encapsulated Helen's lifelong demeanor.

Making up for feeling unappealing, she carried herself well, remained well versed in many areas, and revealed a keen wit. Nellie studied literature, history, languages (excelling in French), and was engrossed with music, her enduring love, which she studied at the University of Cincinnati. She had a serious attitude, strong opinions (which she shared without reservation, and articulately defended), and a fierce determination.

Yet, as an adolescent, many of Nellie's journal notations referred repeatedly to her insecurities. Regarding her nervousness and lack of self-esteem, she wrote: "I would enjoy society if I could only get over my nervousness" and "Anything but one's own nature can be remedied, but from oneself there is no escape. I am sick and tired of myself. I would rather be anyone else even some one who has not some advantages I have." She also fought feelings of depression, confirming: "I am blue as indigo."[1]

To combat her depressive "blues," Helen forced herself to remain active and became an excellent bowler. She enjoyed all kinds of concerts and developed a lifelong hobby of gambling. Playing poker for money became a passion. As Helen's skills improved with continued practice, so did her winnings. When told cigarettes would "lift her mood," Helen soon became an addicted smoker. She also developed a taste for beer. Presumably, she used alcohol to numb her feelings of sadness and inadequacy. Regardless of their origin in her teens, gambling, smoking, and drinking, were all habits Helen sustained throughout her entire life.

Recalling her most cherished childhood memory, she said of visiting the White House while on a two-week vacation during the Rutherford Hayes administration: "Nothing in my life reaches the climax of human bliss I felt when, as a girl of sixteen, I was entertained at the White House."[2]

In 1877, the newly elected president, Rutherford B. Hayes, and his wife, Lucy, were celebrating their twenty-fifth wedding anniversary. As the Herron and Hayes families had remained very close, when Harriet gave birth to her sixth daughter, she named the baby Lucy Hayes Herron, after her good friend Lucy. In addition to having the Herron family celebrate with them, the First Lady also wanted her namesake christened in the executive mansion. From that time on, Helen's desire to live in the White House never waned.

Disapproving of the restrictions placed on the women of her era, and with the women's suffrage movement well on its way, Helen would have made an ideal candidate for her own successful career. She struggled with herself, as well as with her mother's Victorian beliefs. Helen recorded in her journals:

A man is not endurable until he is twenty-eight or thirty and not always then.

I believe my greatest desire now is to write a book . . . write it I must confess for money—not that I think that I could write anything good, but because I do so want to be independent.[3]

Of course a woman is happier who marries exactly right—but how many do?[4]

. . . I have been a good for nothing and useless . . . I am thoroughly disgusted with myself. I am not in the least what I want to be . . . I am not satisfied spending the whole day at home in quiet pursuits. . . . I think it very much better to go to the university than to simply waste my time but I can not persuade Mamma to look upon it in that light . . .

Mrs. Herron was not opposed to her daughter's education; it was her working and the departure of female upper-class Victorian values that she objected to. Harriet wrote to her daughter:

[Is it] wise for you to decide to devote yourself to school teachings as a profession—there being no positive necessity in the case? Do you realize that you will have to give up society, as you now enjoy it . . . I admit the offer is complimentary and the compensation offered seems large. [assistant teacher position at an annual salary of seven hundred dollars] . . . but to think seriously where and how it will all end![5]

After graduation, Helen did teach school for two years in addition to giving piano lessons. Although she was well accomplished, Helen never lost her feelings of insecurity, and her perfectionism nearly wore her out.

At twenty-two, Helen and some friends organized a literary salon to discuss the intellectual and economic issues of their day (an activity reminiscent of the one Mary Todd Lincoln participated in). Invited to the discussions was William Taft, who had graduated second in his class from Yale, and was now a member of the bar. William, the brother of Fanny Taft, a schoolgirl friend of Helen's, was an amiable, gentle man who, like his own father, needed prodding.

Impressed with Helen's intellect, William wrote to her in part: "Your thoughts and speech are marked especially by direction, force, and clearness." Attributes the young attorney admired. As it turned out, Helen and Will were well suited to one another. Her challenging intelligence, strong will, and determination were all qualities that nicely counterbalanced his personality.

Energetic yet frustrated, Helen understood her ambition was far beyond what women's suffrage could help her accomplish. Three years after they met, William had at last persuaded Helen she was the smartest woman he knew; and she was finally convinced of Will's potential for achievement. Turning her determination in the direction of a husband and his career opportunities, at twenty-five Helen married the nearly twenty-nine year old attorney in her parents' home. Maria, Helen's closest sister and Fanny, Will's only sister, were bridesmaids. Horace, Will's youngest brother, was his best man.

Each provided the other with the qualities they were missing. Will's laid-back personality needed the goading Helen could and certainly would provide. Helen required the intellectual freedom and public acceptance she was unable to obtain on her own. They also shared the ability to tease one another, and William often joked that an "obedient husband" was the first requirement for a successful marriage.

The Tafts married in 1886, just two weeks after Frances and President Cleveland's White House wedding, an occasion Helen undoubtedly was keenly aware of.* A three-month honeymoon in Europe followed. Helen's energy for adventure, love of culture—and thriftiness—all contributed to the first of the couple's many wonderful travel experiences.

Reportedly, the one-hundred-day European wedding celebration cost barely a thousand dollars. Helen kept an account of their expenses, while Will documented her financial prudence. For "economical reasons," they not only ascended to the fourth floor for a hotel room, they also traveled in third-class train seats.[6] Forever prideful of

---

* The same year, another presidential spouse's portrait appeared on a one-dollar silver certificate: the picture was of Martha Washington, the only woman to appear on US paper currency.

her frugalness, Helen nonetheless always lived in the most comfortable of environments, with servants for herself and later her children. (A characteristic she shared with Edith Roosevelt.)

It was a balancing act and a way of life she understood well. Always working harder and longer, Helen's father had found himself in constant debt, trying to maintain the lifestyle his wife envisioned for her family. Raised with the expectation of living an upper-class societal existence, Helen was accustomed to living in a certain style, and began expecting the many advantages her mother taught her to enjoy. But forever mindful of her father's continuous struggle to provide those niceties, she also learned the significance and consequences of overspending.

Within a year, William was appointed an Ohio superior court judge. More than delighted, William was heading toward his ultimate target. There was never any secret regarding Taft's fundamental desire to become chief justice of the US Supreme Court. However, Helen was concerned that the bench was "too limiting" and persuaded her unwilling husband to accept President Benjamin Harrison's appointment of US solicitor general.

Moving to Washington, DC, with an infant son, Robert,* Helen was getting closer to her career goal. They lived on Dupont Circle, and it was there William Taft and neighbor Theodore Roosevelt, then US civil service commissioner, became good friends. While they were there, Helen gave birth to their only daughter, also named Helen. Two years later, when President Harrison lost his reelection bid, Taft also lost his job, and the family returned to Cincinnati, where he was appointed to the US federal circuit court.

In 1897, Helen bore her last and undeniably favorite child, Charles. She also found a way to support her love of music: she raised funds, organized, and became president of the Cincinnati Orchestra Association, whose orchestra became one of the finest in the country. Busy

---

* Robert Alphonso (1889–1953), Helen Herron (1891–1887), Charles Phelps (1897–1983)

with her family, and now excelling in what she did best, Helen was temporarily less inclined to poke and prod at her husband's career.

When President McKinley asked Taft to head a commission to establish a new government in the Philippine Islands at the commencement of the twentieth century, Helen was more than eager to move. Once again, she was zealously encouraging her reluctant husband, who opposed the annexation of the Philippines, to accept the position. Helen's love of adventure and desire to never miss a novel experience overshadowed any hesitation she may have felt for moving her children (now ten, eight, and two years old) to a foreign country some ten thousand miles away, where they might encounter cholera or even the bubonic plague.

Prior to meeting Will in Manila, the Philippine capital, Helen first took her children on a several-months' exploration of Hawaii, China, and Japan. She studied the countries' histories and cultures, and was anxious to partake in every possible exciting activity open to her. She rode the Hawaiian surf in a canoe and was received by the Japanese empress. When oldest son Robert contracted diphtheria, Helen remained quarantined with him while the other children were cared for at the Grand Hotel. Years later, Helen wrote of her journey: "I have never shrunk before any obstacle when I had an opportunity to see a new country and I must say I have never regretted any adventure."

At the time the Philippines Islands were in the midst of guerilla warfare, and upon arriving in Manila Helen discovered that her new servant-filled residence was heavily guarded. She read up on the country's history, studied its culture, and learned to horseback ride in order to travel "where no white woman had ever been." She also insisted that the entire family learn Spanish. When Taft became governor of the Philippine Islands, the family moved into the spacious Malacanang Palace. To Helen's delight, Governor Taft held his conferences in the palace, where she was free to overhear all of his discussions. Regarding their partnership, Helen once said: "I . . . always had the satisfaction of knowing almost as much as he about the politics and intricacies of any situation."[7]

During the four years Helen resided in Manila, she experienced the fulfillment of a stature akin to that of the First Lady in the United States. Helen entertained thousands of people, encouraged women of the country to accept medical attention, and when typhus threatened, she brought in cows and worked with the Drop of Milk organization to distribute sterilized milk. In a letter to home, Helen wrote: "The position gives us a great deal of attention which I for one would never have otherwise . . . We are really so grand now that it will be hard to descend to common doings."

Nevertheless, "common doings" in the form of stress and anxiety occurred rather quickly. One particularly difficult period came about when Taft was rushed into surgery for an abdominal abscess, which necessitated a second surgery in the United States. At the same time, Helen's mother suffered a life-threatening stroke. Although the family returned to Cincinnati immediately, her mother passed away before Helen could reach her. Devastated, she was unable to attend her mother's funeral.

After returning to Manila, Taft was then sent to Rome to negotiate the ownership of land between the Philippines and the Vatican. Helen and her children were granted a once-in-a-lifetime audience with Pope Leo XIII. When the family returned once again to Manila, now their adopted country, it was experiencing a devastating cholera epidemic. Witness to overwhelming famine and death, the Taft family fortunately was not infected with the disease.

In 1903 President Theodore Roosevelt offered Taft an appointment to the Supreme Court, his ultimate career ambition. Helen wrote in her memoirs, *Recollections of Full Years*: "I had always been opposed to a judicial career for him, but at this point I shall have to admit I weakened just a little." Believing he had a commitment to his current post, Taft magnanimously turned down the appointment. The following year, when the president convinced his good friend to accept the position of secretary of war in his cabinet, despite the meager eight-thousand-dollar annual salary, Helen again recorded: "This was much more pleasing to me than the offer of the Supreme Court appointment, because it was in line with the kind of work I wanted my husband to do, the kind of career I wanted for him and expected him to have."

Now back in Washington, Helen was not as happy as she had expected to be. Being a mere Cabinet wife did not carry all the advantages of her previous position. It felt like a demotion to her; and she was accountable to First Lady Edith Roosevelt, for whom she had little affection. It was not until many years later that Helen openly confessed: "I don't like Mrs. Roosevelt at all. I never did."[8]

When President Roosevelt announced that he would not be seeking another term, Helen could feel the presidency within her reach. When Roosevelt offered to either appoint Taft to the Supreme Court or support his nomination for president, Helen intervened. Indisputably, Taft wanted the Supreme Court nomination. Helen, needless to say, wanted the White House.

Taft told Roosevelt he would not be "disappointed" if the president were to support another candidate for the presidency. He also announced that "any party which would nominate me would make a great mistake." Helen was more than annoyed and spurred her husband "to display a little more enthusiasm on his own account." According to the National First Ladies' Library Web site, Helen campaigned so vigorously for her husband that President Roosevelt "called her into his office to rebuke her on her unwomanly behavior." In his book *Nellie Taft, The Unconventional First Lady of the Ragtime Era*, distinguished First Lady historian Carl Sferrazza Anthony describes the West Wing conference, a meeting to clarify who Roosevelt's ideal successor might be. Mr. Anthony writes: "A powerful incumbent president conferring with the wife of his potential successor was unprecedented in presidential history."

Finally overruled by his wife and with Roosevelt's support, Taft won the 1908 election. Over thirty years had passed, but finally the determined Nellie Herron had fulfilled her dream of living in the White House.

Retiring president Roosevelt invited incoming President Taft to sleep in the White House the evening before the inauguration—a more than unusual request since the sitting First Lady and incoming First Lady had less than an amiable relationship. Helen later discreetly wrote: "My impression, that neither Mrs. Roosevelt nor I would have suggested such an arrangement for this particular evening, but, it having been made for us, we naturally acquiesced."[9]

The following day, Helen set a new precedent. When Roosevelt announced that he would not accompany his successor back to the White House, as he was immediately leaving the capital city, she seized the opportunity to sit beside her husband on the ride from his inaugural ceremony to the White House. Until now, the outgoing president had always accompanied the incoming president, and many observers saw this as Helen's declaration of her power and position. Helen determined: "No President's wife had ever done it before, but as long as precedents were being disregarded I thought it might not be too great a risk for me to disregard this one. Of course, there was objection. . . . but I had my way."[10] She was also the first to contribute one of her evening gowns when the Smithsonian Institution created its First Ladies Collection, three years later.

Tears of joy and making immediate changes were Helen's first reactions to becoming the new mistress of the White House. She stationed black "formally costumed footmen" at the door to receive visitors, replacing the "gentlemen ushers." A female housekeeper replaced the male steward, because "no man, expert steward though he might be, would ever recognize" the multiple domestic requirements a woman would. (Elizabeth Jaffray oversaw the day-to-day details and White House cleaning for the next fourteen years.)

Replacing their outdated carriages, the new First Lady also purchased the first White House automobiles. Since the First Lady wanted four cars, totaling more than the twelve thousand dollars Congress had appropriated for expenses, she negotiated with the automakers to advertise that the White House drove their vehicles, if they agreed to a reduced price. Naturally they did.

Forever economical, and despite the fact that the president was now earning seventy-five thousand dollars a year, Helen put a cow on the White House lawn (for fresh milk) and purchased food in wholesale lots. She had a special vault built with velvet-lined drawers and installed a silver-cleaning machine for the presidential silver. An extra-large bathtub needed to be installed, because her 350-pound husband got stuck in the existing regular-size tub. Four average-size men could fit into the new custom tub.

A good hostess who liked to entertain, Helen had numerous other ideas to increase the enjoyment of her guests, such as dancing at formal receptions, and erecting a bandstand for twice-a-week concerts at the newly planned Washington Drive along the Potomac.

Washington's now famous cherry trees were also planned and planted under Helen's direction. After Helen ordered all the domestic stock of trees that could be found (approximately one hundred), the mayor of Tokyo was so flattered the First Lady was honoring Japanese custom that he sent her two thousand more, generating the now popular annual Cherry Blossom Festival.

The first two months of Helen's White House tenure were everything she had envisioned. But then—whether you choose to believe in voodoo dolls or the pitfalls of taking on too many projects at once—something contributed to Helen's cruelest misfortune ever. Only ten weeks into her new duties, while entertaining aboard the presidential yacht, Helen suffered a severe stroke. (Earlier that same day she had accompanied her younger son Charles to the hospital to have his adenoids removed.) Unable to speak, and paralyzed on her left side, the First Lady was crippled for nearly a year.

President Taft, who never wanted to be chief executive and maintained that "politics make me sick," was nearly paralyzed himself. Presidential aide Captain Archie Butt later described his boss as "a great, stricken animal. I have never seen greater suffering or pain shown on a man's face."[11] The president acknowledged as much in a letter: "[My duties are] heavier to bear because of Mrs. Taft's condition."[12]

Returning to her summer home in Beverly, Massachusetts, and prevented from participating in public life, Nellie was deprived the full pleasure of her hard-earned position. For the next year, daughter Helen adjourned her studies at Bryn Mawr College to assist the First Lady's sisters with White House social functions.

While the First Lady worked diligently at regaining her speech, she continued to enjoy an activity that did not require dialogue—betting at cards. When her son Charles expressed concern over the possible political damage his mother's gambling could cause, should the press become aware of it, the president's only response was: "I will not forbid any thing, which gives Mrs. Taft any amusement and takes her mind off troubles."[13]

Through sheer determined effort, Helen reclaimed her ability to walk, albeit with difficulty, and speak, with hesitation. Still avoiding dinners and other social gatherings that required conversation, she did partake in receptions where she could offer memorized, formulated greetings.

Although still embarrassed by her facial paralysis, and having not yet regained her full vigor, by the spring of 1910 Helen was beginning to resume her official duties. Regarding those early months of her tenure, Helen wrote: "My own problems became to me paramount and I began to give them my almost undivided attention and to neglect the political affairs which had for many years interested me so intensely."[14]

The social season of 1911 brought Helen great joy and a renewed sense of anticipation and hopefulness. In addition to hosting her daughter's White House coming-out party, the First Lady's love of musical entertainment was widely expressed. A Hawaiian quartet, two Hispano-Filipino composers, and various female pianists performed at the White House. Selections from Beethoven and the *William Tell Overture* were presented, as was Shakespeare (for the first and only time).

Back in command, Helen was soon to oversee the executive mansion's most impressive party ever. The First Lady orchestrated her extravagant twenty-fifth wedding anniversary celebration. An estimated five thousand guests (of the eight thousand invited) attended, plus three times that number of spectators beyond the fences. Former presidential family members—including relatives of Lincoln, Grant, Hayes, Garfield, Arthur, and Cleveland—were in attendance, in addition to four of the Roosevelt children. Although former president Roosevelt and his wife, Edith, sent a silver bowl, they were conspicuously absent.

Circumstances once again nearly prevented Helen from experiencing the glory of her memorable gala celebration. Just five weeks prior to the brilliant event, she once again collapsed from a "nervous attack." Her daughter wrote: "She isn't able to articulate clearly or to find her words. The doctor seems to think that the attack is similar to the first one but much less severe."[15]

With Helen's physicians insisting on bed rest, the White House went so far as to notify the press that the First Lady's daughter would serve as her stand-in hostess. The baton had been passed, and Helen had precious little time to rally. Firmly rejecting the suggestion that she depart to her summer home in Massachusetts, Helen remained in the executive mansion, resolute in her decision to recover. Mercifully she did recuperate, and relatively quickly.

Similar to the Hayes's reenactment at their silver wedding anniversary thirty-four years earlier, the president and First Lady walked arm in arm to the music of the "Wedding March," followed by their three siblings from the original wedding party, Maria, Fanny, and Horace.

An enchanting, mesmerizing fantasyland was created with thousands and thousands of little twinkling lights for the evening garden party on the White House lawn. In addition to red Japanese paper lanterns in the shrubbery and trees, a large red, white, and blue flag of flashing lights hung over the portico.

The presidential couple was inundated with silver gifts. True to her character, Helen had the monograms removed from the smaller pieces and passed them along to others for wedding gifts.[16]

Less than a year after Helen's extravagant anniversary celebration, the largest and most luxurious ship ever built struck an iceberg on its maiden voyage to New York. Within three hours, the "unsinkable"

RMS *Titanic*, representing the best of technology to date, broke apart and plunged to the bottom of the sea.

In addition to poor emigrants traveling from Europe in search of economic and social freedom in the new world, the *Titanic* was also carrying some of the richest, most powerful capitalists of the day. Reportedly, their combined fortunes totaled $600 million in 1912. With over fifteen hundred lives lost, the First Lady led a fund-raising drive for a memorial to them.

Returning to the political front, the wedge between William Taft and Teddy Roosevelt's friendship continued to expand. Roosevelt believed his successor would "back issues for which I have fought" and "in which I most firmly believe."[17] However, even before President Taft took office, he proved to be his own man, and failed to keep the majority of Roosevelt's Cabinet. As time went on, Roosevelt believed that Taft supported fewer and fewer of his policies.

The harsh fallout between Taft and Roosevelt literally split the Republican Party in half. There is little doubt that Helen passionately wanted to remain in the White House. However, considering Taft's misery in a job he was poorly suited for, did not want (he called the presidency an "awful agony"), and was probably ill-equipped to handle, it is logical to assume that he only accepted the Republican nomination out of a commitment to his party.

Roosevelt, by now completely and thoroughly frustrated with his protégé, viewed his ex-friend and now political foe as "weak." The former president called Taft, although "an admirable fellow," an "utterly commonplace leader . . . with plenty of small motive; and totally unable to grasp or put into execution any great policy." When Roosevelt lost the Republican nomination for the presidency in 1913, he ran against sitting President Taft on the Bull Moose ticket. Woodrow Wilson was the Democratic nominee.

As all of the candidates went to Ivy League schools—Yale, Harvard, and Princeton—sportswriters dubbed the election the "Big Three." Roosevelt received a greater number of popular votes than his former friend; however, due to the split in the Republican Party, Wilson won the majority of votes.

The president felt no animosity in leaving the White House. "The nearer I get to the inauguration of my successor the greater the relief I feel . . . I am content with the opportunity that has been mine . . . My tastes had been, and still are judicial."[18] Taft and Roosevelt managed to reconcile their differences, and six years later William attended Theodore's funeral and "sobbed at his grave site."

Helen was disappointed yet resigned; her long-awaited fairytale was coming to a close. Upon leaving the executive mansion, it was time to redefine and redirect her life. Retiring in Connecticut, the former president taught constitutional law at Yale University, while the former First Lady returned to music, substituting concerts, theater, bridge parties, and travel for politics.

When a reporter asked the former First Lady's daughter, Helen, if her mother felt a sense of relief in leaving the White House, she replied: "Well, Mother was never very much for relief. She always wants something to be happening."[19]

Never very interested in the academics of law, for the first time ever Helen found herself on the sideline of her husband's career. Finding her social life in New Haven not to her liking, she had feelings of unhappiness and loneliness, while the now content William spent his time teaching, writing, and giving dozens of speeches each year.

Finding himself taking over his wife's role, William began to prod Helen to write her memoirs. He understood his wife's tendency to depression, and believed mental stimulation was her best approach. As much as Helen disliked pondering over the past, with her daughter's assistance she found writing *Recollections of Full Years* very beneficial. Focusing on her happiest memories, and only briefly describing of her discontent, her published memoirs sold well.

Eight years would pass before Taft would finally achieve his ultimate ambition. In 1921, President Warren Harding appointed Taft chief justice of the US Supreme Court. Overjoyed at returning to

Washington, and now in a position to offer advice to her successors, Helen could once again be at the center of social and political importance.

Additionally, Helen received immense pleasure in seeing all three of her children achieve great success. Although eldest son Robert was an unsuccessful presidential candidate (1940, 1948, 1952) he did become the most prominent Republican senator of his day. Serving in the US Senate for fifteen years, he was known as "Mr. Republican." Daughter Helen not only received a law degree from George Washington University and a PhD in history from Yale, she also became dean of Bryn Mawr College and was an outspoken proponent of women's suffrage. Charles enlisted in the army during World War I (both his parents supported American involvement) and went on to become a successful lawyer. All of her children married, ultimately providing Helen with thirteen grandchildren.

During the nearly nine years that the former president served as chief justice, the Taft marriage remained strong; yet there was greater independence on both sides. It was no longer a partnership where each one was reliant upon the other. Just the opposite: after Helen's stroke William gradually consulted his wife less and less.

Making up for a lifetime of lost passion, William started working himself to death. In a letter to her son Charles, Helen wrote: "Your father has court duties all the time and work in the evenings . . . He says that he is going to take Saturday night and Sunday for recreation, but I don't see any sign of it yet."[20]

Far more relaxed now that her husband was no longer in politics, Helen channeled her time into more pleasurable endeavors. Travel was one and the theater another, as her husband confirmed: "[She] goes without hesitation everywhere, accepts all the invitations that she wishes to accept."[21] Helen would also travel alone, in southern Europe, for instance, sometimes for weeks or months at a stretch.

During Prohibition, William objected to his wife serving and drinking alcohol. Even so, being the wife of the chief justice did not prevent Helen from enjoying her cocktail. "The truth is that Nellie and I differ on prohibition. We might as well face that, because I am utterly out of sympathy with her, and she with me," conceded Taft.

Taft resigned from his dream job just weeks before his death in 1930. Helen had already curtailed all of her own personal desires, remaining by her husband's side to assist and be with him. The original Nellie had returned, with one remarkable variation: she had a new philosophy. She no longer agonized over the things she had little control over. William passed away, with his devoted wife of nearly forty-four years at his side.

Burial at Arlington National Cemetery, with a view of both the White House and the new Supreme Court building, seemed a fitting choice for both Tafts. At Helen's request, the former president was buried wearing his judicial robe, in a private service.

Without appearing to look back, the former First Lady moved ahead with her life. Helen was close to seventy, but, all the same, she still had a great deal of living to do. Shortly after disposing of her husband's personal items, she and her sister Maria left for Lisbon and several other locations. Subsequently agreeing to unveil the *Titanic* memorial, the former First Lady shed her public role and remained a private, self-sufficient, extremely active senior citizen.

As the years passed, several other family members became ill and died, yet Helen always mourned in private. She refused invitations for Christmas and other family celebrations; being on her own soon became her new standard pattern of behavior. It was almost as though Helen no longer wanted to be a part of her former life; moreover, lack of recognition no longer appeared to upset her.

At the laying of the cornerstone for the new Supreme Court building, Helen was turned away from the VIP seating area. "I went alone. They did not call upon me for anything," Helen wrote.[22] The widow of a Supreme Court justice and former president was no longer recognized, and therefore went unacknowledged. Saying nothing, Helen smiled and found a seat in the public gallery with the other tourists.

For the next thirteen years, Helen traveled extensively both inside the United States (New York, Charleston, Connecticut, and Washington, DC) as well as abroad. Like Abigail Adams, who wrote numerous letters to her husband and family describing daily life, Helen too maintained a wonderful descriptive correspondence with her son Charles.

Historian Carl Anthony has done an outstanding job of researching both Helen's letters and Charles Taft's papers. To quote Mr. Anthony: "[Helen] maintained a manic pace," traveling to locations such as the British Isles, China, England, Egypt, Greece, Italy, Jerusalem, Mexico, the Middle East, Naples, Rome, Scotland, Spain, Turkey, Venice, Vienna, Wales, and Warsaw. It is exhausting just to name these locations, let to alone travel to all of them.

After some time, Helen's children naturally grew concerned over their aging mother's frequent, unaccompanied voyages. Consequently, the independent Helen often purchased her tickets before notifying the family of her travel plans. Once she even declined to leave an itinerary, and her children did not know how to contact her.

When Helen turned seventy-seven, the family demanded that she no longer travel alone. Helen agreed to be accompanied on her adventures, so long as she did not have to pay the companion's fare, an expense her children were happy to absorb. She would *not* agree to stay home, or move closer to Charles, who had located a house for his mother across the street from his residence in Cincinnati.

Like thousands of other sightseeing explorers, Helen also enjoyed viewing the cherry blossom trees in Washington every spring (one of her personal contributions) and attending popular musicals like *Gentlemen Prefer Blondes, Showboat*, and *No, No Nanette*. Besides reading extensively, she attended lectures, concerts, and plays such as *Porgy and Bess, Ladies of the Evening*, and *The Czarina*.

Viewing National Geographic Society films, as well as attending movies starring Fred Astaire, Tallulah Bankhead, John Barrymore, Douglas Fairbanks, Greta Garbo, and Katharine Hepburn, some of the most famous actors of their day, were other favorite pastimes.

Life was undeniably for the living and Helen did an incredible job of seeing, doing, and being part of it, including remaining fashionable into her eighties. Unlike her predecessors Sarah Polk and Lucretia Garfield, whose primary mission in life after their husband's death was to keep the former president's memory alive, Helen only looked forward. When it came to her husband's biography, she was content to leave everything in her children's hands. She did not so much as give an interview to the president's biographer.

As she had in her youth, Helen continued to enjoy cigarettes, card parties, and cocktails. She remained informed about politics, and although she believed in women's education, she never outgrew her embedded beliefs regarding female status:. "I am old fashioned enough to believe that woman is the complement of man . . . and . . . the highest mission is the ability to preside over a home."

As much as she approved of women having the right to vote, Helen also believed they should be barred from running for office. Her philosophy was that the "home" would be destroyed. In other words, being informed did not equate to being included.

Helen continued to live in her own home with a housekeeper and eventually a nurse. At eighty-two the feisty, energetic, determined world adventurer died from a circulatory disorder. Entombed next to her husband, she was the first First Lady to be buried in Arlington National Cemetery.

What Helen taught me:

Determined, intelligent, ambitious, and adventurous are all superlative descriptions of Helen Taft. Even with her sizeable aspirations, being a wife was Helen's ultimate gratification.

Societal limitations aside, Helen could not escape from her nervousness and insecurities—two characteristics that ruled her early life and which required modification, rather than mere acknowledgment. If Helen had been as successful in managing her behavioral shortcomings as she was in administering her husband's political career, I wonder if her devastating stroke would have occurred.

Helen taught me that our aspirations, even if fueled by burning desire, may not always be in our own best interest. Confirming the adage, "All of one's wishes are not meant to be fulfilled."

Epilogue

By the time Helen Taft left the White House, history had turned another corner. The United States had hosted the Olympic Games for the first time, in St. Louis, Missouri (1904), Mother's Day was established in Philadelphia on the second Sunday in May (1907), and, two years later, Spokane, Washington, celebrated the first Father's Day.

The North Pole had already been discovered, and while five million people attended motion-picture theaters daily (1909), John D. Rockefeller became the world's first billionaire. By 1911, the aging population had grown so large that the first "old age" home for seniors was opened in Prescott, Arizona.

Thirteen years into the twentieth century, the nation had grown to include forty-eight contiguous states (another forty-six years would pass before Alaska, the forty-ninth state, and Hawaii, the fiftieth, were admitted into the Union), and traveling by train set new time records. The 20th Century Limited, an express passenger train that traveled between Grand Central Terminal in New York, New York, and LaSalle Street Station in Chicago, Illinois, could typically make the 960-mile-journey in sixteen hours. Meanwhile, the first transcontinental airplane flight had been made.

Undeniably, many progressive innovations had occurred since the nation's inception. But as future president Harry Truman so accurately observed, history was destined to repeat itself.

Volume 2 of *Loves, Lies, and Tears* continues with remarkable stories of heartache and triumph against the backdrop of more recent historical events. The extraordinary lives and times of the remaining women who called the White House home will be chronicled, along with the lightening-speed advances that would radically alter their daily lives, their relationships with their husbands, and place them in a more active, prominent role.

Just as Martha Washington and her fellow sisters of the American Revolution courageously stood by and supported their patriot husbands, women of the coming century would be faced with numerous conflicts, not the least of which would include two world wars.

You will discover another woman who, like Julia Tyler before her, was courted by and married a sitting president. After an initial divorce, two more women found love with politicians who went on to become the country's chief executive. Cousins would again marry and occupy the White House. Abigail Adams will no longer be recognized as the only woman both to marry a president and become the mother of another.

Helen Taft married a lawyer who graduated with honors from Yale Law School; eighty-eight years later, a future First Lady would earn the same academic distinction. Mary Todd Lincoln remained secluded and wept in her upstairs White House bedroom for weeks after her husband was assassinated; nearly a hundred years later the nation watched as another First Lady stood—still wearing the blood-stained suit from her husband's fatal head wounds—alongside the new president at his inauguration.

Another First Lady would tragically die in the White House; more would suffer the loss of a child, while still others would publicly survive a mastectomy, breast cancer, and drug addiction. Learn who served liquor to guests during Prohibition, which First Lady spoke fluent Chinese (and why she did so privately with her presidential husband), and who in the early 1900s would be called the first woman president.

Some upcoming White House relationships will essentially be business partnerships, others long and great love affairs. One First

Lady would be suspected of murdering her spouse, and another involved in an accident resulting in a young man's death.

The embarrassment and humiliation of impeachment and infidelity would also occur. However, these First Ladies would have to endure heartache and devastation via the watchful eye of the entire world, under the vigilant spotlight of television and later the Internet.

The amazing women in Volume 2 of *Loves, Lies, and Tears,* witness radical change in almost every area of daily life. Their stories will take you through the history of women's rights, the Roaring Twenties, the Great Depression, the civil rights era, and the transition into the twenty-first century. You will not want to miss the abundantly rich and productive stories of bravery, adventure, scandal, and triumph, as well as the constructive life lessons each First Lady's life demonstrates.

Look for *Loves, Lies, and Tears: An Intimate Look at America's First Ladies, Volume 2* in December of 2008. To sign up for an advance copy of Volume 2, please forward your email address to:

firstladies.lady@verizon.net.

To inquire about my speaking engagements, or if you are interested in a guest speaker for your next conference, symposium, national convention, classroom or fund-raiser, please view my website at www.firstladieslady.com.

Bibliography

Adler, Bill. *America's First Ladies: Their Uncommon Wisdom, from Martha Washington to Laura Bush*. Lanham: Taylor Trade Publishing, 2002.

Allgor, Catherine. *A Perfect Union: Dolley Madison and the Creation of the American Nation*. New York: Henry Holt, 2006.

———. *Parlor Politics: In Which the Ladies of Washington Help Build a City and a Government*. Charlottesville: University Press of Virginia, 2000.

Anthony, Carl Sferrazza. *America's First Families: An Inside View of 200 Years of Private Life in the White House*. New York: Touchstone, 2000.

———. *First Ladies: The Saga of the Presidents' Wives and Their Power 1789–1961*. New York: William Morrow, 1990.

———. *First Ladies:The Saga of the Presidents' Wives and Their Power 1961–1990*, vol. 2. New York: William Morrow, 1991.

———. *America's Most Influential First Ladies*. Minneapolis: Oliver Press, 1992.

———. *Florence Harding: The First Lady, the Jazz Age, and the Death of America's Most Scandalous President*. New York: William Morrow, 1998.

———. *Nellie Taft:The Unconventional First Lady of the Ragtime Era*. New York: HarperCollins, 2005.

Boller, Paul F. Jr. *Presidential Wives: An Anecdotal History*. New York: Oxford University Press, 1988.

Britton, Nan. *The President's Daughter*. New York: Elizabeth Ann Guild, 1927.

Butterfield, L. H. and Marc Friedlaender and Mary-Jo Kline. *The Book of Abigail and John: Selected Letters of the Adams Family 1762–1784*. Cambridge: Harvard University Press, 1975.

Caroli, Betty Boyd. *America's First Ladies.* Pleasantville: Reader's Digest, 1996.

———. *The First Ladies. From Martha Washington to Laura Bush:The Fascinating Lives of the Women in the Influential Role of America's First Lady,* 3rd ed. Garden City: Guild America Books, 2001.

Colman, Edna M. *Seventy-Five Years of White House Gossip: From Washington to Lincoln.* Garden City: Doubleday, 1926.

Coolidge, Calvin. *The Autobiography of Calvin Coolidge.* New York: Cosmopolitan Book Corp. , 1929.

DeGregorio, William A. *The Complete Book of U. S. Presidents: From George Washington to George W. Bush,* 5th ed. New York: Gramercy Books, 2001.

Durant, John and Alice Durant. *Pictorial History of American Presidents.* New York: Castle Books, 1975.

Foss, William O. *First Ladies Quotations Book.* New York: Barricade Books, 1999.

Garrison, Webb. *White House Ladies: Fascinating Tales and Colorful Curiosities.* Nashville: Rutledge Hill Press, 1996.

———. *A Treasury of White House Tales: Fascinating, Colorful Stories of American Presidents and Their Families.* Nashville: Rutledge Hill Press, 1996.

Gerlinger, Irene Hazard. *Mistresses of the White House: Narrator's Tale of a Pageant of First Ladies.* New York: Samuel French, 1948.

Gormley, Beatrice. *First Ladies: Women Who Called the White House Home.* New York: Scholastic, 1997.

Harris, Bill. *The First Ladies Fact Book: The Stories of the Women of the White House from Martha Washington to Laura Bush.* New York: Black Dog & Leventhal, 2005.

Hay, Peter. *All the Presidents' Ladies.* New York: Viking Penguin, 1988.

Healy, Diana Dixon. *America's First Ladies: Private Lives of the Presidential Wives.* New York: Macmillan, 1988.

Hoover, Irwin Hood. *Forty-Two Years in the White House.* Westport: Greenwood Press, 1934.

Kane, Joseph Nathan. *Presidential Fact Book*. New York: Random House, 1998.

Keckley, Elizabeth. *Behind the Scenes*. Chicago: R. R. Donnelley & Sons, 1998.

Kessler, Ronald. *Inside the White House*. New York: Pocket Books, 1995.

Klein, Edward. *Farewell, Jackie: A Portrait of Her Final Days*. New York: Viking, 2004.

Kunhardt, Philip B. Jr. and Philip B. Kunhardt III and Peter W. Kunhardt. *The American President*. New York: Riverhead Books, 1999.

Logan, Mrs. John A. *Thirty Years in Washington*. Hartford: A. D. Worthington, 1901.

Longworth, Alice Roosevelt. *Crowded Hours*. New York: Charles Scribner's Sons, 1933.

Marton, Kati. *Hidden Power: Presidential Marriages That Shaped Our Recent History*. New York: Pantheon Books, 2001.

Mattern, David B. and Holly C. Shulman, eds. *The Selected Letters of Dolley Payne Madison.* Charlottesville: University of Virginia Press, 2003.

Mayo, Edith P. and Denise D. Meringolo. *First Ladies: Political Role and Public Image*. Washington: Smithsonian Institution, 1994.

McConnell, Jane and Burt McConnell. *First Ladies: Martha Washington to Mamie Eisenhower.* Binghamton: Vail-Ballou Press, 1953.

Means, Marianne. *The Woman in the White House: The Lives, Time and Influence of Twelve Notable First Ladies*. New York: Random House, 1963.

Melick, Arden Davis. *Wives of the Presidents*. Maplewood: Hammond Incorporated, 1972.

Mitchell, Jack. *Executive Privilege: Two Centuries of White House Scandals*. New York: Hippocrene Books, 1992.

Morris, Sylvia Jukes. *Edith Kermit Roosevelt: Portrait of a First Lady*. New York: Coward, McCann & Geoghegan, 1980.

Nelson, Michael. *The Presidency: A History of the Office of the President of the United States from 1789 to the Present*. London: Salamander Books, 1996.

Perling, J. J. *Presidents' Sons: The Prestige of Name in a Democracy.* New York: Odyssey Press, 1947.

Ross, Ishbel. *Grace Coolidge and Her Era.* New York: Dodd, Mead, 1962.

Sauer, Patrick. *The Complete Idiot's Guide to the American Presidents.* Indianapolis: Alpha Books, 2000.

Schneider, Dorothy and Carl J. Schneider. *First Ladies: A Biographical Dictionary.* New York: Checkmark Books, 2001.

Simon, John. *The Personal Memoirs of Julia Dent Grant (Mrs. Ulysses S. Grant).* New York: G. P. Putnam's Sons, 1975.

Truman, Margaret. *First Ladies: An Intimate Group Portrait of White House Wives.* New York: Random House, 1995.

Watson, Robert P. , PhD, ed. *American First Ladies.* Pasadena: Salem Press, 2002.

Wead, Doug. *All The Presidents' Children: Triumph and Tragedy in the Lives of America's First Families.* New York: Atria Books, 2003.

West, J. B. with Mary Lynn Kotz. *Upstairs at the White House: My Life with the First Ladies.* New York: Coward, McCann & Geoghegan, 1973.

Whitton, Mary Ormsbee. *First First Ladies 1789–1865: A Study of the Wives of the Early Presidents.* New York: Hastings House, 1948.

Notes

Part One: Women of the Revolution

1. *1776*, 294.
2. *The Book of Abigail and John: Selected Letters of the Adams Family 1762–1784*, 67.
3. Ibid., 86.
4. *Presidential Fact Book*, 5.

Chapter 1: The General's Lady: Martha Washington

1. *First Ladies Quotations Book*, 131.
2. *Profiles & Portraits of American Presidents & Their Wives*, 9.
3. *First Ladies, A Biographical Dictionary*, 4.
4. *The Complete Book of U.S. Presidents*, 6.
5. *First Ladies, A Biographical Dictionary*, 7.
6. *First Ladies Quotations Book*, 99.
7. Ibid., 120.
8. *The First Ladies Fact Book*, 17.

Chapter 2: First Lady of Liberty: Abigail Adams

1. Excerpts from over thirteen hundred letters that Abigail and John exchanged over the years, from *The Book of Abigail and John: Selected Letters of the Adams Family 1762–1784*, unless otherwise stated, 148.
2. Ibid., 86–87.
3. Ibid., 121.
4. Ibid., 53–54.
5. Ibid., 71.
6. Ibid., 79.
7. Ibid., 219.
8. *First First Ladies 1789–1865*, 25.
9. Ibid., 69–70.

10. Ibid., 90.

11. Ibid., 107.

12. Ibid., 107.

13. Ibid., 108.

14. *First Ladies, A Biographical Dictionary*, 14.

15. Ibid., 126.

16. Ibid., 136.

17. Ibid., 139–142.

18. Ibid., 145.

19. Ibid., 144, 147.

20. Ibid., 153.

21. Ibid., 153.

22. Ibid., 163–164.

23. Ibid., 178.

24. Ibid., 178–180.

25. Ibid., 182.

26. Ibid., 203.

27. *First First Ladies, 1789–1865*, 27.

28. Ibid., 212.

29. *America's Royalty: All the Presidents' Children*, 12.

30. *First First Ladies 1789–1865*, 30.

31. *First Ladies, A Biographical Dictionary*, 17.

32. *America's First Ladies, Their Uncommon Wisdom, from Martha Washington to Laura Bush*, 15.

33. *American First Ladies*, "Abigail Adams" by Bryan Le Beau, 23.

34. *America's First Ladies, Their Uncommon Wisdom, from Martha Washington to Laura Bush*, 14.

35. *First Ladies, Martha Washington to Mamie Eisenhower*, 32.

36. *America's First Ladies, Their Uncommon Wisdom, from Martha Washington to Laura Bush*, 15–16.

Chapter 3: Never to Be First Lady: Martha Jefferson

1. The Jefferson Monticello website.

Chapter 4: Bountiful Hostess to All: Dolley Madison

1. Dolley Madison Digital Edition Letters 1788–1836.

2. *Presidential Wives, An Anecdotal History*, 45.

3. *First Ladies Quotations Book*, 23.

4. *Presidential Wives, An Anecdotal History*, 44.

5. Ibid., 41.

6. *First Ladies Quotations Book*, 87.

Chapter 5: European Formal Lady: Elizabeth Monroe

1. *First Ladies, A Biographical Dictionary*, 37.

2. *The First Ladies Fact Book*, 101.

Chapter 6: Foreign-Born Culture: Louisa Adams

1. *First Ladies Quotations Book*, 133.

2. *First Ladies, A Biographical Dictionary*, 44–45.

3. *The First Ladies Fact Book*, 110.

4. *First Ladies Quotations Book*, 175.

5. *The First Ladies Fact Book*, 113.

6. *The First Ladies, from Martha Washington to Laura Bush*, 44.

7. *First Ladies Quotations Book*, 247.

8. *America's First Ladies, Their Uncommon Wisdom, from Martha Washington to Laura Bush*, 24.

9. *First Ladies Quotations Book*, 55.

10. *The First Ladies, from Martha Washington to Laura Bush*, 45.

PART TWO: WOMEN OF THE FRONTIER

Chapter 7: A Scandalous Youthful Blunder: Rachel Jackson

1. National First Ladies Library website.

2. *American First Ladies*, "Rachel Jackson" by Ann Toplovich, 57.

3. Ibid., 58.

4. *The First Ladies Fact Book*, 123.

Chapter 8: Matt's Dutch Sweetheart: Hannah Van Buren

1. *First First Ladies 1789–1865*, 139.

2. *Ladies of the White House*, 346.

3. *American First Ladies*, "Hannah Van Buren" by Virginia A. Chanley, 63.

4. *Profiles & Portraits of American Presidents & Their Wives*, 86.

Chapter 9: Frontier Matriarch: Anna Harrison

1. *First Ladies, A Biographical Dictionary*, 54.

2. Ibid., 55.

3. *First Ladies Quotations Book*, 205.

4. *Presidential Fact Book*, 61.

5. *First Ladies, A Biographical Dictionary*, 56.

6. *Presidential Fact Book*, 327.

PART THREE: WOMEN OF TRANSITION AND EXPANSION

1. *Smithsonian Presidents and First Ladies*, 31.

Chapter 10: Upstairs White House Invalid: Letitia Tyler

1. *First First Ladies 1789–1805*, 182.

2. *First Ladies, Martha Washington to Mamie Eisenhower*, 114.

3. *America's First Ladies, Private Lives of the Presidential Wives*, 51.

4. *First Ladies, A Biographical Dictionary*, 60.

Chapter 11: Downstairs White House Romance: Julia Tyler

1. *First Ladies, A Biographical Dictionary*, 63.

2. Ibid., 63.

3. *America's First Families, An Inside View of 200 Years of Private Life in the White House*, 194.

4. National First Ladies Library website.

5. *The First Ladies Fact Book*, 170.

6. Ibid., 171.

Chapter 12: The CEO's Secretary: Sarah Polk

1. *America's First Ladies, Their Uncommon Wisdom, from Martha Washington to Laura Bush*, 38.

2. *First Ladies, A Biographical Dictionary*, 71.

3. *America's First Ladies, Their Uncommon Wisdom, from Martha Washington to Laura Bush*, 38.

4. Library of Congress, American Memory website.

5. *American First Ladies*, "Sarah Polk" by Barbara Bennett Peterson, 87.

6. Ibid., 87.

7. The Texas State Library and Archives Commission.

8. *First First Ladies 1789–1865*, 208.

9. *Presidential Fact Book*, 72.

10. *The First Ladies Fact Book*, 181.

11. Wives of the Presidents, 35.

12. Ibid., 35.

13. *First First Ladies 1789–1865*, 215–216.

PART FOUR: WOMEN OF THE SLAVERY ISSUE

Chapter 13: The Better Soldier: Margaret Taylor

1. *Presidential Fact Book*, 76.

2. *American First Ladies*, "Margaret Taylor" by Patricia Brady, 93.

3. *First Ladies, A Biographical Dictionary*, 80.

4. Ibid., 81.

5. Ibid., 81.

6. Oak Ridge National Laboratory website.

7. *America's First Ladies, Their Uncommon Wisdom, from Martha Washington to Laura Bush*, 41.

8. *First Ladies, A Biographical Dictionary*, 82.

Chapter 14: Library Matron: Abigail Fillmore

1. *First Ladies, A Biographical Dictionary*, 84.

2. *American First Ladies,* "Abigail Fillmore" by Elizabeth Lorelei Thacker-Estrada, 101.

Chapter 15: The Ultimate Devastation: Jane Pierce

1. *First Ladies A Biographical Dictionary*, 89.

2. *America's First Ladies, Their Uncommon Wisdom, from Martha Washington to Laura Bush*, 45.

3. *First Ladies A Biographical Dictionary*, 90.

4. *First Ladies Quotations Book*, 4.

5. *First Ladies, A Biographical Dictionary*, 91.

6. Ibid., 91.

7. New Hampshire Historical Society.

8. Ibid., 92.

PART FIVE: WOMEN OF THE CIVIL WAR

1. Various Civil War websites, including The U.S. Civil War Center, and Civil War Home.

Chapter 17: Controversial and Unstable: Mary Todd Lincoln.

1. *Behind the Scenes*, 118.

2. *The First Ladies Fact Book*, 225; *First Ladies A Biographical Dictionary*, 96.

3. *The First Ladies Fact Book*, 226.

4. Ibid., 230.

5. *First Ladies, A Biographical Dictionary*, 98.

6. *The First Ladies Fact Book*, 231.

7. *Profiles & Portraits of American Presidents & Their Wives*, 151.

8. *Behind the Scenes*, 87.

9. Ibid., 88.

10. Ibid., 175–176.

Chapter 18: Mountain Woman of Tennessee: Eliza Johnson

1. *The First Ladies Fact Book*, 261.
2. Ibid., 250.
3. *First Ladies, A Biographical Dictionary*, 109.
4. *American First Ladies*, "Eliza Johnson" by Ann Toplovich, 123.
5. Ibid., 123.

Chapter 19: Undeterred Devotee: Julia Grant

1. *American First Ladies*, "Julia Grant" by Carole Elizabeth Adams, 126.
2. *First Ladies, A Biographical Dictionary*, 114.
3. Ibid., 116.
4. *American First Ladies*, "Julia Grant" by Carole Elizabeth Adams, 128.
5. *First Ladies, A Biographical Dictionary*, 119.
6. *Profiles & Portraits of American Presidents & Their Wives*, 176.
7. *First Ladies, A Biographical Dictionary*, 120.

Chapter 20: Lemonade Lucy: Lucy Hayes

1. *American First Ladies*, "Lucy Hayes" by Craig Schermer, 133.
2. *First Ladies, A Biographical Dictionary*, 127.
3. *American First Ladies*, "Lucy Hayes" by Craig Schermer, 135.
4. *First Ladies, A Biographical Dictionary*, 127.
5. *American First Ladies*, "Lucy Hayes" by Craig Schermer, 137.
6. *First Ladies, A Biographical Dictionary*, 129.
7. Ibid., 129.
8. *Inside the White House*, 272.
9. *Presidential Fact Book*, 124.

Chapter 21: First Betrayed, Then Widowed: Lucretia Garfield

1. *First Ladies, A Biographical Dictionary*, 134–135.
2. Ibid., 135.
3. *America's First Ladies, Their Uncommon Wisdom, from Martha Washington to Laura Bush*, 62.
4. *First Ladies, A Biographical Dictionary*, 136.
5. Ibid.,137.
6. *Profiles & Portraits of American Presidents & Their Wives*, 198.

Chapter 22: Never Forgotten Wife: Ellen Arthur

1. *American First Ladies*, "Ellen Arthur" by Sina Dubovoy, 152.

2. *America's First Ladies, Private Lives of the Presidential Wives*, 110.

3. *First Ladies, Martha Washington to Mamie Eisenhower*, 217.

PART SIX: WOMEN OF ACKNOWLEDGMENT

Chapter 23: White House Bride: Frances Folsom

1. *First Ladies, A Biographical Dictionary*, 140.

2. Ibid., 140.

3. *The First Ladies, Their Lives and Legacies*, 88.

4. *Forty-Two Years in the White House*, 16.

5. *The First Ladies, from Martha Washington to Laura Bush*, 139.

Chapter 24: Mother to the White House China: Caroline Harrison

1. *American First Ladies*, "Caroline Harrison" by Anne Moore, 161.

2. *First Ladies, A Biographical Dictionary*, 149.

3. Ibid.,150.

4. *American First Ladies*, "Caroline Harrison" by Anne Moore, 164.

5. *America's First Families, An Inside View of 200 Years of Private Life in the White House*, 206.

Chapter 25: Act II, Wife and Mother: Frances Folsom

1. *First Ladies, An Intimate Group Portrait of White House Wives*, 345.

PART SEVEN: WOMEN OF THE TURN OF THE CENTURY

1. Numerous "turn-of-the century" websites.

Chapter 26: Dearly Loved Epileptic: Ida McKinley

1. White House website.

Chapter 27: Second Wife, First Lady Extraordinaire: Edith Roosevelt

1. *First Ladies, A Biographical Dictionary*, 170.

2. *The First Ladies, from Martha Washington to Laura Bush*, 150.

3. *First Ladies, A Biographical Dictionary*, 164.

4. *Edith Kermit Roosevelt, Portrait of a First Lady*, 4.

5. Ibid., 5.

6. *America's First Families, 200 Years of Private Life in the White House*, 255.

7. *The First Ladies, from Martha Washington to Laura Bush*, 154.

8. *Edith Kermit Roosevelt, Portrait of a First Lady*, 5.

9. *Profiles & Portraits of American Presidents & Their Wives*, 248.

10. *First Ladies, A Biographical Dictionary,* 169; *Edith Kermit Roosevelt, Portrait of a First Lady,* 423.

11. *Profiles & Portraits of American Presidents & Their Wives,* 255.

12. Ibid., 255.

13. *Edith Kermit Roosevelt, Portrait of a First Lady,* 423.

14.,Ibid., 3.

15. Ibid., 414.

16. Ibid., 511.

Chapter 28: Careful What You Wish For: Helen Taft

1, *Nellie Taft, The Unconventional First Lady of the Ragtime Era,* 36–38.

2. Ibid., 22.

3. Ibid., 36–37.

4. *First Ladies, A Biographical Dictionary,* 173.

5. *Nellie Taft, The Unconventional First Lady of the Ragtime Era,* 49–50.

6. Ibid., 84.

7. Presidential Fact Book, 167.

8. *Nellie Taft, The Unconventional First Lady of the Ragtime Era,* 402.

9. *First Ladies, A Biographical Dictionary,* 177.

10. Ibid.,177.

11. *Profiles & Portraits of American Presidents & Their Wives,* 265.

12. *Presidential Fact Book,* 167.

13. *Nellie Taft, The Unconventional First Lady of the Ragtime Era,* 279.

14. *First Ladies, A Biographical Dictionary,* 178.

15. *Nellie Taft, The Unconventional First Lady of the Ragtime Era,* 304.

16. *Profiles & Portraits of American Presidents & Their Wives,* 266.

17. *Nellie Taft, The Unconventional First Lady of the Ragtime Era,* 221.

18. Ibid., 356.

19. Ibid., 358.

20. Ibid., 376.

21. Ibid., 381.

22. Ibid., 397.

Index